A NEW MANUAL OF CLASSIFICATION

A New Manual *of* Classification

RITA MARCELLA
& ROBERT NEWTON

Gower

Published by
Gower Publishing Limited
Gower House
Croft Road
Aldershot
Hampshire GU11 3HR
England

Gower
Old Post Road
Brookfield
Vermont 05036
USA

Rita Marcella and Robert Newton have asserted their right under the Copyright, Designs and Patents Act 1988 to be identified as the authors of this work.

British Library Cataloguing in Publication Data
Marcella, Rita
  New Manual of Classification
  I. Title II. Newton, Robert
  025.4
  ISBN 0–566–07547–4

Library of Congress Cataloging-in-Publication Data
Marcella, Rita.
  A new manual of classification/by Rita Marcella and Robert Newton.
      p.   cm.
  Includes bibliographical references (p.) and index.
  ISBN 0–566–07547–4: $59.95 (est.)
  1. Classification – Books. I. Newton, Robert. II. Title.
Z696.A4M37 1994
025.4'3 – dc20
                                                                94–172
                                                                CIP

Typeset in Century Old Style by Bournemouth Colour Graphics Limited, Parkstone, Dorset and printed in Great Britain by Hartnolls Ltd, Bodmin.

Contents

List of figures

Preface

When Berwick Sayers first produced his *Manual of classification,* in 1926, it was designed as a textbook which would survey and explain a complex subject. When, after Sayers' death, Arthur Maltby assumed the mantle with the fourth and fifth editions, he revised and updated the material while retaining the thrust and purpose of the work. This present text builds upon the work of its predecessors; it hopes to maintain the traditions they have established and fulfil the same aims – that is, to provide a clear and comprehensible overview of classification theory, policy and practice, together with a description of the major general classification schemes, such as would support students of classification in the course of their studies. It is intended as a simple – but not simplistic – introduction to a complex subject. While the more technical and abstruse aspects have not been ignored, they have been treated to the extent that we feel is desirable for the reader at this stage in his or her career. Much valuable material has been taken from the earlier editions virtually unchanged, in particular the excellent review of the history and development of classification. Every effort has been made, however, to make the information as current as possible when discussing work in progress today. In that sense this is very much a 'new' manual. We have borne in mind the present-day reader and tried to convey the ideas which underpin classification, and to illustrate their application, in up-to-date language and examples.

Every effort has also been made to take an objective and nonpartisan approach as far as attitudes to classification are concerned. There is something of an Atlantic divide in this area, perceptions and practice varying quite considerably in the United States of America and Great Britain. So far as is possible – given the authors' nationality, training and experience – we have tried to represent fairly all sides of the issues which are raised.

The text has been arranged in three broad sections:

- Part One, *Principles and systems,* deals with the purpose and the theory of classification, beginning with first principles and ending with an examination of the major general schemes and a discussion of the contribution and development of special schemes. It includes a brief description of the historical development of the theory and practice of bibliographic classification.

- Part Two, *Classification policy and practice*, deals with the way in which libraries select, implement and maintain the classification schemes in use with their collections. It looks at the application of classificatory principles and discusses the ways in which these may be mediated via library policy and applied in working practice. This section considers first the various functions which classification may serve in libraries, then goes on to a pragmatic investigation of classificatory practice.
- In Part Three, *Information technology and classification*, the material has been refined to emphasize the ever more significant inter-relationship between information retrieval, classification and technology and this section has, therefore, grown proportionally from earlier editions of the *Manual*.

Each of the chapters is accompanied by a concluding section which identifies some of the major issues which have been raised.

As in previous editions, the attempt here has been to survey, summarize and comment on the enormous body of work which has been carried out by others rather than to report original research. We have sought to bring together the body of knowledge in a way which would be useful to those coming new to the study of classification. It has, therefore, been considered important and useful, in the pages which follow, to bring to the reader's attention as many of the significant writers and thinkers in the field as could be accommodated. A final section identifies suggested reading, to guide the, hopefully, enthusiastic and stimulated reader to further areas of investigation and study.

The authors extend their thanks to all those who helped in the production of this work: our colleagues David Andrews, Douglas Anderson and David Harper for their advice and support throughout; Ia McIlwaine and Alan Gilchrist for guidance on the progress and future development of UDC; Joan Mitchell for her vision of DC's future; and Michael Moulds for information on the FIAF classification. Above all, however, the authors would like to acknowledge their immense indebtedness to both the late Berwick Sayers and, most particularly, to Arthur Maltby, much of whose original work and thoughts are contained herein: the help, patience and generosity of the latter in advising and supporting the efforts of the authors cannot be over-emphasized.

Rita Marcella and Robert Newton, 1994

Part One
Principles and systems

1 Rationale: why classification?

The whole object of classification, as described in this *Manual*, is to create and preserve a subject order of maximum helpfulness to information seekers. The act of classifying, as practised over the years by libraries and related organizations with an information store in the form of books and other materials, may be defined as:

> The systematic arrangement *by subject* of books and other learning resources and/or the similar systematic arrangement of catalogue or index entries, in the manner most useful to those who are seeking *either* a definite piece of information *or* the display of the most likely sources for the effective investigation of a subject of their choice.

It is a technique designed to facilitate and expedite the fullest possible revelation and use of the knowledge stored in the library or information service's collection.

Classification, in the sense of grouping together (either literally or mentally) things which are alike, goes back to ancient civilizations. In this widest sense, it remains an activity which we all practise in everyday life: we have a mental map or 'classification' in which we associate or dissociate the objects, ideas and impressions that are our experience of the world. Classification systems seek to provide a structure for the organization of materials so that an item may be retrieved according to some aspect of its character. A library is, in the main, a store of documents and we will, therefore, in this *Manual*, concentrate on the classification of documents or, as it is often termed, *bibliographic classification*. It should be noted, however, that the principles which we will apply when considering how to organize and retrieve information from books, journals, pamphlets, reports and so on, apply to the organization of things generally. Systems exist for the classification of fingerprints, blood groups and plants, among others, and although they are based on different types of association they fulfil the same function as bibliographic classification. Fingerprints are classified so that, when a print is lifted, the identity of the person to whom that print belongs can be retrieved from the system. Documents are classified so that, when an individual seeks to locate a document on a particular topic, the identity of the documents which deal with that subject can be retrieved from the system, in this case the library collection.

Before considering *how* we achieve the helpful organization of bibliographic material, we need to be quite clear *why* it is desirable so to do. One of the major tasks of the librarian or information officer is to assist the user in the location of a specific document or set of documents – either from a given collection or from the universe of published knowledge – and to do so in a fast, efficient and effective manner. For very small collections, a fairly simple arrangement may suffice. It is unlikely that many of us would seek to classify our own personal collection of books in a formal manner; the number would probably be too small, the effort too great and our familiarity with the works would render such a process unnecessary. However, as the size of a collection grows so does the need for some method of physical arrangement which will allow us to locate works speedily. Most library collections today are unlikely to be small – a familiar theme which pervades modern librarianship is that of the *information explosion*; as Bernard Palmer[1] reminds us, 'A year's output of books in the mid-twentieth century probably surpasses that of the whole of the seventeenth century.' The volume and complexity of material to be found in even a fairly small modern library makes it essential that we organize it systematically in order to have any hope of retrieving information quickly. Without such organization, every book in a collection must be examined in order to gather information for any particular subject enquiry. For the majority of library users, the time taken to find material is a very significant factor in their evaluation of the effectiveness of the service.

Classification also allows us to manage and control ideas so that they can be used. In a recent novel of philosophic exploration, Robert M. Pirsig[2] describes the necessity, whether for individual research or on a larger scale, of some form of systematic subject categorization of ideas:

> When information is organized in small chunks that can be accessed and sequenced it becomes much more valuable than when you have to take it in serial form . . . Before long he noticed certain categories emerging. The earlier slips began to merge about a common topic and later slips about a different topic. When enough slips merged about a single topic so that he got a feeling it would be permanent he took an index card of the same size as the slips, attached a transparent plastic index tab to it, wrote the name of the topic on a little cardboard insert that came with the tab, put it in the tab, and *put the index card together with its related topic slips* . . . It was fascinating to watch this thing grow.

The idea of the imposition of a structure upon human understanding is one which has long delighted philosophers. Pirsig here describes an individual's discovery of the value of classification. Let us consider in more general terms the role of classification.

In housing and maintaining collections of material, we have a responsibility to ensure the maximum exploitation of these resources. That responsibility involves not just satisfying the user who comes to the collection knowing that he or she wants a particular item, but also in showing what other similar works are available and of potential interest. Classification has a promotional role, then, which, like the stock layout of a department store, draws attention to the materials available and seeks to sell these to customers who may have only the vaguest notion of the kind of purchase they wish to make. It would be possible to accomplish this task in one of two ways:

- Staff assistance

  or

- A form of display which gathers material together in a helpful and, where possible, self-evident way.

The first option relies very heavily on the staff's personal knowledge of the collection and, like all activities which are heavily reliant on manpower, is very costly. The second option has greater administrative appeal and is the norm in most open access libraries.

Having decided, then, that the documents in a collection should be arranged, the next question is *how* best to arrange them. Basically we seek an end result in which items are physically brought together on the shelf if they are similar and are separated if they are dissimilar. Classification is the formal process by which a mechanism is established to translate these similarities and dissimilarities into a *place* in a physical sequence. Documents display a number of attributes which can be used to determine likeness. One may be quality. John Ruskin[3] tells us that, 'All books are divisible into two classes; the books of the hour and the books of all time.' While a perfectly valid distinction, this is not likely to be a helpful criterion in arranging a physical sequence, quite apart from the literary and critical debates which would most likely ensue. Another attribute may be shape – all the long thin books could be shelved together; another may be colour – all the red books could be held in one section. Such aesthetic considerations might very well influence us in organizing our own personal collections. However, with a collection which is going to be accessed by a number of people, the guiding principle should be that arrangement which is the most *helpful* to the greatest number of users. This being the case, we might expect that the form of arrangement chosen would be affected by the type of library or information service in which it was to be used, the type of users who most commonly use the service and the typical way in which they look for information as a group.

Documents possess four attributes by which they may be grouped:

Author by the person or persons intellectually responsible for the creation of the work
Title by the title of the individual work
Form by the physical form in which the document appears
Subject by the content of the work, the subject matter which it contains.

While users will frequently seek works by a specific author and, less frequently, works in a particular form – for example, a report or a conference paper – the most common way of seeking documents is by subject. Even when an individual is interested in the works of a particular author, or a specific title, such a request may disguise a subject need and the reader's search may be perfectly happily concluded by the provision of other materials on the same subject. (It is in very specialized circumstances that a slide set is sought and the likelihood is that it would be a slide set on a particular subject.) Documents are, too, largely a means of conveying intellectual subject or thought content. For the author their subject matter will be their most significant attribute, as it is for the reader. In an arrangement of non-bibliographic items, such as an arrangement of archaeological artifacts for example, another attribute may be deemed more significant, such as size or date or material. Subject order is, however, the most significant and helpful way in which we can order a collection of documents.

The final alternative to subject searching, in terms of the approach to documents, is that of the *known item search* or title search, where the library user looks for items which have been identified by some mechanism other than classification; it may be a work which has been brought to their attention by recommendation, by review, by reference in other works and so on. Apart from the significance of the assurance of quality in the work sought, this, as has already been stated, may be simply another way of conducting a subject search. It may be resorted to because the user has difficulty in understanding the system of classification or, perhaps, be due to the inadequacies of the classification scheme in use or to the way in which the library organizes the scheme. Research, carried out by Ray Larson[4] in the early 1980s, suggested that users were conducting a greater proportion of subject searches than known item searches, though his more recent work[5] has shown a reverse in that trend. Such research, however, has drawn inferences from the behaviour of users – via the logging of actual searches on online public access catalogues – rather than from the analysis of original need. We are on safer ground in relying upon research into the reference process and information need. Micheline Hancock-Beaulieu[6], for instance, examined searching at the catalogue and at the library shelves, and one of her major findings was that the subject enquiry is proportionally predominant.

When we seek to apply the principles of helpful bringing together of related materials to subject grouping in a collection of materials of any significant size, we have basically two objectives in mind. Firstly, we want an infallible way of locating material on any given theme (for example, monetary economics). Secondly, we want this material to be sympathetically related so that closely associated topics (for example, banking or taxation) are helpfully represented nearby. We cannot display all possible subject relationships of this kind on the shelves of a classified library or in a classified catalogue, but we can seek to show the most significant ones and, indeed, classification can be judged by the success with which this proximity of like subjects is achieved. Classification is not only the grouping of things for location or identification purposes; it is also their display in some sort of rational, progressive (usually subject) order so that their chief relationships may be ascertained. In the world of information management the latter task is crucial, for while we can rapidly rearrange our mental maps of subjects and ideas to suit new purposes and situations, we cannot rearrange, with any degree of economy, a classified library or resources collection. It becomes vital then that the subject relationships displayed are the most useful ones. As we shall see, subject associations of less significance to our users can be picked up by means other than the classification.

Such systematic arrangement starts with broad subject areas or categories and moves, step by step, to specific themes within each. Classification has been described as a pre-coordinated system because themes are arranged in a preferred subject order before information searching takes place. (We shall contrast it with post-coordinate systems later.) It is clear that if we arrange things in a definite subject order and we know what that order is we have a very good key to (our map of) these things. A stock of resources for recreation, learning or information provision itself comprises a very basic class, or category, in relation to other things, but unless that stock is suitably sub-arranged we cannot find out – without immense loss of time – what items, if any, this basic category contains on, for example, physical chemistry, the history of France, fluid mechanics, opera or road transport. If we glance briefly at alternatives to an organized, general through to special, subject order, we see immediately that arranging stock by size or colour clearly will not do in terms of functional efficiency. Nor will some chronological order by date of publication or accession number suffice. Physical format certainly has a part to play in determining the arrangement of stock on shelves (as opposed to the catalogue entries representing it), but the criteria of needs and use point firmly to systematic subject arrangement as the dominant factor. Thus, even in a multimedia collection, if someone wants the poetry of Louis MacNeice, say, we can find it in the specified place within the system of subject classification employed, with critical works and the writings of his contemporary poets nearby; and if there are, say, relevant audio or video tapes these will be at the same specified place in the classification, although (because of format) probably in a parallel arrangement to the sequence of printed materials.

One possible arrangement of a collection, as we have seen, is by author. This will almost certainly be sufficient for fiction, although even here a certain element of subject classification has crept in with the idea of categorization; it is common for there to be separate sequences for romances, detective novels, thrillers, science fiction and westerns, for, even when choosing fiction, the reader is often likely to have a subject preference. Bibliographic aids, such as *The fiction index*, also support this approach, albeit in a slightly different way, by allowing users to identify books set in Russia, say, or which have as their hero a civil servant, perhaps. However, with fiction it continues to be accepted that the author is the most significant element in retrieval for the major part of the collection. More readers come into the library looking for a novel by Ruth Rendell than for one about the Civil War in America.

For factual material, the author has a place in sub-arrangement, but could only serve as the major factor in displaying stock if users already knew all the authors on their chosen subject. With the enormous and increasingly rapid growth in the amount of published information in the past two hundred years, this has clearly become ever more difficult and even the specialist in a subject area will not be able to keep up with all the authors in their field. The predominant need of most users of any non-fiction collection is for a helpful subject arrangement. Author order is thus best left to a catalogue, for even in the case of students with a pre-determined reading list which cites the authors required, the emphasis will be upon a subject or a cluster of related subjects. Much effort is saved in grouping stock accordingly rather than sending students to various parts of the collection – the physical distance between them being determined by the accident of alphabetical distribution of authors' names.

So subject arrangement is infinitely preferable, but it must be systematic subject arrangement which moves in stages from broad general themes to specific ones, and a system which groups themes with the aim of making items support one another. It might be thought that the simplest approach is to identify the subject matter of a work and then to organize the subjects alphabetically. An alphabetical subject order, however, which places 'abbeys' near to 'accidents' and separates materials on 'baseball' or 'golf' from each other, from other sports and from 'sport' in general, cannot possibly generate what H. E. Bliss used to call 'maximal efficiency'. So-called classified telephone directories adopt this rudimentary approach and are excellent examples of the irritation and confusion which ensue for the user. For, in lifting one down, we may find 'stockbrokers' next to 'stevedores' which in turn has 'sterilizing services' closely juxtaposed, but 'stockbrokers' is very far removed from 'financial advisers' and 'investment consultants', although most of us would be hard pressed to distinguish the niceties of difference between these three closely related services. It should be reiterated that traditional bibliographic classification – and we need not confine this accepted term to the organization of printed media – goes beyond the location of material on any specific theme, such as golf, highly important though that is. It seeks also to display the most significant relationships between subjects: to lead one also to other ball games, for example. This means that it relies on the idea of relative location. Stock is not assigned to a fixed and unchanging position on the shelves, as often happened in the days when libraries forbade shelf access to the public, and a librarian would fetch the book for the reader. Rather, the stock is moved about on the shelves so that new material can be accommodated in the appropriate place within the chosen classified order. When a brand new book on golf arrives it is placed alongside those works on golf already in the collection instead of being added to the end of the sequence as the newest book in the collection. Fixed location saves some space, in that room does not have to be allowed for new additions to stock – such new items being simply filed at the end of the sequence – and it may be used in storerooms or wherever browsing for material on a subject is extremely rare, but it is the antithesis of true classification.

Relative location of subjects is the great time-saver, for it places together the items likely to be used together. It is an aim of all the classification systems which we will study to so collocate subjects and it allows that chosen arrangement to be preserved, despite the fact that the collection is growing and new materials are being added. Relative location allows new works on existing subjects and new works on new subjects to be placed at the correct point in the classified subject arrangement on the shelf. This physical and linear sequence is achieved by a device known as *notation*. Notation is a brief code used to represent the classes in the system and to ensure that the desired subject order is achieved when works are filed in a linear sequence; it establishes the order of the works on the shelf. To take a very simple example, let us imagine that we have a collection of gardening books which we wish to arrange in a logical sequence so that we have all the books on roses together in a helpful manner. We might begin by identifying the groups:

Roses
    shrub
    hybrid tea
    patio
    climbing

These would then require some sort of code to keep them in that order. The simplest would be an alphabetic or numeric code, thus:

1   Roses
2   shrub
3   hybrid tea
4   patio
5   climbing

The code here clearly shows the place of the materials in the sequence on the shelf and however complex the code may become – and inevitably in anything but the very smallest of collections it will become much more complex – as we add books on damask roses, on miniatures, on pests and diseases, and so on, it remains the essence of notation. One early writer in library classification history, E. W. Hulme,[7] described the process as 'a mechanical time-saving operation for the discovery of knowledge . . . by the shortest route'. It is notation which strives to display readily for us the chosen sequence of the classification system we employ and to make its maintenance a relatively 'mechanical' task.

The ultimate aim of the classification sequence is to provide a physical arrangement where similar materials are closely located on the shelf and, within subject groupings of like subjects, an order of *general to specific* subjects is observed. Where a well-designed classification system exists and is well guided – to make its helpful but unfamiliar order intelligible – the user can see items which are preliminary to, or the foundation of, a chosen specific subject. Following these are items on the specific subject itself and, following them in turn, items on themes which develop from that subject. So we might have an arrangement whereby 'card games' was followed by 'bridge', which in turn was followed by 'contract bridge'. Thus, the linear and horizontal physical arrangement will attempt to cater for the hierarchical and vertical relationships of subjects. The subject relationships may be represented as a tree:

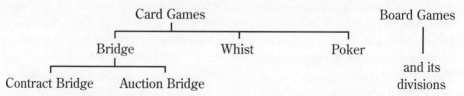

However for the purpose of physical arrangement the classification must translate this schema into a single line of subjects:

Card Games > Bridge > Contract Bridge > Auction Bridge > Whist > Poker

The use of classification is not limited to arranging materials on shelves. If classification is applied to a subject catalogue or bibliography, the entries will be in the equivalent systematic subject order. The result is that if we find little available on the chosen theme of 'bridge', then we might consult the works on card games in which there might be a useful section, or we might be content with the more limited work on 'contract bridge'. We might not have found specifically what we were looking for but we have found supportive material in the works which are located nearby. Searches can be broadened or narrowed down as circumstances dictate. This is useful in that we cannot always predict what the collection will have on offer or, indeed, upon which subjects works may have been produced.

Classification is thus seen as organizing stock for effective service. Melvil Dewey once said that piles of bricks and mortar are no temple, nor are heaps of type Shakespeare's works, it is only when they are 'set, each in right relation to the rest' that the transformation occurs. This analogy with the process of classification may seem extravagant, but the message is very clear. A collection is an amorphous and unrevealing entity without the guiding light of classification. Naturally, there are also actual and potential weaknesses to combat as well as strengths in any classified sequence, and these will be considered in due course.

There are five general bibliographic classification schemes now in use and they share the basic aims which have been outlined. The five are: the Dewey Decimal Classification (often known as DDC or just DC, in line with its creator's, Melvil Dewey's, known predilection for maximum abbreviation); the Universal Decimal Classification (UDC); the Library of Congress Classification (LC); the Bibliographic Classification (BC) originally compiled by H. E. Bliss; and the Colon Classification (CC), the brainchild of S. R. Ranganathan. Apart from schemes such as these which attempt to span all human knowledge, there are an increasing number of *special* classification schemes, which restrict themselves to one area, such as engineering, law or music.

Looking at the history of general schemes in particular, it will be found that many attempts have been made to imbue such a systematic ordering as they provide with a philosophic respectability. Classification in a sense reflects the deep human desire to create order from disorder. Other schemes have been much more blatantly pragmatic. The *mark and park* ethos, for instance, contents itself with finding a suitable location for works and providing a system whereby library users will be able to locate works on a subject. The test of all systems of classification, finally, is in the end product: how reliable, effective and up-to-date is the system of classification being used? We should end by reiterating the basic aim of classification: that it should create a physical arrangement of documents by subject, in the manner most useful or helpful for an individual seeking information. The classification system is, therefore, a means to an end; it is a process and it is the helpfulness of the order which is ultimately achieved and not the excellence of the system designed to obtain that order, which must be judged. As librarians, we should always bear this caveat in mind, otherwise we are in danger of ceding the justice of a comment by Umberto Eco[8] a great observer of the idiosyncrasies and preoccupations of librarians:

> The maximum of confusion achieved with the maximum of order: it seems a sublime calculation. The builders of the library were great masters.

ISSUES FOR CONSIDERATION

At the end of each chapter there is a short checklist to which one can return, if need be, after reading on. These may prompt thought about key issues and assumptions because classification, like our other technical operations in the library, should never be above criticism; it must be judged by the impact and economy with which it contributes to the total task of organizing and retrieving the subject information stored in the collection it is serving. So, at the very outset, some questions can be put for preliminary consideration: they will be developed in greater detail later.

1. The fundamental purpose of any library or resources collection may determine what the classification should seek to do, or where priorities should lie. Is a detailed arrangement of books and other materials on the shelves necessary? Or could this be counter-productive for browsing purposes, for which it might be argued a simple marking and parking arrangement could suffice? We might ask ourselves if there is a maximum size at which classification becomes necessary, or if there are factors in the user group for which the collection is housed, which might affect the desirability of a detailed and potentially complex scheme of arrangement. In certain circumstances it might be argued that a classification

could actually reduce the effectiveness of a collection by attempting to provide, within the one scheme of things, for both the shelf arrangement of materials and for a detailed catalogue or bibliography.

2. It is recognized that knowledge and its relationships are complex; that standpoints and approaches are diverse, and that no classification can be perfect. Support is therefore necessary, for even if a scheme picks up major subject relationships quite well, the classification requires alternative means of accessing information via catalogues and bibliographical aids of a variety of types. Subject indexes will also be necessary, if all subject information is to be retrieved, because works are comprised of smaller units of subject information. A search for information on badgers, say, may only be answered by a chapter in a book on nocturnal animals and classification may not reveal its existence. Such problems suggest that a complementary approach to total retrieval strategy is necessary, that the classification cannot and does not stand alone, but is one element in a phalanx of tools which can assist the user in the search for information. Such tools may include the subject index for alternative subject approaches; the catalogue for author and title searches and for complex subjects; and the help of the reference librarian or readers' advisor in guiding the user through the collection. We will return to this complementarity of subject assistance in Part Two when we consider classification in practice.

These questions will be discussed in more detail later in the book, but hopefully they may whet the critical appetite of readers. It may be worth repeating that a well-structured classification scheme should bring a high degree of system and benefit to the display of materials and to the provision of effective information services. It should do a great deal to display resources on any subject and to save time and effort both in allowing purposive browsing and searches for information within any specific field. The larger the collection, the more evident these gains will be.

NOTES

1. Palmer, Bernard, *Itself an education: six lectures on classification*. London: Library Association, 1971.
2. Pirsig, Robert M., LILA: *an inquiry into morals*. New York: Bantam Press, 1991.
3. Ruskin, John, Sesame and lilies. In *Two lectures: 1. Of kings' treasures; 2. Of queens' gardens*. London: Smith, Elderr and Co., 1865.
4. Larson, Ray R., Managing information overload in online catalog subject searching. In *ASIS '89: Managing information and technology; proceedings of the 52nd Annual Meeting of the American Society for Information Science, Volume 26;* edited by J. Katzer and G. B. Newby. Washington: Learned Information, 1989.
5. Larson, Ray R., The decline of subject searching: long-term trends and patterns of index use in an online catalog. *Journal of the American Society for Information Science,* 42 (3), 1991, pp. 197–215.
6. Hancock-Beaulieu, Micheline, Evaluating the impact of an online library catalogue on subject searching behaviour at the catalogue and at the shelves. *Journal of Documentation*, 46 (4), 1990,

pp. 318–338.
7.   Hulme, E. W., *Principles of book classification*. London: Association of Assistant Librarians, 1950.
8.   Eco, Umberto, *The name of the rose*. London: Secker and Warburg, 1983.

2 The theory of classification

Having decided that there is a necessity for systematic subject arrangement in most situations, how can a bibliographical scheme – that is, a scheme designed for the subject arrangement of physical items and possibly the catalogue records which represent them – best be constructed? All classification schemes are made up of *classes* or categories. If we browse through any of the widely used general schemes, they appear to be gigantic maps of knowledge. They begin with general works in what is called a *generalia* class. This class is designed to accommodate general collections of essays, multi-topical encyclopaedias and other works too wide in scope to be linked with any one discipline; these are works which deal with, or attempt to deal with, all knowledge. In some schemes generalia also embraces any theme deemed to serve all of the various disciplines, one obvious example being librarianship or information science, a science which may be applied to any subject discipline. Other examples include computer science and publishing. There are those who feel that the inclusion of such subjects in the generalia class is not appropriate, for they are not truly general – the documents themselves do not deal with all subjects. It might be argued that other subjects, such as accountancy, apply to a wide range of working environment and subject areas, but few of us would seek to suggest that accountancy is therefore general and belongs with truly multidisciplinary works such as encyclopaedias. In such ways, the generalia class in certain systems has become something of a catch-all for subjects which have no clearly definable place in the overall structure of knowledge – those which do not clearly belong to any of the other main classes.

After the very necessary generalia class come the major broad subject fields, for example:

Arts
Literature
History
Science
and so on . . .

Each of these broad subject fields is subdivided, via a step-by-step progression, until specific themes are reached, moving thus from general classes and categories of subject to gradually more and more specialized ones. This is a logical progression; for most of us it is a natural progression and one to which, as users, we can readily relate.

Main class	First division	Second division	Third division, etc.
	Poetry	English	20th century
			19th century
		French, etc.	20th century, etc.
			19th century, etc.
Literature	Prose	English	20th century
			19th century, etc.
		French, etc.	20th century
			19th century, etc.
	Drama	English	20th century
			19th century, etc.
		French	20th century
			19th century, etc.

Some schemes offer much more actual or potential detail than do others. It is no disparagement of the late 19th-century pioneers – Dewey and Cutter in the USA for example – to say that, in the earliest applications of classification in open access libraries, when for the first time the shelves were open to the public, that classificatory practice forged ahead of theory. In many respects, perhaps of necessity, it did so for a long time. The description of theory which follows is a concise overview of a process which developed at first very gradually. From about the middle of the present century there was acceleration; Ranganathan in particular, and later his disciples, began to perceive how a fully developed theory could be put together. Various special schemes were produced, some clearly intended for use and based on user needs, others more experimental in outline. In the United Kingdom, a Classification Research Group was set up. By the time one British enthusiast, Jack Mills, produced a textbook in 1960, it was possible to present principles which had been thought through, were linked to recorded knowledge, and were seemingly quite different from the early years when some enthusiasts had looked to the history of science, philosophical principles and logic for inspirational guidance.

In more recent years, the pace of theoretical innovation has slowed; much of what could be argued and demonstrated had so been done by the late 1960s. Nor are there now likely to be radical new developments in theory, as distinct from changes wrought by new technology. The theories developed have been accepted much more enthusiastically by some people than by others and, generally speaking, much more enthusiastically in some countries than in others. Perhaps, with some risk of over-simplification, two reasons can be suggested for this. Firstly, two of the three very widely used general classification schemes, the

Dewey Decimal Classification (DC) and the Library of Congress Classification (LC), both created in the nineteenth century, have a basic framework which does not harmonize too easily with the full application of the recent theory. The widely used DC, in particular, while it has not shirked the incorporation of the newer ideas and features which it deems advantageous, has to beware of implementing too rapid a rate of change. For the more widely used a scheme is, the more difficult radical change becomes; there are simply a greater number of users who will complain at being forced to reclassify their collection. Secondly, many practitioners feel that, however intellectually satisfying the full flowering of the theories appears, practical advantages in terms of effectiveness may be marginal, especially for shelf arrangement. Such critics would probably argue that efforts to achieve precision in specifying subjects and to provide for minute provision of detail in that sphere are blunted by the inescapable fact of different physical formats of the materials in the collection or by the relentless limitations of any attempt to show subject relationships in a display which presents them in a continuous line rather than as a family tree.

The order within a catalogue might be a somewhat different matter, but in some countries, subject catalogues arranged alphabetically by verbal subject headings or keywords, rather than in a classified sequence, predominate. This is very evident, for instance, in the United States and, relatively speaking, there is little interest in classification theory, as opposed to the practice, there. In an endeavour to explain or to justify this situation, it may be noted that one American writer, J. K. Feibleman, in a work on the history of ideas, claims of his fellow countrymen, '. . . we are not an intellectual country. At our best we are simply not much interested in ideas.'[1] Some would say that in the context of classification such lack of interest, if indeed true, was no bad thing. The focus in the United States could be said to be on realism and on the day-to-day performance of the classification scheme as a working tool in the library. This pragmatic approach asks, what is feasible and what works? We need not ponder the different stances further at this stage, but it is useful to know before examining the theory in more detail, that it is received by some with great enthusiasm, by others with relative indifference. It is also worth bearing in mind that, when the older established schemes draw on modern classificatory theory, they apply it to a structure which predates the full articulation of some of the ideas and which is not susceptible to rapid change. The extent and status of classification within the curriculum for pre-service and in-service training of librarians and other information professionals from country to country also reflect what has been said above. The emphasis in education on theory may be radically different for librarians in different countries, and even in different educational establishments in the same country. But let us turn to the theory, via a consideration of the structure of schemes; the seeking of a helpful order; and the requirements of notation.

THE STRUCTURE OF SCHEMES

Before looking at the forms which classification has taken, it is useful to pause and consider the nature of the subjects with which such systems will have to deal. It will then be possible to examine and evaluate the manner in which such subjects are treated in the various classification schemes. Three types of subjects exist: *simple*, *compound* and *complex* subjects.

- A *simple subject* is one which deals with a whole main class or with a single aspect of a class. 'Surgery' as a subject treated as part of the 'medical sciences' would be a simple subject. Other examples might be 'politics' or 'the Democratic Party' or 'political campaigns' – to illustrate but a tiny fraction of the possible examples of simple subjects in a single class.

- A *compound subject* is one where two or more simple subjects are combined, or treated equally in a text; an example might be 'cats and dogs' or 'painting and drawing'. Ranganathan described compound subjects as interactions of two or more simple subjects from the same main class. Although in the examples above the simple subjects which are combined come from the same subdivision of their class, compound subjects may also be multi-faceted, such as 'monetary economics in France' or 'campaigning in the Democratic Party'.

- A *complex subject* is one where the combined simple subjects emanate from two or more main classes. Again there are limitless possibilities, but examples might include 'market research in book publishing' or 'surveys and their impact on political campaigning'. With complex subjects the two or more subjects which are brought together may not be equal in treatment; they may rather have a relationship to each other, as in 'the impact of income tax changes on the life style of old age pensioners'.

The older general schemes begin with recorded knowledge in its entirety, divide that universe of knowledge into main classes, and then into sub-classes, which are subsequently divided again and again until the most detailed necessary subject has been specified. At each stage a particular characteristic of division is used, as, in the example seen above, we can divide literature first by literary form, then by language, then by chronological period and so on, although the division need not necessarily be in that order. The way in which subjects are divided has significance in terms of the material which will be kept together on the shelf. In the first instance all poetry will be kept together, but French material will be scattered amongst poetry, drama and so on. In the second instance all French material would be together, but French poetry would be separated from English poetry and so on.

This process of division proceeds then until eventually the scheme has listed all the topics it wants to specify, in a sequence which moves from the general to the specific in a series of gradual, regulated steps, so that we might have:

Literature
  English
    Prose
      1945 – date
        Criticism
          Feminist

The approach is that of building up a *family tree*, where at each stage the parent may have a number of offspring each of which might produce a further number of progeny. There are strong links with the approach taken historically by philosophers and logicians such as Francis Bacon, and occasionally such philosophic arguments are called into play in support of the schemes. Because these longer established systems of classification tend to list or enumerate subjects in this way, predicting and setting out subjects in a continuous line and providing notation in the form of a ready-made classmark to represent each of the identified subjects, they are sometimes called *enumerative classification*. This mapping out of existing subjects is reflected in DC and, most particularly, in LC.

The newer method, developed in the mid-twentieth century, relies on synthesis, the fitting together of components in order to specify a subject, rather than on the enumeration of subjects as such. To take the example of the Literature main class again, it recognizes that *language* is one facet of literature, but that all languages will find expression in the same basic literary forms – poetry, prose and drama. It should only be necessary, therefore, to list these once and the classifier can simply take the notation from the facet for the required *form* and add it to the notation for *language*. Synthetic classification is often associated with the Indian librarian and theoretician, S. R. Ranganathan (1892–1972) and was developed in his Colon Classification (CC) in its first edition in 1933. The main principle to be considered in synthetic classification is one which can be seen evolving in some of the older schemes, but which was developed and made a central principle of classification by Ranganathan. In DC, the schedules had provided a listing of certain recurring concepts at just one point in the schedules and these could then be added to other classmarks, rather than repeating the concepts on each occasion, potentially limitless, upon which they might be required. DC had provided a single listing for forms of presentation, such as dictionaries or journals, and for geographical areas, both of which might be used with any subject. Similarly in the Universal Decimal Classification (UDC), recurring division had been used to represent time periods, racial groups and points of view, among others. Ranganathan's work in seizing upon this policy of building numbers to form a classmark, however, is often seen as the essential expression of the theory which has been developed considerably by others since about 1950.

The theory is based upon the argument that, instead of attempting to list all

19

subjects, a classification should first identify main classes or distinct disciplines. Then, within each discipline, it need only enumerate basic concepts, or elements, arranging these within the appropriate category. Each category represents a *facet* of a subject. Most subjects are compounds made up of two or more elements from the various facets of a subject field or from facets common to all subjects, such as form of presentation, place and time. To classify an item, we analyse it into its facets and then focus on the appropriate element in each. We then employ what is called notational synthesis, by linking together in a specified order and manner the symbols representing these elements, or *foci*,[2] thus building up an appropriate classmark.

The differences between the two approaches may be illustrated, thus:

In an enumerative scheme

The classifier would consult the schedules, find the literature section, within which he or she would locate English literature, then poetry and there would be the classmark listed.

Subject	Classmark
Literature	L
English	LE
Poetry	LE41
Sonnets	**LE415**

In a faceted scheme

The classifier again consults the schedules, but this time collects the pieces of notation to represent the Main Class, then from the appropriate facets, such as Language, he or she would collect the required notation to represent the various foci, in this instance English in the language facet.

Main Class	Literature	L
Language Facet	German	D
	English	E
	French	F
	Italian	G
Form Facet	Poetry	41
	Sonnet	415
	Ballad	416

The classifier then consults the schedules for the *facet order*, that is the order in which the pieces of notation are to be fitted together to build the final classmark. This might simply be a listing in a pre-ordained order, or one might be given a choice.

Facet order
Main Class   →   Language   →   Literary Form

The pieces of notation, representing the subjects, from the facets are then assembled in the specified citation order:

L → E → 415

and combined to give a final classmark:

= **LE415**

These are much simplified examples. In order to illustrate more broadly the two approaches to classification, let us consider an extended example. The following are summarized listings of the schedules for the Class *Architecture*, first as they would appear in an enumerative and then in a faceted classification scheme:

Architecture schedules in an enumerative scheme
(based upon the Dewey Decimal Classification)

720	Architecture		726.5	Christian buildings
.1	Philosophy and theory		.6	Cathedrals
.2	Miscellany		727	Educational and research buildings
.8	For special groups			
.9	History, geography		.3	University
721	Architectural structure		.5	Laboratories
.1	Foundations		.8	Libraries
.2	Walls		728	Residential buildings
.3	Columns		.3	Housing
.5	Roofs		.37	Detached houses
.7	Ceilings		.373	Single-storey houses
722	Ancient architecture		.5	Hotels and motels
.2	Egyptian		.8	Large private dwellings
.8	Greek		.81	Castles
723	Architecture (300–1399)		729	Design and decoration
.3	Saracenic		.1	Elevation, facades
724	Architecture from 1400		.2	Plans and planning
.2	Classical revival		.4	Decoration in paint
.3	Gothic revival		.7	Mosaic
.6	1900–1999		.8	Ornamental glass
725	Public structures			
.1	Government buildings			
.5	Health and welfare			
.6	Prisons			
726	Religious buildings			
.3	Synagogues			

This is a summary of the schedules; far more detail is provided at many of the classmarks shown, for example, in the section on health and welfare buildings. The full schedule listing is:

725.5	Health and welfare buildings
.51	General hospitals
.52	Psychiatric hospitals
.53	Institutions for persons with mental handicaps
.54	Institutions for persons with physical handicaps
.55	Institutions for the poor
.56	Institutions for persons in late adulthood (presumably the elderly – but a more politically correct form)
.57	Children's institutions (welfare and hospital)
.59	Other
.592	Veterinary hospitals and shelters
.594	Homes for veterans
.597	Morgues and crematorium

In an enumerative scheme, we are dependent upon our scheme having provided a ready made classmark for the subject we seek to classify. Compound subjects may not have been catered for and if we have such a compound then a choice may have to be made as to which is the most significant aspect, otherwise the subject is classed at the point which comes first in the schedules or according to the instructions given in the schedules.

The following are some examples classified using this enumerative schedule:

1. **The design of bungalows**
   - This is an example of a simple subject, which presents no great difficulties for the classifier;
   - identify the subdivision of the schedules in which one would expect to find bungalows, in this instance 728 – residential buildings;
   - the divisions of 728 are examined;
   - the next stage of division is that for conventional housing at 728.3;
   - conventional housing contains the subject separate houses;
   - within separate houses, we find single-storey houses at 728.373.

   classmark = 728.373

2. **Skyscrapers**
   - Here we have a slightly more difficult example, for from the outline of the schedules listed above it is not immediately apparent where skyscrapers might be found. The categories which are identified in terms of type of building relate to the building's function and not its style. Skyscrapers are in fact located at 720.4 in a group helpfully entitled *special topics*;
   - within 720.4 we have the subdivision buildings by shape at 728.48;
   - as we might expect since its shape is the major characteristic of the skyscraper, we find here a classmark for tall buildings 728.483 at which we may classify a work dealing with skyscrapers.

classmark = 728.483

There is a final complicating factor for upon examination of the schedules there is an entry for apartments (flats) which includes tenements under residential housing, but tenement is as far as we are allowed to go here. Were we dealing with a work on residential skyscrapers we might have some difficulty in deciding where it should be placed.

3. **Ornamental glass in churches**
    - Here we have a compound subject, where the two concepts combined each have a separate place in the schedules; ornamental glass is at 729.8 and cathedrals at 726.6. These two cannot be combined and the schedules instruct the classifier to class decoration of specific types of building with the type of building;
    - we turn first then to the number for churches 726.5 and find that at the subdivision 726.52 decoration in specific media are to be classified;
    - therein 726.528 signifies ornamental glass in churches.
      classmark = 726.528

We are fortunate in this example that provision is made for specific media in church; this would not be the case if we were seeking to classify ornamental glass in government buildings. When an enumerative system fails to list a compound, then the specific work is housed at the general number and so ornamental glass would in this instance be lost amongst works in general on government buildings.

If we now look at a faceted schedule for the same subject area (table on p. 24), we shall see the differing manner of constructing a classmark and of treating compound subjects.

The following are examples of the classification of compound subjects, based upon the faceted scheme above:

1. **Chinese rural architecture**
    - Identify elements of the compound subject

      Chinese   +   rural dwellings

    - locate notation for elements in the compound from the various facets

      Chinese = NA41   +   rural dwellings = 33

    - establish the facet citation order

      place > type of building

    - check whether any facet indicators are necessary
      none   none

Architecture schedules in a faceted scheme
(based upon the Colon Classification)

Facet 1 Place & Period		*Facet 2 (cont.)*	
NA41	Chinese	7	Office building
NA42	Japanese	8	Sepulchral monument
NA44	Indian	8(a)	Other buildings
NA46	Saracenic	*Facet 3 Parts of building*	
NA5	European	3	Floor
NA5,D	Romanesque	4	Support
NA5,F	Gothic	41	Wall
NA5,J	Renaissance	45	Pillar
NA51	Greek	5	Stairway
NA52	Italian	6	Roof
NA56	British	65	Dome
NA561,J	Tudor	67	Tower
NA563	Scottish	7	Window
NA564	Irish	91	Cornice
NA677	Egyptian	99	Decoration
NA74,F	Aztec	996	Stained glass
Facet 2 Type of Building		*Facet 4 Activity*	
2	Building	1	Location
3	Dwelling	2	Composition
31	Urban	3	Plan
33	Rural	4	Elevation
35	City	5	Section
37	Castles	6	Perspective
4	Hotel	8	Model
5	City Hall		
6	Museum		

- assemble notational chunks.
  ### classmark = NA4133

2. Towers in Tudor castles

- Identify elements of the compound subject

  towers   +   Tudor   +   castle

- locate notation for elements in the compound from the various facets

  towers = 67   +   Tudor = NA561, J   +   castle = 37

- establish the facet citation order

  place   >   type of building   >   part of building

- check whether any facet indicators are necessary

  none   none   , (comma)

- assemble notational chunks
  classmark = NA561, J37,67

3. **Models of Scottish urban dwellings**
    - Identify elements of the compound subject

      models + Scottish + urban dwellings

    - locate notation for elements in the compound from the various facets

      models = 8   +   Scottish = NA563   +   urban dwelling = 33

    - establish the facet citation order

      place > type of building > activity

    - check whether any facet indicators are necessary

      none   none   : (colon)

    - assemble notational chunks
      classmark = NA56333:8

There might also be symbols, as we see above, to indicate the beginning of each facet, producing a classmark such as L/E(415), where the slash (/) indicates that the next piece of notation will represent language, and brackets ( ) enclose the notation for physical form. Ranganathan likened this approach, very aptly, to a Meccano set where simple pieces can, according to a plan and with the help of nuts and bolts, be formed into the representation of a complex whole. A fully faceted classification scheme does not then list subjects but provides a kit from which any needed subject can be specified, even when such a subject might never have been predicted at the time of the compilation of the schedules. Ranganathan called this an *analytico-synthetic* approach, in that it consists of two stages: first, subjects are analysed into their individual elements; secondly, these elements are synthesized or brought together to form a classmark.

The distinction between the two types of scheme can also be seen in the following example. Consider the specific and highly complex subject: 'the doctrine of Grace in Methodism in Britain during the eighteenth century'. A completely enumerative scheme, if it could cope with such a specific subject, would try to provide the classifier with a complete classmark for this as for all other subjects. The extensiveness of the listing which would be needed to identify all such subjects, as can be imagined, would be enormous. It may be noted that even the most enumerative of schemes are rarely enumerative to this degree, but the method of listing all topics is essentially the major principle they try to follow.

A completely synthetic, or faceted scheme, within the main class Religion, would instruct the classifier to divide the subject into its component parts and then to build up the classmark by linking together the notation representing Methodism (as a branch of Christianity) from one facet, with the notation representing Grace (from the Doctrines facet). These would then be combined with the notation representing Britain (from the Place facet) and that for the eighteenth century (from the Time facet). The branch and doctrines facets would be unique to the Religion main class, but the Place and Time facets would be applicable to all main classes and would be listed only once. The saving in space in the schedules should be evident and considerable.

As we have seen, classification has to deal with simple, compound and complex subjects. Ranganathan spoke of compound subjects as drawing their elements from the facets of a single subject field (plus facets common to all subjects like time and place); when this is the case they display an inter-facet relationship. Compound subjects may also draw their elements from within the foci of a single facet; in which case they are said to display an intra-facet relationship. It may be helpful to consider an illustraion. Here if we first look at a specific facet in CC, the Personality facet in Psychology, we find listed the types of persons who can be classified:

Personality

1	Child	5	Sex
11	New born	51	Male
12	Toddler	55	Female
13	Infant	58	Eunuch
15	Pre-adolescent	6	Abnormal
2	Adolescent	61	Genius
21	Boy	63	Insane
25	Girl	64	Sick and infirm
3	Post-adolescent	65	Criminal
35	Middle-age	69	Deaf and dumb
38	Old age	68	Blind
4	Vocational	6916	Left-handed

Intra-facet relationship may draw together foci which are quite different, as in 'left-handed toddlers' from the Personality facet in CC's Psychology class; or they may be foci of equal rank, as in 'the psychology of the genius and the insane' in which case the compound is said to display an intra-array relationship. Another example of intra-array relationship might be 'the poetry of Larkin and Hughes', where both are English poets of the same era.

Ranganathan also spoke of complex subjects as requiring *phase analysis* to determine the nature of the relationship between the component elements. As we have seen, in enumerative schemes, simple, compound and complex subjects either must be listed – or there will be no place for them. It is uneconomic for all possible compound and complex subjects to be listed; it is much more difficult for enumerative schemes to distinguish complex subjects with such nuances of relationship indicated. However, these are much more rare in literature: they spring from interaction between distinct subject areas – the influence of A on B; a work on C with a bias towards users in field X, and so on. If we have a simple two subject work, say 'electricity and magnetism', the solution is simple. The scheme should have provided us with a classmark. In an enumerative scheme, we classify under the dominant subject, or if this dominance cannot be ascertained, we classify under the first named in the schedules of the classification scheme in use – in order to maintain general to specific order. An extra subject entry can be made in the catalogue for the subsidiary subject. But phase analysis, as devised by Ranganathan in order to display phase relationship in a classmark, caters for much more complex examples than this, such as:

The influence of psychology on the world's stock markets

Keeping fit: a guide for the physically handicapped

and so on. Older schemes might ignore such themes, or enumerate them when the flow of publications compels their recognition, but they cannot predict or guess at new complex situations. UDC tackles this problem by allowing the linking of numbers for two distinct subjects by means of its general relationship sign, the colon (:). Ranganathan went much further in his CC, distinguishing between different kinds of complex subjects and defining various types:

The *general relation phase* which denotes a comprehensive interaction between two topics in which two subjects are examined in terms of their similarities, their differences, their influence on each other and so on. Such a work would examine the full interrelationship between, let us say, 'the Christian and the vivisectionist'.

The *bias phase* indicating a subject treated exclusively for experts in another subject area, such as 'computing for nurses'.

The *comparison phase* which is used for the comparison of the similarities between two subjects. We might thus imagine a work entitled 'The scholar and the sleuth' or a work 'comparing methods of research in the FBI and in librarianship'.

The *difference phase* which as one might expect concentrates on the factors that differentiate two subjects, as in a study of 'the concept of sin in Calvinism and Roman Catholicism'.

The *influence phase* for a work in which one subject is dealt with only in so far as it has an effect on another subject, as in 'the influence of the Finnish language on Tolkien's prose'.

The *tool phase* is used for works which deal with a subject when it is being used in the exposition of another subject, such as 'the investigation of the imagery of thought processes as illustrated in Joyce's *Finnegan's wake.*' Here a work of literature is being used as a tool in the study of psychology.

These are nice distinctions and potentially valuable, although there may be some debate as to the difficulty of their application and interpretation, particularly in distinguishing between the comparison and difference phase. The radical revision of BC in its second edition, known as BC2, also permits such detailed analysis and exact specification. How valuable it is depends again on the purpose to which we put classification and our having clear objectives or priorities in what we require from it. But phase analysis, like the much more common method of facet analysis, needs to be known as an essential part of the apparatus of the analytico-synthetic classification which breaks a subject into parts and then seeks to specify and connect these.

In any classification scheme, general or special, we can look for the facets of a subject field. Our recognition of them and the way in which elements from them are to be combined are the clues to the way in which that classification has organized the subject field concerned. As already indicated, among the general schemes the two forerunners, DC and LC, are basically enumerative; DC has incorporated a number of synthetic features over the years and this is increasingly evident with each new edition which appears; LC has remained profoundly and unrepentantly enumerative, hence the enormous size of its schedules. As for the other general schemes, UDC was designed for the detailed arrangement demanded by highly specific items such as reports, rather than for shelf arrangement. Because of this need for detail and in order to be able to represent highly complex and compound subjects, UDC typifies the synthetic approach, despite the fact that its original outline framework used as its base the adoption of the enumerative structure provided by DC. The Bibliographic Classification (BC), in its second edition and, of course, Ranganathan's CC are fully faceted classifications and a number of special schemes have been created on these lines.

As we have seen, a scheme may be basically enumerative and yet have some opportunity for synthesis. Originating at a time when these ideas of subject analysis had not been thought through, DC relies largely on the enumeration of compound themes. Despite this, it does give scope, increasingly over the past forty years, for some synthetic classification. Indeed the most recent major revision in DC – to the Music class – adopts a basically synthetic approach. Melvil Dewey called the operation of adding notation from standard tables to the enumerated classmark found in the schedules, 'number building', and developed the base upon which the theory of synthesis developed. To illustrate this process, let us consider the journal title *European training: a professional review of theory and practice.* Such a serial publication is presented in a frequently used format which might have to be specified for any topic from sewage to skiing. 'Journal treatment' is one of a host of such aspects listed once only in DC, in what is there termed a *Table of standard subdivisions*. The number or notation in that Table for periodicals or serials is **05** and so, by adding this to our basic classmark for industrial training and education **658.3124**, listed in the main schedules, we have our final *synthetic* number – **658.312405**.

DC also considers geographical divisions or place to be applicable to all subject areas. We can have economics in France, scientific research in France, French philosophy and architecture, etc.; any geographical area is a potential addition to any subject as such and the notation for place can be added to the classmark for any specific subject without a special instruction in the schedules. Thus in DC there is a common geographical facet called the *Area Table*, which lists all places and regions thought to be necessary; there is even notation for Outer Space. We can add the regional numbers from this table to any subject number from the main schedules, either directly with the addition of the notation for place alone, when we are so instructed in the schedules, or at any point in the schedules with the interpolation of **09**. If we consider the subject 'Magnetic surveys in the United States of America', our basic number for magnetic surveys, **538.78**, is found in the Physics class of the main schedules. By adding the Area Table notation for the USA, **73**, as instructed in DC, our completed classmark becomes **538.7873**. Geographic division might be added to subject terms at any stage in the process of division or at any level of detail of specification and so we might have:

	Notation
Animal husbandry in France	636.0944
French dogs	636.70944
French sporting dogs, hounds and terriers	636.750944
French hound dogs	636.7530944

In UDC, the idea of arriving at any compound by fitting together its elements has been carried much further. True, the enumerative base of DC was used in the initial creation of UDC, but UDC went much further and recognized from the start that place, time, race, language and points of view must all be established as facets common to all subject classes. This emphasis in a scheme which originated at the end of the nineteenth century is undoubtedly due to the fact that, from its inception, UDC was concerned with the highly specific subjects that are the themes of journal articles, patents, conference papers and reports literature, rather than with the arranging of books on the shelf. This emphasis on pinpointing or analysing subject information content for subsequent retrieval has always pervaded UDC. Thus if we had a specific subject 'Patent applications for vending machines in European countries in 1992', we could analyse the subject first by identifying the core theme, that is vending machines, and find this in the schedules at **681.13**. We then find and add the other facets:

	patent applications	(088.8)
	Europe	(4)
and	Year, 1992	"1992"

Having established the order in which the notational pieces should be combined, our full classmark would then be **681.13(4)(088.8)"1992"**. This classmark is cumbersome, lengthy and difficult to interpret, but it specifies the subject absolutely precisely. Later we will consider the question of the citation order, or the order in which facets are combined. However, we should note that the classmark unambiguously indicates the facets to which the elements in the notation belong. For example, time period is always introduced by inverted commas, a form of presentation is always enclosed in brackets and its notation invariably begins with a zero, and notation for place is again enclosed in brackets but the number there begins with a digit other than zero. To the initiated, therefore, (4) is totally unambiguous in UDC, in the sense that it always means, and can only mean, the concept or element Europe, whenever it appears as part of a piece of notation. This means that (4) or Europe can be picked out of a mass of classmarks to identify all the material which relates to Europe very readily, either by the human eye or by an automated system.

Nowadays, whatever terminology we use, even schemes which are primarily concerned with arrangement on shelves, where minute specification may not be deemed so necessary, often consider and make some use of the faceted, or analytico-synthetic, approach, but there is clearly much more synthetic potential in UDC than in DC. At the other extreme, among the general schemes, is the highly enumerative LC. Looked at in a different way, we could say that given such highly specific subjects as the vending machine example or one such as 'flexi-study methods for the teaching of modern languages in the Australian secondary curriculum', an entirely enumerative system would try to list all such specific subjects if it possibly could; unless of course it remained at a very broad level of classifying and deliberately ignored the attempt to deal with more detailed subject provision. An entirely synthetic scheme would build up a classmark gradually after the comprehensive application of facet analysis. A mid-way system would enumerate to some degree and then offer limited further development via synthesis; although it might not permit the full expression of the specified theme in the classmark.

The advantages claimed by the advocates of the fully faceted approach are that this is the best way to provide detail and accuracy in a system. It also enables the scheme to keep pace with the growth of knowledge and the concomitant development of the need for greater provision of detail in rapidly growing disciplines, much more readily than can an enumerative scheme. The latter has a certain built-in obsolescence: any subject which has not been predicted simply cannot be accommodated and many new subjects, which the enumerative scheme has not listed, may simply involve fresh combinations of existing elements. Faceted schemes tend to be slimmer; once we have specified a recurring element like 'Europe' (4), we do not need to list it repeatedly in every context in which it might possibly be needed. Moreover the aid to memory or mnemonic value of such a device is extensive. Through repeated use of geographical divisions we come to know that Europe is perpetually shown as (4); through similar use of the forms of presentation we discover that dictionaries are invariably (03). This is true of other common facets and of course of the other form and geographical divisions, which we readily come to recognize and can easily remember.

We have yet to examine the quest for a helpful order, but clearly this depends to a large degree on the sequence in which facets are cited or combined. A clear facet structure may remove muddle and repetition; it also builds in predictability, as we can see which facets have been given precedence and which are cited later, being deemed relatively minor by the *classificationists* (Ranganathan's term for the creators of schemes to distinguish them from the classers or classifiers who merely apply a scheme to their collection). In our earlier example if, in the Literature class, Language takes precedence in the facet order, then the relationship between literature in any form and of any period is collected together for *English* literature. The language relationship is the one which is deemed of primary importance, because this is the way in which literature is studied as a discipline. The scheme does not display the relationship between prose novelists in different languages, however. The relationship between Flaubert, Tolstoy and Henry James is one which the shelf order ignores and which would have to be investigated via some other mechanism, such as the Subject Index (more of which later). Form is a minor facet in the literature class, and this is to an even greater extent true of time period. Were a researcher interested in the 1890s as a period, then they would have to search in all of the different language sections on the shelves and amongst all of the forms to pick out relevant material. Their subject interest would not be reflected in the shelf order and material would not have been collocated, or brought together, to reveal that relationship.

The extent to which facet analysis is used is not, therefore, the only criterion by which a classification may be evaluated. It leaves unresolved, as we have seen, the issue of whether the classifiers, implementing the scheme, will agree that the classificationist has the facet citation order right and has, for example, chosen to display the most important relationships. No classification, faceted or otherwise, can fully display in a one-dimensional or linear sequence all subject groupings. The ultimate test of all schemes lies in their practical application and in their responsiveness to the most common approach of users. Faceted notation is not simple, as we shall see. Faceted classification is often, rightly or wrongly, associated with very detailed order and the world of information science and documentation. Some critics think that the problems found in these areas are better dealt with through the use of alphabetical indexing vocabularies rather than by a classification scheme. Various specialists in the information field may contest these matters, but we can at least say with certainty that if classification is used, then we must constantly keep in mind the objectives which we wish to achieve and the system's limitations, using it as is most appropriate. For years to come and despite the fluid nature and the clarity of synthetic systems, shelf arrangement in established public and academic libraries and for many new collections will be dominated by classification schemes which are largely enumerative in their structure. These have other, more immediately practical advantages to their implementation and continued use, and are stubbornly resilient, refusing to be cast on the fires of Gehenna. A grasp of the principles of faceted classification is nevertheless important for an understanding of UDC, an examination of BC and CC, and for the grasping of new developments in DC. It also leads us into the study of specialized schemes, the role of classification in information science and the appreciation of much of the research of recent years. Finally, in order to classify consistently using any scheme, an understanding of the significance of citation order and of the eventual filing order is essential.

THE SEARCH FOR THE MOST HELPFUL ORDER

Classification represents pre-coordinate indexing rather than post-coordinate indexing. By this is meant that it links concepts in a fixed and pre-selected order, which is one of the many possible orders in which they might be combined. For example:

Villains in science fiction in British cinema in the 1950s
Concepts
Cinema
Villains
Science fiction
Britain
1950s

The resultant shelf order is likely to be Cinema – Science Fiction – Villains – British – 1950s and is preordained by the scheme; the searcher for information has no input into the equation. Classification identifies the order in which the concepts would be combined and hence the order in which they will be found on the shelf. When we consider post-coordinate indexing we shall see that this is not classification as such, though it may use classificatory principles, nor does it attempt to provide the physical display of stock in helpful sequence. Essentially it employs concept coordination as does faceted classification, but it keeps the concepts separate and uncombined until the actual time of particular searches, at which point the user might specify Villains and 1950s or British science fiction, and still locate readily the desired information. Classification for shelf arrangement selects an order and displays that relationship, at the expense of the other possible orders. Because knowledge is complex, multi-dimensional and constantly developing, this order can never be perfect and there must, of necessity, be many possible orders or groupings not displayed. The purpose of classifying is served by an order which is as helpful as possible to the majority of users, while catering for legitimate alternatives by other means. There are some who contend that since no single order serves all customers equally well, the search for helpful order is a fruitless one and might as well be abandoned. This argument will not stand examination. It is a pseudo-egalitarianism that says that, because all cannot be equally served, we should be equally unhelpful to all.

There are, however, genuine problems for an international system striving to serve a number of different kinds of institution of varying sizes and with widely ranging needs and emphases. Some organizations primarily in the public library sector, far from totally satisfied with the general system in use, have experimented with *reader interest order* for the shelves. This is in effect simply another kind of classification and is based upon home-spun categories designed to serve best the local clientele. Again a more detailed description must wait, but it has been applied in variant forms in both public and academic libraries. The question of whether it has decisive advantages in terms of costs or genuine benefits is unsettled. Certainly it introduces a note of personal flair into subject arrangement. It might, for example, be tempting for a college or school to model classes on its own faculty or departmental structure. Too close a fit may be a mixed blessing, since inhabitants of the realms of academe sometimes need to be reminded that knowledge cannot be rigidly departmentalized – investigative studies and innovative thought often demand the crossing of disciplinary boundaries. Thus the use of a conventional classification, perhaps with some concession to local needs via the use of authorized adaptations, such as are offered by the major general schemes, may well be a better choice. But how do such classifications design their sequence?

Classification schemes usually adopt a discipline-based rather than topic-based approach to subject treatment. Schemes have to take into account not just what might appear to be the *core* subject of an item, but also the discipline or intellectual environment in which that core subject is being treated. 'Water', for instance, may be thought of as a basic subject or concept, but there can be no one place for it in the classification scheme, for it can appear in many diverse contexts, such as 'water engineering', 'water beds', 'water divining', 'water gardening', 'waterfalls' or even 'the use of water in religious rites and ceremonies'. Likewise 'the moon' can fall within the contexts of astronomy, astrology, space exploration and primitive religion. The first stage in classification involves the identification of the context or main class to which the particular treatment belongs. It is customary to take into account the environment into which a topic falls to carry out accurate subject specification and placement within the system. We distinguish between, say, 'transport by boat' and 'boat building'. Many subjects are unaffected by this problem of discipline or intellectual context, but the examples above should show that there are some cases where the distinction is essential to avoid impractical or even ludicrous results. This correct discrimination is called *classification by discipline*: its reverse has been called *classification by attraction*. The end-result of a discipline-based system is that the works on 'water' are not all together on the shelves, but appear under engineering, religion and so on. Ideally, we also need a place for the rare work which treats all the aspects of a topic in a thematic study, that is 'the uses of water throughout the ages', and to an extent DC has tried to cater for this in its provision of the *interdisciplinary number* which is to be used for a topic treated in a number of different environments such as this.

Having noted this at the outset, we can explore ideas for establishing or evaluating a helpful order. Some guidelines may include consideration of how the experts in any subject field would expect their material to be organized; this is what Bliss called the consensus of opinion. Another possibility is to base one's approach on the way in which customers, who may not necessarily be subject experts, demand and use information when making subject requests; or we can look at the pattern and character of published material itself, in which case we are working with the documents as they are produced rather than attempting to force published literature into an ideally conceived scheme. The latter method is often denoted by a term chosen for it long ago by E. W. Hulme – *literary warrant*. This suggestion that the schedules of a system should be moulded to fit published material is based, therefore, upon what the literature justifies or warrants. It may be considered to be an important corrective to an over-theoretical approach. It also ensures that for each piece of literature which exists there will be a corresponding place for it in the classification. However, a recent piece of research by Leslie Morris,[3] in which he analysed the number of works classified in each of the classmarks used in LC and DC on centrally created catalogue records, suggests that the existence of classmarks in schedules does not relate to the amount of literature published. He found that in 1 303 300 MARC records, 80 per cent of the records were classified in 20 per cent of the classmarks. Morris recommends that very many classmarks could therefore be discarded while the remainder are expanded to accommodate the number of works which they are to house.

This is a very pragmatic suggestion but one that is unsupportable in fact. We cannot control the number of publications that will be produced on a subject – if there are hundreds of books on the general subject of electronics, then we cannot artificially subdivide these or we would misrepresent that subject content; nor can we say that just because only a few or even a single writer has written on a subject the subject therefore does not exist. Literary warrant is related to the existence of documents and to the transmission of thought content on a subject. Classification cannot convey the extent of the information that exists on a subject.

Beyond such preliminaries, there are other separate, but related, matters to consider in a review of the helpfulness of order. These are the sequence of the major disciplines or main classes (the *macro order* of a scheme); the more specific *micro order* of subsidiary subjects within the main classes; the problem of creating a filing order through the use of the notation, in which the sequence of compound subjects accurately reflects the most helpful final sequence on the shelves; and finally the conscious use of the A–Z index in order to bring out subject associations which the classification scheme neglects. We shall now consider these topics in turn.

MACRO ORDER: THE ORDER OF THE MAIN CLASSES

Classification schemes, as we have seen, must first list and arrange the principal disciplines of knowledge. The sequence of these main classes or principal disciplines has caused much heart searching among some people. Clearly in using a large collection it will be of value for certain disciplines, which are studied together or closely associated, to be found in proximity physically in the library. Certain fairly obvious examples might suggest themselves to us, such as 'language' and 'literature'. The main class order has been seen by some as important in relating the broad areas of knowledge in a philosophically sound manner and reflecting scholarly thought. H. E. Bliss argued, for example, in evaluating the general systems which preceded his own *Bibliographic Classification* (BC), that they failed to dignify the profession of librarianship in the eyes of the learned. Others have paid less attention to main class order, concentrating on what we might think of as micro-order, the sequence within the individual disciplines or main classes. The argument would seem to be that if there is only a handful of main classes, the user can be simply directed to the broad area of the library in which that discipline is situated and it does not really matter whether the works on 'psychology' are next to those on 'medicine' or 'religion'. Bliss' order at the broad level is undoubtedly good and it also offers the flexibility of alternatives which may be chosen to suit particular library needs.

A more modern effort, the *Broad System of Ordering*, which is an attempt to provide a roof classification for various systems in that it takes the best parts of all the general classification schemes, has chosen a main class order which is certainly very heavily based upon Bliss' model. In DC, the order of the principal classes has been criticized and indeed they seem somewhat arbitrary and haphazard in their arrangement, with history separated from the social sciences and literature from philology; it is based upon the order of an earlier scheme with dubious philosophical origins. Perhaps surprisingly, Ranganathan, working later, was also fairly casual about macro-order, but relentlessly serious about the micro-order within classes. But some of Melvil Dewey's contemporaries were much more fastidious than he on the subject of main classes. So strongly did he feel about its significance that C. A. Cutter asserted that 'nature itself is classified' and both he and E. C. Richardson, looking back to the work of philosophers and scientists for guidance, thought that a lasting classification should adhere to true scientific order. The LC classification, in many other respects so distinctively utilitarian and pragmatic in approach, owes a fair part of its scholarship to Cutter's philosophical explorations.

Another complicating factor in the attempt to achieve an excellent main class order has been the manner in which the relationships between disciplines have changed with time. The link between language and literature, referred to above, is largely one that has been fostered by the manner of organization of academic institutions and there may not be as intrinsic a relationship as contemporary attitudes would suggest. The search for an enduring order of nature has, however, been one of perennial interest in the history of bibliographic classification. Returning to the stance taken by Dewey and Ranganathan, we may ask ourselves whether main class order is really so significant. Subject searches are usually far more specific. Few users come into the library looking for books about science; if they do so, our response would usually be either to attempt to negotiate a narrowing of the search or to provide an overview at a very basic level. Certain main classes do benefit from close association on the shelves; an example might be 'chemistry' and 'chemical engineering', where the user needs to move easily from material on pure research to its application.

Another problem lies in the difficulty of defining a main class with precision. It would be naive to suppose that it is coincidental that a classificationist designing a scheme with an alphabetical notation, fully employing all the characters from A to Z, just happened to find that all knowledge conveniently divided itself into 26 main classes; yet this is precisely what we must accept that Ranganathan found when designing CC. Interestingly, Colon Classification has recently added new main classes and these are represented by a numeral, the alphabetic notational base having already been fully utilized; it is, however, relatively unusual for new main classes to be added to general schemes. DC and UDC are based upon the decimal ten numerals, which may give the impression that there are only nine main classes – the 0 division being used for generalia. Research has shown that there are in fact between thirty and forty main classes. In effect a main class is simply any subject area large enough to lend itself to systematic subdivision or, in the parlance of modern classification theory, to facet analysis, and so to equate main classes with the breadth of any one notational base is an illusion. It is an interesting experiment to attempt, without preconceptions and bias, to list all of the disciplines which are studied or practised or might be reflected in the literature, via perhaps publishers' catalogues, and to compare the results with the main classes identified in the general classification schemes.

MICRO ORDER: SEQUENCE WITHIN CLASSES OR CITATION ORDER

The problem of the sequence of specific subjects within a single main class or discipline is at the core of all classification; if it is avoided, the result is merely a pigeonholing device which may locate topics accurately, but does not systematically relate them. The primary part of the problem concerns the sequence in which a scheme moves from very general topics to very specific ones. To use a simple example, again from the class 'architecture', should an item on 'stained glass in cathedrals' have its elements cited in the order stained glass → cathedrals or cathedrals → stained glass? The first grouping will collect information on stained glass in different types of building at the expense of keeping together all of the data on cathedrals and all of their constituent elements, such as stained glass, spires and so on; the second option separates, by individual type of building, material on stained glass, thus scattering material widely on the shelves dependent upon whether the glass is to be found in cathedrals or castles or office buildings or houses.

Likewise the maker of a specialized classification scheme for the Arts had to decide between citing the facets in the order:

Medium – Period – Style – Country

or

Medium – Period – Country – Style

Whichever facet is cited first will represent the major concentration in terms of grouping, in this example the Medium will be of primary importance and all material in a particular medium will be collocated. There would be a little scattering under Period, more under Style and even more by Country. The following illustrates the grouping and scattering effected if the first citation order is chosen:

Shelf order

Medium 1	1
Medium 1 – Period 1	1a
Medium 1 – Period 1 – Style 1	1a1
Medium 1 – Period 1 – Style 1 – Country 1	1a1a
Medium 1 – Period 1 – Style 1 – Country 2	1a1b
Medium 1 – Period 1 – Style 2 – Country 1	1a2a
Medium 1 – Period 1 – Style 2 – Country 2	1a2b
Medium 1 – Period 2	1b
Medium 1 – Period 2 – Style 1	1b1
Medium 1 – Period 2 – Style 1 – Country 1	1b1a
Medium 1 – Period 2 – Style 1 – Country 2	1b1b
Medium 1 – Period 2 – Style 2	1b2
Medium 1 – Period 2 – Style 2 – Country 1	1b2a
Medium 1 – Period 2 – Style 2 – Country 2	1b2b
Medium 2	2
Medium 2 – Period 1	2a
Medium 2 – Period 1 – Style 1	2a1

Medium 2 – Period 1 – Style 1 – Country 1	2a1a
Medium 2 – Period 1 – Style 1 – Country 2	2a1b
Medium 2 – Period 1 – Style 2 – Country 1	2a2a
Medium 2 – Period 1 – Style 2 – Country 2	2a2b
Medium 2 – Period 2	2b
Medium 2 – Period 2 – Style 1	2b1
Medium 2 – Period 2 – Style 1 – Country 1	2b1a
Medium 2 – Period 2 – Style 1 – Country 2	2b1b
Medium 2 – Period 2 – Style 2	2b2
Medium 2 – Period 2 – Style 2 – Country 1	2b2a
Medium 2 – Period 2 – Style 2 – Country 2	2b2b[4]
etc.	

All works about Medium 1 will be kept together on the shelves, but the material about Country 1 will be scattered all over the Arts class, not even limited to the few occasions illustrated in this example. Of course, modern classification theory regards it as axiomatic that the alphabetical index should display possible groupings which the classification has been forced to ignore, thus complementing the work of the scheme, but these should be relatively minor relationships, a good scheme having displayed the major ones. The alphabetical subject index would in this instance collect together all appearances of Style 1. In DC this is referred to as the collocation of distributed relatives, as can be seen in the example below:

Entries in an alphabetical subject index (a relative index)
Germany,
  Drawing
  Painting
  Sculpture

Good shelf order, then, depends upon the citation order of facets, or, if we prefer the language of older theory, the order in which the characteristics of division are applied. Consider again the familiar subject area of Literature. Different schemes have adopted different approaches. In DC, the class is first divided by Language then Literary Form, then by Period. In LC, on the other hand, Literature is first divided by Language then by Period and, and only if necessary, by Literary Form. DC then collects everything in one place on French Literature, but French drama is separated from drama in other tongues and the literature in all languages of a particular epoch is scattered according to both Language and Form. The second arrangement may suit serious students better, as it tends to reflect the content of syllabuses and to mirror the way in which research takes place in literary studies. It collects and distributes subject groupings on a rather different basis from DC, but the inevitable showing and grouping of certain subjects while ignoring other possible ones is the same. Both are perfectly workable systems and both have operated well in academic collections. There are in both instances likely to be *distributed relatives*, scattered on the shelves, which have to be brought together in the subject index, as we have seen. The important considerations from the viewpoint of helpful order are that the relations shown should be the ones most useful to users of the collection served and that collocation should be consistent. So, to change the subject field, if 'tutorials in higher education' are separated from the use of 'tutorials in secondary schools', this should be because it is more user-friendly, or more likely as a typical user approach to emphasize the age group of those being taught, rather than the teaching method; if 'maths in higher education' is separated from 'maths in schools' this should again be because the age group or level of study is more important than the curricular area. This educational example indicates a more clear-cut instance, in that the age group facet is clearly the most significant element for both students of education and for practising teachers, but there are many occasions when the issue will not be as readily resolved, where the users' needs may be variable and where schemes have adopted variant approaches.

The faceted scheme may be much more fluid than its enumerative counterpart in specifying compounds of this type, many of which may be omitted in a more rigid enumerative structure, which has simply failed to predict all of the possible compound subjects. However, the problem of collecting some related themes and scattering others is an insuperable problem in any classification scheme, whether it be faceted or enumerative. This is determined essentially not by the individual classifying but by the classificationist in constructing the scheme. In modern parlance, it depends upon the citation order of facets; using older terminology it depends upon the order in which the characteristics of division are applied in the schedules. The most important facet must be that which is cited first or that which represents the first characteristic of division. In the last example the 'group educated' must be cited before 'curricular subject' or 'teaching method'.

MICRO ORDER: THE ORDER OF COORDINATES WITHIN A SINGLE FACET

Although not as important as facet citation order, this is not without significance. How do we order foci in an array of equal rank? In the 'teaching methods' facet, should 'tutorials' come before or after 'lectures'; should 'French, German, American or Indian' etc., come before or after 'English' in the language facet of the Literature class? It is difficult to establish priorities among such a group, where the question is essentially one of which should be first among equals. This is a perennially difficult question, whether it is a question of etiquette or of subject classification, as witness the elaborate rules which apply to the former. Sometimes the best way of achieving an order in such an instance will be obvious; sometimes it is almost impossible to determine. In the first example one might work from the largest group situation to the smallest, in which case 'lectures' would come before 'seminars' which would come before 'tutorials', but there may be other complicating factors such as the distinction between 'group and individual tutorials'. Various methods can be used as appropriate and where a logical justification for their application may be found, for instance:

- *geographical order*, where the geographic relation of places determines their sequence;
- *chronological order*, which has many applications apart from the historical;
- *evolutionary or developmental order*, these may relate to the stages in a process or to life stages;
- a *traditional* or *canonical order*, such as is found in the literature of the subject and which has been accepted as a general rule or orthodoxy;
- an *order of increasing complexity*, moving from broader, more general to more specialized foci;
- *order of serial dependency*, which holds that where a subject depends for its existence upon the existence of another, then it should follow that subject in array;
- and *favoured category order*, which is sometimes considered to reflect a bias but may be justifiable in the attainment of an ultimately helpful sequence.

These are all possibilities. The method must be chosen to seek the best possible order in the context concerned and again the needs of the user group to be served must be borne in mind.

FILING ORDER

An important question which must concern any general or special system with at least an element of synthesis is that of filing order. How do we file compound themes consistently so as to reconcile detail with helpful order? How does 'eighteenth century English drama' file on the shelf in relation to 'eighteenth century English Literature' or 'English drama' (in general)? How would the compound theme 'administration of libraries' stand in relation to 'the administration of manuscript collections in British academic libraries in the 1990s'? The key to the answer again lies in the citation order of the scheme used. The order required is that of the most helpful, for the majority, which is a general to specific sequence, where we move from the works dealing with most of the subject area to those dealing with smaller aspects of it. We would, therefore, as users expect 'English drama' to come before 'eighteenth century English drama', within the broad section dealing with 'English Literature'.

Facets are cited so that the most concrete, significant or important facet comes first; remaining facets in any example are cited in diminishing order of importance. It is, as we have seen, in the facets which are cited last that scattering of related material most occurs and where it is presumably most tolerable to the user. Hence our citation order – as has already been established – must ensure that the final linear sequence on the shelves, or in catalogues, brings together ideas or concepts from the facets which are deemed to be most significant and appear early in the citation order, confining scattering to those facets cited later.

As well as such collocation, we also seek to attain a general to specific order within the subjects as so displayed. How do we achieve this effect? Paradoxically, and odd as it must seem on first acquaintance, it is done by filing facets on the shelves in the order which is the exact reverse of the order in which they were cited. The notation of course must be designed to permit this, and we will examine how this is achieved later. This rule of faceted classification is termed the *principle of inversion*.

Let us consider the two examples above and a further notated example from UDC to demonstrate the principle in operation. For the literature example, we shall assume that the citation order chosen is that of:

Language > *Form* > *Period*
English   > Drama > Eighteenth century

In order to file correctly, the citation order is reversed or inverted, to Period > Form > Language. We would then have a general to special order, as follows, for six hypothetical examples:

Eighteenth century literature (in various languages)
Drama (in various languages)
Drama: eighteenth century (in various languages)
English literature: Eighteenth century
English Literature: Drama
English Literature: Drama: Eighteenth century

In this example the Period facet files before form, which in turn precedes language. The Period facet has its material scattered, there is less scatter in the Form facet and none at all in the most significant facet, that of Language. Period is actually filed before Language, when it stands alone, but the result is that the most significant relationship, that of language, is reflected in the gathering together of material by language. Horizontally in determining the citation order, language is cited first; vertically, in determining the filing order on the shelves, period files first. The most important effect of the principle of inversion is that the order achieved on the shelves is one of increasing specificity. What often confuses novices is simply the fact that the most important facet does not file first on the shelves, where we might logically expect it to – but rather comes last. However, this is essential if the most specialized material is to be found at the end of the sequence. Another and more extended example may help to clarify the process.

If we consider the topic 'methods of storing audiovisual material in British public libraries in the 1990s'. Library Science, clearly, here represents a main class and within it we have no less than five facets appearing. These would be cited in the following order:

Type of library	> *Material*	> *Operation*	> *Country*	> *Period*
Public library	> Audiovisual	> Storing	> Britain	> 1990s

These should appear in the reverse order on the shelves:

Libraries in the 1990s
British libraries
British libraries in the 1990s
Storing materials in libraries
Storing materials in libraries in the 1990s
Storing material in British libraries in the 1990s
Audiovisual material
Audiovisual material in libraries in the 1990s
Audiovisual material in British libraries in the 1990s
Audiovisual material storage in British libraries in the 1990s
Public libraries
Public libraries in the 1990s
Public libraries in Britain in the 1990s
Public libraries: storage in Britain in the 1990s
Public libraries: storage of audiovisual materials in Britain in the 1990s

The sequence thus begins with the most general material in 'libraries in the 1990s' and ends with the most specific possible theme in the range of combinations. The sequence also shows again the greatest scatter occurring in the least significant facet, Period, and that everything on Type of Library, the most important facet, is gathered in one place. Of course you may not agree with the order of significance chosen for this or for the previous literature example. If you were creating a scheme you would select what you thought was the best citation order: in evaluating an existing scheme, it is usually a matter of appraising the citation order pre-ordained by its maker. But a faulty citation order does not change the fundamental truth of the *principle of inversion*, that is, that the vertical filing order of individual elements must be the exact reverse of the horizontal citation order. If your citation order is right, strict adherence to it must always give the best results: if you adhere to the principle of inversion and the results look unsatisfactory, it is the citation order, not the idea of inversion, that requires critical review.

A notated example yields the same results. If we recall the earlier UDC example on the theme, 'patent applications for vending machines in Europe in 1992', the filing order for various possible combinations for all or some of the elements shown here is:

681.13	Vending machines	(1 concept)
681.13"1992"	Vending machines in 1992	(2 concepts)
681.13(088.8)	Patent applications for vending machines	(2 concepts)

681.13(088.8)"1992"	Patient applications for vending machines in 1992	(3 concepts)
681.13(4)	Vending machines in Europe	(2 concepts)
681.13(4)"1992"	Vending machines in Europe in 1992	(3 concepts)
681.13(4)(088.8)	Patent applications for vending machines in Europe	(3 concepts)
681.13(4)(088.8)"1992"	Patent applications for vending machines in Europe in 1992	(4 concepts)

We should again have the best possible grouping, the most tolerable distribution of subjects and a move from general to specific. Of course, we may not be classifying to this level of detail but the examples serve to show how a general to special order is achieved and how the various possible themes then relate to the position of others within the desired sequence. The effect of the principle of inversion is achieved mechanically by the notation and its designated filing order: the classifier who is merely implementing the scheme may well be in blissful ignorance of its operation, but as a principle it is important that we understand why and how we achieve the eventual order on the shelves.

THE INDEX TO THE CLASSIFICATION SCHEME

An important auxiliary in the revelation of the order of the scheme is its alphabetical subject index. Each classification scheme needs an index as a guide to the place of subjects in the schedules themselves. This is in addition to any subject index which might be provided in a library as a guide to its collection on the shelves. The index to the classification scheme is essentially a guide for the classifier to find the appropriate section(s) of the schedules where the subject concerned may be found. It lists topics, locates them and includes all necessary synonyms. Essentially it should do two things:

1. Locate subjects within the systematically arranged classification, and
2. show related aspects of a subject which are distributed beyond a single class, often due to the problems, noted earlier, caused by classification by discipline.

The index thus rescues from oblivion subject relationships which the classification has been forced to ignore in order to display its own favoured relationships. The index is an essential tool for the classifier, showing these relationships and guiding the classifier's choice of possible locations for a work. The published index to a classification scheme is not intended as an index for library users or clients; it is intended to be a key or guide to the schedules, rather than to the works on the shelf of the library. It will of course contain entries for all subjects dealt with by the classification scheme; possibly all knowledge will be represented in the schedules to a general scheme and in its index and this is likely to include a significant amount of material that would not be held in any but the very largest of libraries.

Because of its display of these alternate relationships an index which seeks to perform this function is referred to as a *relative index*. In DC, therefore, the index shows the various locations where information on, say, 'drugs' can be found. The classifier will choose the most appropriate context for the particular work from the selection available; the information searcher will be directed to the right context or location, or if necessary to more than one of the locations, if for example the work is multidisciplinary. Some subjects which appear in a variety of different disciplines may have a large number of entries in the relative index. The entry for 'drugs' in the index of the latest edition of DC is, therefore:

Drug abuse	362.29 (interdisciplinary number)
medicine	616.86
personal health	613.8
social theology	291.1783229
Christianity	261.83229
social welfare	362.29

This effectively displays the context in which the various entries are treated and brings together the *distributed relatives*; it also indicates the interdisciplinary number to be used for multi-topical works where no aspect is deemed to be dominant. Some themes will have only one entry, but others, arising as they do at various points in the schedules, will have several. This is rather similar to a reference work, such as a multi-volume encyclopaedia, where for some of the subjects the index may show that the topic has been dealt with in a number of the volumes and that relevant information can therefore be found in various parts of the work.

A few further points may be made about the index to a classification scheme. It is really, simply expressed, the path from the familiar, but generally unhelpful order of the alphabet to the unfamiliar, but hopefully well structured and helpful order of the classification system itself. It should not be used alone, but in conjunction with the schedules; that is to say, despite the temptation, the classifier should not simply classify from the index alone; the index should be used as a guide to points in the schedules at which their topic will be found, and the classifier should then turn to the schedules in order to investigate fully the detail, the special instructions and possibilities available.

The relationships displayed in the index should not duplicate those brought out by the scheme itself. At 'personnel management', for example, material is brought together in the DC schedules on the various aspects of personnel management. It would, therefore, be uneconomic and pointless for the index to reproduce this effect, by listing:

Personnel management   658.3

education and training	658.3124
induction	658.31242
interviewing	658.31124
promotion	658.3126
selection	658.3112
etc.	

Instead, the index covers the spread of treatment, complementing the scheme by picking up on those aspects which it has elected or been compelled to neglect, such as:

Personnel management	658.3
executives	658.407
libraries	023
museums	069.63
public administration	350.1
central governments	351.1
local governments	352.0051

The index is an essential auxiliary, an important feature of a classification, but it is no substitute for a good scheme, despite Melvil Dewey's justifiable pride in the excellence of his original index to the Decimal Classification. It cannot entirely compensate and atone for the fault of defective order in the system it supports: to suggest otherwise is to be guilty of the *subject index illusion*; that is, to assume that an alphabetical key is as good as the main systematic order. As Bliss pointed out, 'no index, however convenient or necessary, can convert an arbitrary or disordered arrangement into a systematic classification'.

NOTATION

Notation is the group of symbols, technically applied, which as a code represent the subject contained in the schedules of a classification scheme in order that these subjects will be filed at the correct point in a physical sequence of subjects.

Notation too is an auxiliary or feature of all classification schemes. Since references to it thus far have been quite sparse, it must now be considered in some detail, as it is the essential representation of the preferred, classified order; it is the mechanism by which this order is achieved on the shelves. Its function is not only to indicate concisely the subject content of materials via a code but also to show and help maintain the chosen order of materials on the shelf. Notation is just one device amongst many; however it is interesting to note its perceived significance for the classificationists as reflected in their naming of their schemes, which in many instances emphasizes notational features. We can see this phenomenon in, for example, Dewey's *Decimal Classification* and Ranganathan's

Colon Classification, so named for the use of the colon – originally the only punctuation mark used – to divide facets in the notation. Given that classification is the technically applied device that translates the aims and functions of the classification into reality on the shelves, we must acknowledge the significance of its role, but it is wise to bear in mind Bliss' cautionary comment that 'notation does not make a classification but it might mar it.'[5]

A notation may be made up of: numeric figures, either Arabic or Roman numerals; letters, either in upper or lower case; various other signs and symbols, such as the colon (:) or the decimal point (.) or inverted commas (" "); or it may be a combination of some or all of these. If a notation uses only one kind of symbol it is said to be a *pure notation*; if it uses a mixture of types then it is a *mixed notation*. The outstanding example of a pure notation can be seen in DC, where only Arabic numerals are used. There is no automatic, inherent advantage in this strict purity beyond simplicity, as most of us can deal with and are used to dealing with a mixture of symbols. However, it is evident from the eschewing of letters from phone numbers that this approach is popular with users. Numbers are relatively simple, familiar to users, fairly easy to remember, convey an ordered sequence very effectively, and are internationally acceptable.

A potential drawback of DC's pure use of numbers is that it may seem to impose a restrictive pattern upon knowledge: a pattern which makes it appear that classes divide neatly into nine or ten parts and no theme has more subdivisions than this. This is equally true of a pure alphabetic notation, but there the base is 26, as opposed to nine with the decimal notation (ten if the zero is used). An early commentator described this feature of DC as the stranglehold of notation, where the structure of subjects is arbitrarily forced into the restrictive decimal base. The base of division is likely to affect the length of notation for detailed subjects. An alphabetic notation has greater capacity to house subjects at each stage of division, without becoming lengthy. However, alphabetical notation does have the disadvantage of being less universally acceptable, the significance of alphabetic characters not being the same internationally. Many schemes do use mixed notations, despite the complications for the user, particularly in terms of establishing clearly filing order, for example, LC, BC, CC and even UDC, if we take its use of symbols such as brackets into account.

THE QUALITIES OF NOTATION

What do we expect of these symbols which we call notation and which stand in place of the terms, so as to represent their order in the classification scheme? There are various qualities to consider; they are identified below in six categories. Some of these qualities are essential, for example that a notation should express and establish a filing order and that it should be capable of accommodating new subjects as these develop; others of these qualities, while not essential, may be highly desirable.

1. Notation must convey order

Notation *must* establish shelf order. It is in the ease with which that order is conveyed that notations may vary. This is supremely important for, unless the sequence of the system is quickly demonstrated by the notation, it will be impossible to locate classes readily on shelves or in the classified catalogue. Since classification is the link between the user and the shelves and between the catalogue and the shelves, the importance of its ordinal, or filing value of the notational symbols, cannot be overemphasized. If we, as users, are uncertain of the filing order of notation, if we do not know which comes first in the sequence we will find the shelves very hard to negotiate and the task of finding materials in a collection will be aggravated; for example, with a mixed notation we need to know whether AB123 files before or after 123AB. Largely this is why notations are composed of numerals or letters of the alphabet or a mixture of both, because their sequence is so well known to the vast majority of users. The greatest proportion of schemes designed for use by a wide user group use a notation which is relatively easy to follow. There may be rules to be learnt, but generally speaking these are obvious and few in number. We find, nevertheless, that classification designed for the analysis of subjects in depth and the subsequent full specification of their subject content often does use symbols, the order of which must be deliberately learnt by the user of the scheme and which may be very abstruse. A bookmark happens to be to hand which provides guidance on the use of a library classified by UDC. This tells us how filing order applies in the Science class and illustrates the complexities which may be entailed for the library user. (In UDC Science is class 5.)

Science Class number filing order

Numbers joined by /	5/6	**File before**
Simple number	5	**File before**
Numbers joined by :	5:321	**File before**
Numbers joined by =	5=	**File before**
Numbers with ( )	5(03)	**File before**
Numbers with " "	5"324"	
and so on.		

Such depth analysis which enables us to specify the form or language of a scientific item, the time period it covers, or other such facets, and even allows the specification of a work's relationship to another subject, has been touched upon already and clearly has great value in the search for specific information. (It should also be remembered that this filing order is the reverse of the citation order used in specifying in full the theme of a multi-faceted item, thus displaying the use of the principle of inversion.) Here, our concern is with the effect of such a filing order on the intelligibility of the scheme and in particular the effect of its notation on the user of the collection. Clearly the filing order has several problems: it is far from obvious; somewhat arbitrary in the sense that there is no parallel from the user's experience upon which he or she can draw; not easily remembered; and likely to result in confusion on the shelves, when material is wrongly replaced by users unfamiliar with the system, and in the minds of the users. Of course, it may be argued that customers lift items down from the shelves and replace them at random in any case, even with the simplest of systems. Yet such habits only underline the need for the shelf to be checked and restored by staff, and the seemingly arbitrary order of symbols certainly demands more effort from staff too. Such a system may also be discouraging to the user who has found a work in the catalogue, whether by author or title or subject, and wishes to locate that item on the shelves. Demotivation will result in many instances. These two examples from UDC and DC illustrate the variety of approach:

Elizabethan drama
   In DC – 822.3
   In UDC – 820-2"1558/1603"

We should bear in mind, however, that, despite the fact that it is used in open access libraries, UDC was not originally intended to be used as a shelf classification and this again raises the issue of the purpose of a scheme. In DC, a system designed primarily for use in open access libraries, the notation is pure and composed entirely of numerals, for most of us an order even more familiar than the alphabetical. Shelf order ideally requires a notation, the sequence of which is clear and/or familiar: classification in depth will emphasize somewhat different priorities.

2. Notation may indicate hierarchy

Some schemes have developed a notation which reflects within itself the relationship of subjects in a hierarchy or family tree. The extent of the notation may represent the level of subject within the scheme, so that a class, represented by one single symbol, when divided into its subdivisions is represented by two symbols and when these are again subdivided they will be represented by three symbols. In the example below we can tell immediately from the notation that CE is a subdivision of C and that CE is divided into foci of equal rank, CEL, CEM and CEP, among others:

Architecture	C
Domestic buildings	CE
Villas	CEL
Bungalows	CEM
Flats	CEP

The word *may* is used advisedly here, for the display of hierarchy is not an essential quality of notation. Equally at times, schemes are, perhaps deliberately, inconsistent in this respect or even eschew completely the attempt to display hierarchy. Users often look for an indication of hierarchy from notation and they may assume that the notation always does this; they think that 753 represents a class which is a subdivision of that represented by 750 or that DHA must automatically convey a subdivision of DH. It would thus often be assumed that 751, 752 and 753 or DHA, DHB and DHC, and so on, must automatically represent an array of topics of equal status. If notation does this consistently then it is said to be a *hierarchical notation*, showing the structure of the scheme as well as conveying its chosen order. Synonymous terms used to describe such a notation are *expressive* or *structural*. Such notations clearly have value for the users of the scheme, in displaying the relationships between subjects not just horizontally along the shelf but also vertically up and down the family tree. DC, UDC and CC all attempt to convey the hierarchical relationship between subjects in their notation often with quite meaningless results in the prevalence of subdivisions such as 'specific types of buildings' at which no work is likely to be classified but which maintains the hierarchical structure of the notation.

The arguments against providing a hierarchical notation and in defence of non-structural schemes which do not do so consistently, include the fact that it is often difficult for mixed notations to reveal the hierarchy effectively and that it is indeed difficult for any notation to be completely and consistently hierarchical. The display of hierarchy is destined eventually to break down in any classification as new subjects are accommodated, for the notational space available may not allow these to be assigned an expressive classmark. An equally strong argument against hierarchical notation is related to the need for notation to be brief and simple. With regard to brevity consider the following imaginary example, endowed here with two notations, one expressive and the other purely ordinal, that is only concerned with showing order on the shelves.

Hierarchical or expressive notation	Subject	Non-structural notation
A	Technology	A
AB	Chemical technology	AB
ABR	Metallurgy	AX
ABRG	Non-ferrous metals	AXD
ABRGL	Light metals	AXN
ABRGLP	Magnesium	AXW

The structural notation on the left lengthens by one symbol at each step of progression or division in the subject chain; the other, which shows order but is indifferent to the expression of hierarchy, does not necessarily lengthen. Thus it can assign a much shorter classmark to the specific theme 'magnesium'. Likewise the notation on the right allocates to a branch of the subject represented by AB the notation AX. The classes may look coordinate but they are not in fact equal. Thus, we are not constrained by the notation as to how many coordinate topics can be specified in a notational array; as we recall this would be a maximum of nine in a fully expressive pure notation of numbers, a maximum of 26 in a similar notation of letters. We can provide as many or as few as are dictated by the subject in a notation which is intentionally non-expressive.

A hierarchical notation may assist the guiding of the user around the shelves of a collection by allowing the searcher to broaden or narrow his or her search easily, as can be seen in the following example from Colon Classification:

D	Engineering
D5	Vehicles
D51	Land vehicles
D515	Railways
D5153	Railway carriages
D51533	Passenger carriages
D515332	First-class carriages (or higher class carriages as it is in CC)

This allows the searcher, who has gone to the shelves for material on passenger carriages, to move to any works which are held on first-class carriages or to railway carriages in general, in which one might confidently expect to find material on passenger carriages. Notational expressiveness is very important in facilitating effective and structured browsing.

An expressive notation also provides a guide to the creation of a subject index to the classified catalogue, as we shall see later. However, in addition to the problems of the brevity of notation and of the flexibility allowed by the notational base which we have already examined, a hierarchical notation may often be wasteful of notational space. For example, do we really need 26 subdivisions of light metals? The BC in particular among the general classification schemes offers good examples of planned non-expressive notation, but the other schemes also have examples of non-expressive notation whether this is deliberate or not. Often the display of hierarchy fails in schemes which attempt to display rank via notational length and one can find many examples where more than nine subdivisions in DC are forced into a non-expressive form. The following example shows the breakdown of hierarchy in UDC's common geographical table.

Australasian territories	(93)
New Zealand	(931)
Australia	(94)

Here the rank or status of the subjects is shown not by the allocated numbers but, as in the 'chemical technology' example, by indentation in the schedules. However the schedules are not available to the library user and other forms of guidance may be necessary to display the structure of a class to the user where a non-expressive notation is in use. The following illustration from the Bibliographic Classification – which we should remember does not employ an expressive notation – illustrates a somewhat unfortunate example where, despite our knowledge that the notation does not express a relationship, we as users feel convinced that there is some intended significance in the length of the respective notations:

JHN	Female teachers
JHN P	Male teachers

The main reason for the breakdown of hierarchy relates to the limited number of potential notations that are available of equal length.

Numeric (10)	Alphabetic (26)
521	ASA
522	ASB
523	ASC
:	ASD
528	:
529	:
	ASY
	ASZ

Ranganathan, as ever unwilling to acknowledge defeat, invented two methods of overcoming this problem – the *octave* or *sector device* and *group* or *centesimal notation*. With the octave or sector device we can extend the array thus:

521	ASA
522	ASB
523	ASC
:	ASD
528	:
5291	:
5292	ASZA

The **9** and **Z** symbols are only used to extend an array of equal subjects. However, the hierarchical display and its significance must be assumed to be lost to the vast majority of users.

Centesimal notation provides **2** symbols at each division, thus providing notational space for a far greater number of equal subjects.

5	S
521	SAA
522	SAB
:	:
529	SZZ

The argument in favour of expressive notation has been much strengthened in recent years by the advent of automatic or online catalogues. In these the ability of the system to expand upon a classmark relies for its value on the notation being expressive, as we shall see in Part Three; it is only in a hierarchical system that all of the expansions of a classmark will bear a subject relationship to the notational root.

3. Notation should be brief and simple

The importance placed upon this in the design of a scheme may again reflect the purpose of the system or the uses to which it is to be put, but these qualities are obviously always advantageous. Simplicity is often linked with conveying order clearly; it depends upon brevity to some extent, and also upon the type of symbols used and the way in which they are combined. If symbols are used in an intelligible manner, that is one which we as users can recognize and respond to, then the notation will be easier for us to handle. For example, XYC(4) is a group of symbols which we can retain mentally, because we are used to seeing brackets used in this way; XYZ(4" is much more difficult for us to translate mentally, either by putting it into words or as a visual image.

Brevity again has obvious advantages, for reading, memorizing and recall. It represents an interesting aspect of notational theory. In fact there are no fewer than four ways of promoting notational brevity or briefer classmarks. One, as we have seen, involves adopting a casual approach to the reflection of hierarchy in the notation. Another would involve the choice of letters rather than numbers as notational symbols; while numbers may score heavily in terms of simplicity and international appeal, letters do give us more symbols to use. The notational base in a classification of Roman letters is 26, while for Arabic numbers the base is ten. A mixed notation would accommodate possibly 35 subjects in array, for 'O' would be capable of confusion with zero. A pure notation of letters, if extremely non-hierarchical and fully employed, might accommodate 17 000 topics while scarcely ever exceeding a three letter maximum; if employing numbers, we would use at least six digits to represent these topics. The best example of brief notation, which is purely alphabetical, appears in the relatively modern, but neglected, general system cast on staunchly traditional lines, *The International Classification* of Fremont Rider (1961). A third way to achieve brevity would be to sacrifice detail, to permit only broad subject grouping. For shelf classification, and for browsing by relatively non-sophisticated users, this is a process which certainly has its advocates. It has sometimes been argued that the detail should be there as an option for those who want it, but the problem with this is that those who do not want the full detail available in a scheme are in a sense paying for extra unused material in the schedules. Again the *purpose* of classification is thrust to the fore in any evaluation or debate.

The fourth factor affecting brevity concerns the apportionment of notation, that is the manner in which blocks of notation are assigned for use with certain subject areas. If the classificationist has allocated notation to subjects in a manner commensurate with their present (and likely future) importance, the result will be briefer classmarks than would otherwise be the case. A classic example of seemingly ill-judged apportionment is seen in the way Dewey allocated as much notation to Philosophy as to Technology, when DC was devised; the result today is that in the Philosophy Class, 100, there is still ample room for development and most subjects housed there have relatively brief notation because the numbers have not had to be extended as new developments appeared, while there is severe overcrowding in the Technology Class, 600, and often very long classmarks. For example, the base classmark for Electronics is 681.381 and all subdivisions have at least a seven figure classmark. We find therefore examples of very long notations commonly appearing in the 600 class:

Measurement and testing of radio receivers	621.38418027
The use of psychotherapy in the treatment of bulimia	616.852630651

While the entire schedule for the notational range 160–169 in DC consists of seven subdivisions:

Logic	160
Induction	161
Deduction	162
Fallacies and sources of error	165
Syllogisms	166
Hypotheses	167
Argument and persuasion	168
Analogy	169

When first producing BC, Bliss gave attention to all four measures mentioned here concerning brevity in the design of the scheme in order to produce the best possible results.

4. Notation must be hospitable to new topics

An attribute, or quality, without which notation would be quite valueless and schemes would be incapable of developing and responding to changes in disciplinary nature, is hospitality, that is the ability to accommodate new topics and concepts in their correct place. Without this the maintenance of the chosen order would be impossible, because new topics could not be housed at the appropriate point to reveal their true relationship to other subjects. Perfect hospitality should mean that any new theme can be accommodated in the most appropriate place. In practice schemes can always find a way of fitting in fresh topics if necessary, but sometimes the new topic cannot be inserted into the most logical or helpful place for it, so the notation cannot be said to be completely hospitable.

There are various ways of achieving hospitality. A crude one is to leave gaps between numbers as they are being allocated, for example we might have in use for a group of coordinate subjects such as varieties of modern dance:

7273	disco
7274	jazz
7276	jive

When a new type of dance appears on the scene, the classificationist has available to them without disturbing the rest of the scheme a piece of notation, 7275, for say, 'hip hop' dancing. However it might be felt that this new type of dancing has more in common with disco dancing than with either jazz or jive and that it is therefore not placed in the most helpful position for those browsing. The other problem with the leaving of such gaps is that they tend to be fairly quickly filled in fast developing subject areas and that the classificationist very soon will find themselves with an inhospitable block of notation. In fact this method does not represent true hospitality; as gaps are filled the notation ends by dictating the order of subjects.

In looking at better methods of achieving hospitality, it is useful to introduce two more technical terms – *chain* and *array*. A chain is a line of subjects moving from general to specific in a series of steps – from the Chemical Technology example above, a chain of subjects would then be:

Technology
  Chemical technology
   Metallurgy
    Non-ferrous metals
    Light metals
    Magnesium

In a chain topics display a ranked relationship to each other. Each topic has its place in the chain. There may be more general topics higher in the chain; these are termed *superordinate* and are said to show greater *extension* of subject, in that they extend over a wider subject range. There may also be topics below our chosen topic in the chain: these are termed *subordinate*, and are said to show greater *intension* in that they focus upon a more specific aspect of the topic.

An array of subjects is a comprehensive group of themes of equal rank, that is a group with a similar level of generality or extension. Thus in an array with magnesium we would find coordinate topics such as:

Magnesium
Titanium
Aluminium

The nature of a chain will be dictated by the sequence of a scheme, that is by the facet citation order. For example in Education the subjects 'Schools > Mathematics > Worksheets' would represent the facets 'Educational Institutions > Curriculum > Learning methods and materials', displayed as a chain. An array in the Curriculum facet would be 'Mathematics > English > Science'.

A major step forward in the provision of notational hospitality in a chain was introduced in the early history of classification by Melvil Dewey with his far-sighted grasp of the possibilities for decimal subdivision of notation. A chain can, using decimal notation either of numerals or letters, be infinitely extended, as can be seen if we examine the following example. Let us suppose that we have a schedule which includes the following subject group:

787.8	Plectral lute family	NJA
787.83	Lutes	NJB
787.84	Mandolins	NJC
787.85	Flat backed lute family	NJD
787.86	Vihuelas	NJE
787.87	Guitars	NJF
787.88	Banjos	NJG
787.89	Ukuleles	NJH

Were acoustic and electric guitars to be added, this would be an addition by extension of the chain and this could be achieved at the correct point without affecting the expressiveness of the notation by the decimal extension of the notation and we would find in the next edition of the schedules:

Arithmetic notation	Decimal notation	Subjects	Extendable alphabetic notation
5616	787.8	Plectral lute family	NJA
5617	787.83	Lutes	NJB
5618	787.84	Mandolins	NJC
5619	787.85	Flat backed lute family	NJD
5620	787.86	Vihuelas	NJE
5621	787.87	Guitars	NJF
	787.853	Acoustic guitars	NJFA **new addition**
	787.855	Electric guitars	NJFB **new addition**
5622	787.88	Banjos	NJG
5623	787.89	Ukulele	NJH

However the arithmetically applied notation 5616–5623 is not capable of accommodating the new additions, unless it suddenly becomes decimal to give us 5621.3 for example. Were a new coordinate member of the plectral lute family to appear, this too could appear at the most appropriate point in the scheme next to the type of instrument with which it has most in common – let us say between vihuelas and guitars at 787.865 or NJED – but the notation would not be expressive of rank.

Decimal notation represents a great improvement on the gap idea and it is also superior to notations of the integral or arithmetical kind, as adopted by LC when it was created. With an arithmetic notation, there would be no space for interpolation of new subjects between the integers 5621 and 5622. There is far more scope for hospitality in thinking of 5621 as a division of 562 and allowing it to be further extended to form the new notation 56215. Arithmetic notations are therefore obliged to rely upon the leaving of gaps, with all the consequent problems which, as we have seen, are likely eventually to ensue as knowledge grows.

Although a fully faceted classification is subject to all of the difficulties of hospitality in array as are encountered in enumerative schemes, it has the advantage of being capable of growth in more than one way. Each facet is capable of being extended independently to house new foci and new combinations of facets can be created when needed. Often new subjects are just a new combination of existing topics. In CC:

R4.56'N	Ethics in 20th century Britain	**can become**
R4.56'N9	Ethics in Britain in the 1990s	**or**
R42.56'N	Family ethics in 20th century Britain	**or**
R4217.56124'N9	Marriage ethics in London in the 1990s	

At each stage it is the notation for the individual facet which is extended and indeed the topics illustrated can be extended thus in a variety of ways. The CC notation is wonderfully hospitable. It does not rate so highly, of course, for brevity or simplicity and this is indeed always a problem for one feature may negate another in notation.

What we really want from notation is such flexibility that we can not only extend a chain of classes as we may wish, but also insert new topics within an array of coordinates. The latter is often more difficult if we wish to indicate the equal rank of the new topic via the notation. Such true hospitality implies not merely extrapolation or extension – that is the power to add on at the end of an array of subjects. It also signifies interpolation – that is the power to insert a new theme anywhere in the array, at the most helpful place in the existing order. The best way to move towards this, although not without some disadvantages, is seen in an idea already discussed, that of non-hierarchical notation. If we know a notation is largely non-expressive and we see a sequence such as:

$$A \rightarrow AK \rightarrow AN \rightarrow AT \rightarrow B \rightarrow BG \rightarrow BL \rightarrow BV$$

then we know the order of the eight subjects thus represented, but we do not know from the symbols alone if AK, for example, is subordinate to or coordinate with the theme represented by A. Suitable planning in constructing any new scheme, most likely to be for a special area of knowledge in the future, could provide for such hospitality by careful notational planning and allocation. Thus, if a letter notation is used, the subdivisions of K must begin at KB rather than KA, to allow for interpolation between K and KB. This, in turn, if it occurs, might be at KAL, to allow further scope for insertion between this new theme and either K or KB. Notation then expresses the order of subjects but does not necessarily reveal their rank. A numerical notation would be subject to the same kind of planning, if used in a purely ordinal sense rather than hierarchically, and with maximum hospitality as a primary goal. It is often in coping with the addition of new subjects that schemes, which in general attempt to be hierarchical such as DC, are forced to ignore the expression of rank, as the following example shows.

799.1	Fishing
799.12–799.14	Specific methods of fishing
799.2	Angling
799.13	Net fishing
799.14	Other methods of fishing
799.16	Saltwater fishing
799.17	Fishing for specific kinds of fish

There is not a single stage of division applied here; angling and saltwater fishing are not two equal and mutually exclusive themes. The hierarchy has broken down and this is signified by the interpolation of the stage of division which is not reflected notationally in the hierarchy for 'specific methods of fishing' and which only applies to part of the division of fishing, that is for 799.12 to 799.14. Equally, in the section on communication in management we have:

651.7	Communication
651.73	Oral communication
651.74	Written communication
651.75	Correspondence
651.7	Minutes
651.78	Reports

where correspondence, minutes and reports are rather a subdivision of written communications. The virtual impossibility of attaining a truly consistent hierarchical notation, suggests that it is in fact unachievable.

5. Notation may have mnemonic qualities

Some notations are rich in actual or potential memory value. The main type of memory aid employed in notational planning is *systematic mnemonics*, where the same group of symbols is always used to denote the same subject concept and can only denote that subject. Systematic mnemonics are very closely associated with synthesis and so it follows that synthetic or faceted classifications have the greatest potential in this respect. Thus, as we have seen, in UDC (4) always denotes Europe. Two advantages arise from this fact: it is easy for the classifier to remember the notation for Europe, a mnemonic aid; and when (4) is spotted within a piece of notation then the classifier, user or system immediately knows that the work has some relevance to Europe.

With such a system, then, repetition helps the classifier to remember the symbol for a frequently recurring concept. This is, however, only one of numerous similarly mnemonic divisions within the geographical facet of UDC and other recurring aspects in the system – for Time, Place, Race, Language, and so on – have the same potential as common facets applicable to the whole scheme. In DC, recurring forms of division also throw up mnemonics, but rather more arbitrarily. We know that if we are dividing a subject geographically and the geographical area we want is France, our symbols are almost certain to be 44. However, the 'almost certain' in the above statement should be noted, because the piece of notation may have to be introduced by linking pieces of notation or may in some instances be quite different. Similarly, if in DC we are dividing a theme to show that it is treated historically, we soon grow to expect, with familiarity with the scheme, that the appropriate DC number will be 09; dictionaries appear at 03 whether general or attached to any particular subject. The difference from UDC's treatment is that these symbols are not distinctively introduced as they are in UDC by the brackets and indeed as they would be in CC. It is also the case that in DC when we spot the numbers 44 and 09 in a DC classmark, they might be appearing in a quite different context and they may mean something quite different from France or the historical form of treatment or a dictionary.

Another type of mnemonic device is the use of meaningful letters to signify a subject and this is known as *literal mnemonics*, for example the use of CT for Chemical Technology and HB for the Human Body in the Bliss Bibliographic system. These have to be used with care: there can be no justification for distorting the scheme's helpful order to accommodate them. Sometimes, too, they may seem ambiguous, while the randomness of their application may be confusing rather than helpful to the user. Ranganathan tried to enrich his Colon Classification scheme with a third type of mnemonic aid, which he called *seminal mnemonics*. Here the idea was to help the classifier to anticipate and cope with the future growth of the scheme, by associating certain themes with each other and with a particular digit. In CC, for instance, money and finance are linked to the digit 6; problems and illness, among other themes, associate with digit 4. This is really simply a clue or a pointer for the classifier in anticipating classmarks for new subjects. Seminal mnemonics are unique to CC and literal mnemonics can only occur where a scheme has a letter based notation, and as noted should only be employed when the order permits them. It must therefore be reiterated that the most common form of mnemonics are associated with synthetic classification. It is through the constant association of particular symbols with regularly recurring ideas that memory aids are systematically built into a scheme.

6. Notation may need to indicate each change of facet or may seek to reveal the nature of phase relationships

We have already caught sight of this in action in systems like UDC and CC and clearly it will only be necessary in faceted schemes. Very commonly punctuation marks are employed in this role. One facet of UDC requires a bracketed number beginning with a zero to indicate a form of presentation, for example (05) represents periodicals as the form of presentation of a subject, (09) indicates some kind of historical treatment of the subject. In CC each facet is introduced by a distinctive punctuation mark, as follows:

Personality	indicated by	, (comma)
Matter	„	; (semi-colon)
Energy	„	: (colon)
Space	„	
Time	„	' (apostrophe)

In CC, when we know the system well we can see how many facets have been specified in a given classmark and we will recognize some of them at least, through this knowledge of the scheme's structure and the significance of the punctuation marks, without necessarily knowing what the precise subject specified is. For example, we would recognize the apostrophe in the following classmark – **BX,3;57'M** – as indicating that there is some form of treatment by period without necessarily knowing which period was represented by M in the time facet; however, given that the time facet is quite a small one we might also remember that it was the nineteenth century which was treated in a work so classified. (Incidentally the subject is solar eclipses in the nineteenth century.) The symbols of UDC and CC are essential to those systems. It is not 4 which denotes Europe and Europe alone in UDC; it is (4). Likewise in CC, R4.56 is quite different from R4:56. It is .56 and :56 which are unique, not just number 56. The facet indicators are the price paid for thorough, often minute, subject analysis and its specification in the final classmark. They are not easy to say and their filing implications have to be mastered. They thus clash with the aim of notational simplicity, with the result that we must ask again what exactly we want our classification scheme to accomplish. Facet indicators can also be regarded as empty symbols in the sense that, while adding to the length of the notation, they do not add to the specification of the subject. It is interesting to speculate on whether it is possible to build up a classmark for a multi-faceted theme without them. A classmark **Bck806** might indicate a four faceted subject in the following way:

B	capital letters
ck	lower case letters
8	numerals
06	numerals introduced by zero

However, we may have subjects with more facets than this, especially if we also want to specify concepts applicable to all subjects like Place, Time and Form of Presentation. These alone would account for three of our potential four facets.

A more revolutionary and interesting attempt to do away with the use of punctuation marks as facet indicators and the seemingly arbitrary nature of their filing sequence is found in the idea of *retroactive notation*. This depends upon notation being allocated so that the principal facets in a subject field follow the minor facets in the notational sequence; with retroactive notation the introduction of a new facet is represented in a classmark by a retroactive step backwards in the natural sequence of the letters or numbers used. If a pure alphabetical notation is used for instance, the primary facets will be allocated notational blocks from towards the end of the alphabet and each facet can be qualified by any or all of the facets preceding it. Each facet change is shown by a reversion to an earlier letter. If we know the notation is fully retroactive and we see a classmark SXLMHRY, we know that there are three facets in this imaginary example and that the elements drawn from them are represented by the following individual blocks of notation:

SX → LM → HRY

It is relatively simple to spot these changes of facet and yet the notation remains simple and the filing order is not complicated. However the full use of retroactive notation requires care in design and allocation. We will return to this topic later in the discussion on BC, for J. Mills, in directing its revision for the second edition, has been a great advocate of the idea. Some examples from early BC2 drafts illustrate the use of retroactive notation perfectly:

DD	Astronomical bodies	1 facet
DDF	Stars	1 facet
DDJW	Dwarf stars	1 facet
DDK	Variable stars	1 facet
DDKJW	Variable dwarf stars	2 facets
or		
VWCO	Military music	2 facets
VWL	Instrumental music	2 facets
VWLCO	Military instrumental music	3 facets

This method appears in embryonic form, if at all, in the other systems, but through it the expression of compound subjects via notational synthesis is greatly encouraged. The idea of major facets coming last in the sequence as allocated, in other words an inverted schedule, also harmonizes with the principle of inversion and the whole question of the maintenance and preservation of a general to special order, which is the most helpful order for the majority of users, which can be found.

The reiteration of this concept, which underlies all of these theoretical explorations, is a convenient point on which to draw consideration of notation to a close. In some contexts brevity will be of paramount importance; in other situations different needs may override it. The ability to convey order clearly is always helpful and hospitality too is necessary whatever the context in which the scheme is to be used, for no subject area is ever static. Mnemonics may help the classifier and there are both pros and cons in having notation closely reflect the chosen hierarchy of the classification's structure. Notation is generally decided for us by the classificationist in the design of a scheme, although it is important for those who apply it to understand its features, scope and limitations. The nature of the organization in which a classification scheme is to be used and the users of the scheme will influence the manner in which it is applied in practice. For example, do we want full and detailed specification of topics and if so will our users tolerate long and complicated classmarks? Classification schemes must be our servants not our masters and, as their representative, notation too must be judged by the service it provides.

There is one further point about notation to be mentioned which may seem prosaic after the various points already raised for discussion, but it is an intensely practical and significant one. A completed classmark is not synonymous with a *shelfmark* or *call number*, which assigns a specific position to each text or document on the shelves. A classmark specifies only the subject and there may be a large number of books or documents on the same subject in the collection, the shelfmark differentiates each of these individually. At least it is common in medium sized and large established libraries to provide a unique shelfmark for each of the works appearing at the same classmark. Thus, if there are six items with the same classmark, an addition usually indicating the surname of the author or some other feature is usually made. This serves three purposes: it gives a distinctive shelfmark to each item which may be very useful in assisting in the location of material sought by author or title and not as subject material; it is also useful where material is not on open access and staff have to locate and fetch specific items; and finally it enables alphabetical sub-arrangement to take place within each specific classmark. We realize that **BG7 Smi** comes before **BG7 Ste**, although both notations appear on items dealing with exactly the same topic. Sometimes as shown in the example just quoted, the classmark is translated into an individual and precise location for each item simply by the addition of the first three letters of the author's surname. However, this still leaves us with problems if there are several works in a collection by the same author on the same subject or perhaps several editions of a work by the same author. There we still do not have unique shelfmarks giving a precise place in the sequence for each of these.

In the United States more elaborate systems have been conceived to deal with this problem which involve the extension of the subject classmark into *call numbers,* such as the *Cutter-Sanborn* numbers. These involve the provision of a table by which the names of authors may be translated into a sequence of figures. We shall return to this subject briefly when we consider the applications of classification in practice. However the essential objective is always the same, that is to identify each item distinctively – and the broader the classification the more important this is likely to be – and to provide a subarrangement alphabetically within each specific theme that has been identified by the classification scheme.

MEASURES OF EFFECTIVENESS IN CLASSIFICATION

Before leaving pure theory to look in more detail at the characteristics of the individual systems in general use, it is useful to review the features which may be evaluated in a classification scheme. Helpful sequences, predictability as to what is collected and what is scattered, appropriate notation and a supportive index are all to be prized. But there are other virtues of a rather different, more down to earth kind to be sought too. These include the financial viability of the scheme itself. Does it have financial support in terms of sales which will allow the employment of classificationists to continue the work of revision and the production of new editions of the schedules? The speed of the revision process, keeping pace with the development of knowledge and the regular publication of schedules are important too. Whether the work is in the hands of a national or international editorial team or just a small core of zealous advocates may also affect its development and utility in libraries.

There is also the question of how well the system is laid out and guided for ease of use by classifiers. Yet another point is that the scheme should deal with all subjects without bias, although there is something to be said for the potential to provide extra attention to the home country and culture. In a general scheme this should however be an option rather than a bias dictated by its structure. Adaptability may also be important; we should consider not only what the classification has achieved but also what the classifier can make of it faced with the needs of his/her own individual situation and the fact that a scheme is far more likely to have been inherited by the present classifier, often from an original decision as much as a century before, rather than having been selected for its present day qualities. The acceptance of the scheme as an international standard with the consequent provision of ready made classmarks in many cases could be very important. The purpose of use again looms large: do we want a highly precise retrieval system or would we be content with a broad arrangement? Have we the needs of a classified catalogue to consider? Perhaps the very nature of searching on shelves with its emphasis on browsing and the serendipity factor, where we happen almost by chance on the very work which will answer our needs, suggest that shelf arrangement is not susceptible to the same kind of classification as might be required for a classified catalogue or bibliography. The idea of a multi-purpose classification may well in itself be a false grail. This is not an argument against the indubitable benefits of appropriate, purpose-related, subject order in the arrangement of materials, but it is indicative of the fact that, in the shelving of items, sophisticated methods which pay much attention to details may run fairly quickly into the law of diminishing returns. Helpful order may mean rather different things in the context of different collections; facet and phase analysis still leave an item shelved only according to its principal theme and complicated notation may be self-defeating when it is considered that junior personnel do much of the shelving and filing.

The impressive body of theory now available gives pleasure and satisfaction to some observers, who like things to be thoroughly thought through. It provides an intellectual credibility that Bliss and others thought so important. It has yielded benefits, perhaps especially in terms of the development of depth classification schedules for specific subject fields, in the creation of special schemes. Yet this section on principles began with a caveat: theory has not been, nor will it be, fully effective as opposed to merely efficient, for it has not been translated fully into widespread general practice and is still only, as it were, 'seen through a glass darkly', or relatively so, in DC. Some regard theory with scepticism, feeling that its practical benefits are slight or unproven – certainly not justifying the travail of extensive and expensive change – and that an evaluation of an author mark system in use for one's own collection may well prove a more useful exercise than a study of, say, retroactive notation that does not relate to immediate need and opportunity.

Sceptics might thus legitimately say of modern theory that it has made little impact on many people's day-to-day practice: enthusiasts might retort that if you ignore it, then impact cannot be made. If you sit on the fence, you vote, in effect, with the unbelievers for you endorse the status quo. Some enthusiasts for the theory must be vexed at the slow rate of its incorporation into general application. They might argue that there is a danger of the constant consideration of the costs and effort involved in change or reclassification leading to a resigned inertia and that there is a danger of entering the 21st century with tools that exhibit all too clearly their 19th century roots. Yet, in a curious way, one could possibly argue that sceptical stances, particularly in the United States, represent the influence of philosophy just as much as the ideas of Cutter or Bliss did, for they echo the voice of American pragmatists like William James that, if something works well from day to day, is reasonably economic and suitably undergirded in terms of finance and editing, then it has its own kind of enduring 'truth' and vitality. Some writers, Perreault in a UDC context some years ago comes to mind, have reviewed the ignoring of theory in a distinctive way. He suggested that American librarians see classification solely as a shelving device and then – because they do not regard their main systems, LC or DC, as wider purpose information retrieval tools – tend to dismiss classification altogether in reviewing the challenge of that seemingly much more demanding context. It then perhaps becomes a matter of professional philosophy and has different emphases in different countries. Again we return to the question, what do we want classification to do? A much more recent reference by J. B. Young from North America comments, most interestingly, on the ageing of the mainstream general systems, which of necessity 'require periodic reinvestment and renovation'.[6] They are seen as representing an accumulation both of 'great wealth' and of 'inconsistency'. Despite the preference in his country for alphabetical subject catalogues, the writer understandably sees some aspects of this accumulation, and consequent growth in the size of catalogues, as gradually undermining the effectiveness of subject headings. The growing significance of the international exchange of information is also undermining this traditional dependence upon the alphabetic keyword approach; for classification can transcend national boundaries and the limitations of individual languages.

ISSUES FOR CONSIDERATION

1. Consider and weigh, in terms of their importance to a classification, each of the following:

*   detailed schedules
*   a good and financially secure revision programme
*   a helpful sequence
*   a brief and hospitable notation
*   adaptability and the provision of alternatives
*   clear definition of and attention to a particular aim or market for the scheme.

Would you want to add to this list of *desiderata* or desirable features?

2. Thinking of a particular context of application, how valuable is the study of the theory of classification as opposed to the study of particular systems?

NOTES

1. Feibleman, J. K., *Understanding philosophy: a popular history of ideas*. New York: Horizon Press, 1973.
2. From the verb 'to focus', Ranganathan used the word *focus*, plural *foci* as a noun to describe each of the elements when organized within its appropriate facet.
3. Morris, L. R., The frequency of use of Library of Congress Classification numbers and Dewey Decimal Classification numbers in the MARC file in the field of library science. *Technical Services Quarterly*, 8 (1), 1991, pp. 37–49.
4. Note that the notation applied in this example would not work if extended in practice: it is included only to illustrate the way in which documents representing these facets would be placed upon the shelves.
5. Bliss, H. E., *The organization of knowledge in libraries and the subject approach to books*. New York: H. W. Wilson, 1939.
6. Young, J. B., Crisis in cataloguing revisited: the year's work in subject analysis, 1990. *Library Resources and Technical Services*, 35 (3), 1991, pp. 265–282.

3   General classification schemes

In this chapter we trace the history and development of general systems of classification, that is those which attempt to cater for all knowledge, to the present day. The major emphasis is upon those schemes which have been established and continue to retain a practical function in libraries. From their description, it is hoped that the reader will emerge with a broad understanding of the principal features of each scheme and the manner in which they are used, as well as a sense of their contribution to classification in theory and practice.

THE EARLY HISTORY OF CLASSIFICATION

It is only possible here to sketch an outline of the history of classification before Dewey. Those interested in investigating further, and it is an intriguing subject, are recommended to consult Richardson's excellent account of the early systems in an Appendix to his book *Classification, Theoretical and Practical*,[1] which contains 'an essay towards a bibliographic history of systems of classification'.

Earlier attempts at classification were really attempts to organize human thought: they were designed to aid the mental plotting of the universe of thought and objects, rather than serve as practical methods of document arrangement or library systems. These can be traced, somewhat tentatively, from Plato's *Republic* to the late 19th century classifications, via Aristotle, Pliny and others. Libraries, too, have a history of developing schemes. We are assured that the clay tablets in the Assyrian library of Asur-ban-i-pal were divided into at least two main classes; those dealing with knowledge of the earth and those dealing with the heavens. Aristotle, too, is said to have 'taught the Kings of Egypt how to arrange a library'.[2]

The earliest recorded scheme was that designed by Callimachus for the library of the Pharaohs at Alexandria (260–240 BC). The main classes have been identified by Richardson as:

Poets
Law makers

Philosophers
Historians
Rhetoricians
Miscellaneous writers

While we have little concrete information on medieval classification, Umberto Eco's[3] atmospheric and soundly based evocation of a monastic library in the thirteenth century provides us with a mystery, the solution to which hinges upon a form of classification, where the villain – that is of course the classifier – has abstracted – i.e. classified, and denied access to humorous and hence dangerous works. In fact the whole tenor of this work suggests an atmosphere in which helpful order was to be explicitly avoided; information being deemed dangerous to the maintenance of the status quo.

The first more modern scheme devised specifically for the arrangement of books in a library was one designed by Aldus Manutius in France in 1498. It developed into what was called *The French System* or *The System of the Paris Booksellers*, which became the most influential and widely used of all bibliographic schemes, especially in Europe. Further developed by Gustave Brunet, the System of the Paris Booksellers has only five main classes:

1. Theology
2. Jurisprudence
3. History
4. Philosophy
5. Literature

and some 11,000 subdivisions are listed. It is not, apparently, available in English, but has had great popularity in France. The Bibliothèque Nationale bases its arrangement upon Brunet and it has been expanded and used with great success in other libraries. It has dated, possesses a mixed and cumbersome notation and is unlikely to be adopted, or even considered, by libraries today. Its interest is largely historical and also lies in the fact that the system was used for the arrangement of several important French bibliographies.

Alongside the development of practical schemes, a number of philosophical classifications appeared, for the pure ordering of knowledge, most notably by von Gesner and Bacon. Konrad von Gesner (1516–1565) classified knowledge according to definite principles, based upon the concept of the progressive order of studies. He divided both the Arts and Sciences into two kinds: 1) those which are primary or preparatory; and 2) those which are fundamental. He envisaged the primary or preparatory arts and sciences as a progression of studies through *divination and magic, geography and history* to the *illiterate and mechanical arts*. From these the prepared mind could move on to the great class 2, the *fundamental* arts or *substantiales*, which holds the great forms of knowledge, all of which are types of philosophy – metaphysical, natural, moral, civil, economic, political, legal, medical and theological.

Francis Bacon based the framework of his treatise on *The advancement of human learning* (1605) on a chart of knowledge. He proceeded upon a definite principle of division to identify three distinct mental faculties – *memory, imagination* and *reason* – and these he saw exemplified in the three classes, *History, Poetry* and *Philosophy*. The structure of the scheme might be illustrated, thus:

Memory	History	– Natural history
		– Civil history
		– Ecclesiastical history, Theology
Imagination	Poetry	– Literature
		– The Arts
Reason	Philosophy	– The Sciences
		– Civil philosophy, Sociology, Politics, Economic Science

Although this reflects the state of knowledge of the age when it was created, Bacon's chart has been profoundly influential. It influenced the early classification of the Bodleian Library; it was the outline of the first classification applied in the Library of Congress; and, via the classification of Dr W. T. Harris, it strongly influenced Dewey's Decimal Classification.

Other schemes of interest appeared in the eighteenth and nineteenth centuries; for example Leibnitz, who produced an early form of faceted classification and anticipated much more recent work, tells us that the classifier is often 'in suspense between two or three places equally suitable',[4] a comment that still holds true and often provides the classifier with his greatest mental challenge. All of these schemes, and those of others such as Comte, have played a part in establishing an effective order of classes, but otherwise have had little direct impact on modern bibliographic classification.

The real beginnings of classification as we know it today took place in the nineteenth century in America with the growth of the Congress Library. Originally arranged by the size of its volumes, the collection grew so rapidly – from 964 volumes in 1802 to 3 076 in 1812 – that some form of subject arrangement was felt necessary. This was not until after the original library was burned in 1814 during the war – the Revolutionary War, as it is known in the United States, or the War of Independence, as it is known in Great Britain – when the private library, of nearly 7 000 volumes, of ex-President Thomas Jefferson was sold to Congress. Jefferson himself classified the collection and his arrangement consisted of 44 divisions, based upon Francis Bacon's divisions of knowledge, within each of which works were sub-arranged alphabetically by title. This scheme, with minor alterations, was used for the next hundred years.

It is interesting to note the state of classification just prior to the appearance of Melvil Dewey's Decimal Classification. Many schemes had been devised which had used numerical, even decimal notation, but they had all operated upon the principle of fixed location in that the numbers had been applied to the shelves and bays as physical entities rather than to the subjects that might be placed upon any shelf. Of course in growing libraries, which by the end of the nineteenth century it was clear libraries would always be, such a system is impossible to operate in a meaningful way. It is far more useful to be able to move the books around or insert new books at the appropriate point in the sequence rather than to specify a number of shelves to a subject.

In 1874, when Dewey became librarian at Amherst College, there was little of use to the classifier in the way of schemes. The British Museum and the Bibliothèque Nationale were working with systems based upon Brunet, the Bodleian Library used a series of partial classifications never developed into a coherent whole and the Library of Congress used an arrangement which was essentially a variant of Francis Bacon's early 17th century framework. There was, for Dewey, a clear need for some more competent classification; the answer was obvious, he devised his own. The most evident influence on Dewey's scheme was that of W. T. Harris, devised for the public school library of St Louis in 1870.

The following table of classes illustrates the relationship between Bacon, Harris and Dewey. Harris took Bacon's basic outline and inverted it to form:

Bacon	Harris	Dewey
History	*Science*	General works
	Philosophy and Religion	Philosophy, Religion
	Sociology and Politics	Sociology
	Natural sciences and	Science and
	Useful arts	Useful arts
Poesy	*Art*	Fine Arts
	Fine arts	Literature
	Poetry	
	Pure fiction	
	Literary Miscellany	
Philosophy	*History*	History
	Geography, travel	Biography
	Civil history	Geography and travel
	Biography	
	Appendix	
	Miscellany	

This basis on Bacon's structure helps to explain some of the criticisms which have been made of Dewey's main class order in DC. The separation, for example, of Sociology from History can be better understood in this context. This then takes us in our survey of the historical development of classification to the appearance of Melvil Dewey's scheme in 1876.

GENERAL CLASSIFICATION SYSTEMS: HISTORICAL MILESTONES FROM 1876 TO DATE

After our necessarily brief examination of the early history of classification, let us now turn our attention to an overview of the eight general systems in their historical setting. The scene is then set for a more detailed consideration of the five general schemes that are in use today.

1. The Dewey Decimal Classification (DC)

Devised in 1873 and published (anonymously) in 1876, the first edition of DC with schedules and index totalled only 42 pages. And yet it was thought by some to be too detailed! Its creation and publication were extremely timely, coinciding with the switch by public libraries to open access for their users, at which point it became evident that they would require some form of relative location by subject. DC was practical, simple, and its notation gave it universal appeal. A promise in the second edition of 'integrity of numbers', that is, that there would be no drastic changes in the allocation of numbers to subjects, may well have restricted subsequent endeavours at radical revision, but it provided a much needed assurance of stability of the basic structure of the scheme for libraries considering the adoption of DC. This was to be no theoretical scheme, changed at the whim of the classificationist. DC went from strength to strength and is now in its twentieth edition. In a historical review, Ranganathan paid DC's creator, Melvil Dewey (1851–1931), the dubious compliment of saying that the scheme was so good that it inhibited further creative thinking on the subject.

2. The Expansive Classification (EC)

This scheme was devised by another librarian from the United States of America, who was some 14 years older than Dewey – Charles Cutter. Appearing between 1891–1893, the Expansive Classification was much more inclined than DC to seek philosophical justification for its sequence of classes and claimed that an evolutionary order of progression was used. Its notation was mixed, but consisted mainly of letters. Its name derives from the fact that it consisted of seven separate classifications of increasing degrees of detail, the idea being that as a collection grew, it could readily move from a broad arrangement to a more detailed one. This interesting idea proved difficult to translate into practice. The scheme was never quite completed. It is described in the past tense here because, although Cutter's place in the history of librarianship in the USA is secure, it is largely for his achievements in other fields. His classification lives on only through its ideas and the influence it had on two later systems.

3. The Library of Congress Classification

Developed as a 'team enterprise' in the first few years of the twentieth century to provide a scheme for use with the vast Library of Congress collection, it has nevertheless been applied to several other collections in various parts of the world, mostly in universities or other academic institutions and in some special libraries. This is largely because its detail and emphasis are deemed by some to render it more suitable than DC for the arrangement of large, scholarly libraries. Each class is published separately and can be used on its own as a special classification. It bears the mark of Cutter's influence in many parts of its basic structure, but it is strenuously pragmatic in its outlook. It has a mixed notation and its date of origin and desire for detail, to reflect the *literary warrant* of a huge library, combine to make it the most enumerative of the classifications in general use.

4. The Universal Decimal Classification (UDC)

The origins of UDC lie in Europe. It was developed by the predecessor of the organization now known as the International Federation of Documentation (FID) at the end of the 19th century. The first full edition was published in French in 1905. Subsequent editions, some of which have been abridged versions, have appeared in various languages. Its creation was a conscious attempt to develop – with permission – and redesign DC, in order to meet the needs of precise classification for highly specific themes, such as might be the subject matter of periodical articles, patents, standards, conference papers and similar literature, rather than books. It allows for a very wide range of what we would now call facets, accommodating in its own distinctive way such nuances of emphasis as Time Periods, Form of Presentation and the Language employed by the item to be classified. It developed from DC, but in a very different way, and in some respects pointed the way forward to CC and synthetic classification.

5. The Subject Classification (SC)

First published in 1906 and designed by the influential British librarian J. D. Brown as a simple system for British public libraries, the Subject Classification has sometimes been criticized for defective subject analysis through its ignoring of the principle of classification by discipline. In attempting to bring together material on topics like 'money', 'ships', 'the human body' and 'speech', Brown ignored the valid distinctions for the information seeker which exist between, for example, 'numismatics' and 'monetary economics' in searching for information on money; between 'ship building' and 'sea transport' in treating ships; the huge difference in discussion of the human body in 'physical exercise' and 'funerals'; and of speech as it is of interest to the 'orator' and the 'ventriloquist'. The one place per subject index to SC is similarly defective. Yet the scheme has a spirited and in some ways far-seeing introduction, some interesting examples of synthesis, and some useful collocations of pure and applied science. It is salutary to reflect that its final demise came about not because of deficiencies in order or lack of revision, but because local government organization merged the few users of the scheme into larger, and hence Dewey-favouring, units. This would have been particularly galling for Brown, who had rejected DC because of its American bias.

6. The Colon Classification (CC)

The Colon Classification was first published in 1933, the work of a restless, insistent and uncompromising Indian librarian, S. R. Ranganathan (1892–1972). It adopts a main class structure, but thereafter within each main class operates on fully faceted lines. Each class has a (varied) number of facets and the order in which these are combined or cited is controlled by means of a facet formula based upon Ranganathan's view of the fundamental categories. The scheme is little used, especially outside India; it has, however, been immensely influential, both on the development of theory and on the making of new special classifications. The ideas and even indeed the language of CC are also percolating into the other general schemes, to a greater or lesser extent.

7. The Bibliographic Classification (BC)

Henry Evelyn Bliss (1870–1955) believed for many years that libraries needed a more erudite system than DC to win more intellectual respectability in the eyes of subject specialists and of educators. His long evolving system was eventually published between 1940–1953. BC special features include alternative location for certain themes where expert views might differ, short notation, and some selective linking of pure and applied sciences. BC has been used mainly in Britain and the Commonwealth countries. It is now being revised as a faceted classification within the much praised original BC outer shell or structure; this process too has been long evolving, from 1969 to date.

8. The International Classification

Produced by the distinguished American librarian, Fremont Rider, in 1961 in a reaction against synthetic classification, this system is unused and deserves mention only because of the boldness of its conception and because all the general schemes have a potential contribution to make to the evaluation of what classification should or does seek to achieve. Rider produced a broad classification which was up to date in detail but deliberately *archaic* in the sense that he returned to the original principles of enumerative classification. He felt that a scheme aimed at ordering materials on shelves was better without too many refinements. IC, therefore, simply enumerates some 16 000 topics, without any synthetic features. He suggested that, because of the cost and effort of reclassification, libraries should only adopt his system if profoundly dissatisfied with what they had already – shrewd advice, but hardly the best possible marketing ploy. As an admirer and biographer of Dewey, he tried to provide a new start, for anyone wanting it, in the original spirit of Dewey, although for brevity of classmarks he selected a pure notation of capital letters. No one seemed interested! Even the theorists have ignored IC. In its own way, this very neglect may be seen as an instructive commentary. It may be difficult to succeed if your system is different from DC: it seems it is even more difficult if it is a scheme fundamentally of the same type as Dewey's.

Because of their lack of current use and the fact that they are unlikely to further develop, we shall leave the *Subject Classification*, *Enumerative Classification* and *International Classification* and, instead, look in more detail at the *live* schemes, which are being used today and display some vitality in their development.

THE FIVE MAJOR GENERAL SCHEMES

1. THE DEWEY DECIMAL CLASSIFICATION (DC)

The first modest edition of the Dewey Decimal Classification, consisting in total of only 42 pages, appeared in 1876. In 1989 the 20th edition was published in four volumes: Volume 1 the introduction and auxiliary tables; Volumes 2 and 3 the schedules; and Volume 4 the index with – for the first time – a manual of practice.

DC appeared on the library scene at a time when libraries were about to change from closed access – with their reliance on often purely arbitrary arrangement by, for example, accession number, by size or by some other artificial and meaningless feature – to the open-access principle, where users would have freedom to browse amongst the stock and where a subject arrangement would be likely to be of greater value. This happy coincidence of timing was a major reason for DC's initial popularity and is a factor in its continuing success. Indeed today DC remains the most heavily used of the general classification schemes, used as it is in all five continents and having been translated into over thirty languages. In the introduction to the 20th edition[5] we are told that DC is used in 95 per cent of all public and school libraries, 25 per cent of all college and university libraries and 20 per cent of special libraries in the United States. Usage has clearly decreased since the figures given in 1951, when in the United States 89 per cent of all college and university libraries and 64 per cent of all special libraries used DC. There has been an acknowledged shift to the Library of Congress Classification in the academic library sphere. However, in 1992 Russell Sweeney's[6] analysis of the application of DC showed that it was used by over 200,000 libraries in 135 countries and has been translated into 30 languages, so its popularity overall is still enormous. Not only is DC extensively used for physical location of materials, it has also been used in many bibliographies and abstracting services, for example the British National Bibliography uses DC for its classified sequence. This has undoubtedly reinforced the popularity of the scheme, ensuring that DC classmarks are available on all records created by the British Library and hence on purchased catalogue records.

The first edition of DC established the basic structure and the principles upon which it was to develop. DC regards knowledge as unity which is to be divided into nine large classes with a tenth general class.

0	General works
1	Philosophy and psychology
2	Religion
3	Social sciences
4	Philology
5	Natural sciences and mathematics
6	Technology
7	The Arts
8	Literature and rhetoric
9	Geography and History

Each of these classes is further broken down into nine divisions, for example:

300	Social sciences
310	General statistics
320	Political science*
330	Economics
340	Law
350	Public administration
360	Social services
370	Education
380	Commerce
390	Customs, etiquette, folklore

These divisions are, thereafter, further subdivided into nine sections, for example

324	The political process
324.2	Political parties
324.22	Leadership
etc.	

In this manner, DC uses its decimal notation to display the hierarchy of subjects. This is a desirable end but leads to anomalies in the practical development of the schedules, in that options are restricted to nine places at each stage of division and if a concept has more than nine equal subdivisions, then the hierarchy breaks down. The notation is simple and purely numeric, which has limitations but enhances DC's international appeal.

The original apportionment of notation at the three digit level has since been criticized, resulting in the overcrowding of certain classes with their lengthy notation, as, for example in electronics where a six digit number is the base, while in other more static classes the notation is underused and classmarks are correspondingly short. This is particularly so in class 200 Religion.

Some of these problems have been compounded by the policy of *integrity of numbers* which had assured users that no major notational relocations would be made and that no three digit number would be reassigned. This assurance added immeasurably to the popularity of DC amongst libraries reluctant to endure the upheaval of massive reclassification. It also increases familiarity with the basic notation for users and classifiers. However recent editions have broken away from this policy and have completely recast parts of the schedules to conform with modern needs. The growth of DC from its initial 36 pages of schedules and tables to its present near 2 000 pages illustrates the expansibility of the scheme and its hospitality to new and developing subjects.

Synthesis has always been present along with enumeration in DC, but has often appeared only in embryonic form. The schedules themselves are chiefly enumerative but incorporate a number of synthetic devices. These include:

● The seven Auxiliary Tables to be used in conjunction with base numbers from the schedules.

1. Standard Subdivisions – a miscellany of recurring concepts, forms etc.
2. Geographical areas, historical periods, persons.
3. Subdivisions for individual literatures, including methods for dealing with literary forms, individual authors and collective works.
4. Subdivisions for individual languages.
5. Racial, ethnic, national groups.
6. To specify the language in which a document appears.
7. Groups of persons.

Only Tables 1 and 2 can be used with any number in the schedules, the others can only be used when instructions to do so appear in the schedules.

● The 'add to' instruction which allows relevant notation from other subjects to be added to particular base numbers. For example at 359.325 we are told to add to the base number the numbers following 623.82 for specific kinds of naval ships. Therefore the number for naval cruisers is 359.3253 within the discipline Military Science.

● 'Add Tables' are provided in sections of the schedules, for example in 362–363, social problems and services, there is a fairly extensive listing of concepts such as residential care which may be added to appropriate categories, such as veterans, where instructed.

● Special classes where synthesis has been built into their design, such as Law, 340, and more recently Music, 780. The Literature class has also increasingly depended upon number building for detailed specificity.

Clearly then synthesis has grown with the development and revision of DC, although because it has evolved in a haphazard and 'grafted on' fashion we are left with a somewhat confusing mixture of devices.

DC's Relative Index which appeared in the first edition was originally a much lauded feature of which Melvil Dewey was very proud. It brought together the various aspects of a topic which had been scattered throughout the disciplines in the schedules thus complementing the shelf order, for example:

Fur clothing	391
commercial technology	685.24
customs	391
home-sewing	646.4
see also clothing	

Today the Relative Index seems fairly conventional and all the other general schemes offer some similar form of index (or indexes). It includes, as can be seen, cross references and in the 20th edition has introduced a new mechanism for dealing with multidisciplinary works, the interdisciplinary number, which is the recommended number to be chosen, where parts of a work might be classified at a variety of points. In the example above, 391 would be chosen for a work which dealt with the customs relating to fur clothing and its manufacture at home.

A degree of flexibility is built into DC. Broad classification is comparatively easily implemented because of the hierarchical nature of the notation and the degree of truncation is left to the discretion of the classifier. There is an abridged edition of the schedules available for school and public library use. Another feature which reflects awareness of the individual library's needs is the provision of options at various points in the schedules. These are often necessary to counter the admittedly Western/Christian bias of the scheme and allow classifiers to give preferred treatment to, for example, a specific geographic area, a language or a religion.

Another new and welcome feature of the 20th edition of DC has been the incorporation of instructions, which previously appeared scattered throughout the text, into a discrete manual of practice. Arranged to mirror the order of the schedules the manual explicates and illustrates the notation and instructions to be found in the schedules and auxiliary tables. This is a helpful feature in that it has removed extensive discussion and explanation from the schedules. However it does mean that often in order to classify a work one is forced to consult the schedules, the Index (to check alternatives), the Tables, the manual and even the Introduction to the schedules for assistance, particularly if one is a novice classifier. The size of the manual and the number and detailed nature of the instructions found throughout the schedules are evidence of the problems which the scheme has encountered due to its lack of a sound theoretical base.

Revision and administration of DC

In the space of 116 years DC has gone through 20 editions and the 21st is scheduled for 1996 – a new edition every six years approximately. Over that period there has been a growth in the size of the schedules and in the detail it is possible to specify. The growth has not always been steady however and the 15th edition in 1951 attempted to introduce a fairly drastic restructuring of the scheme, in an effort to modernize the scheme overall. However the 15th edition was regarded by many users as virtually a new, and thus highly unpopular, classification and edition 16 returned to a traditional pattern, dropping most of the relocations and restoring much of the detail its predecessor had rejected. Since then subsequent editions have followed a more conservative course of moderate revision of areas in which the necessity for change is agreed and of steady expansion to accommodate growing subjects. In addition sections of the schedules where considerable revision is demanded are periodically identified and receive a thorough overhaul. These recreations were known as *Phoenix Schedules*, an appropriately figurative term, but are now termed more prosaically, by DC, *complete revisions*.

The actual responsibility for the development and revision of DC lies with the Decimal Classification Division at the Library of Congress, whose work involves the classification of works for which MARC records and Library of Congress catalogue cards are being prepared. This ensures that the scheme is based upon literary warrant, reflecting the literature which is being published, and devising numbers which correspond to subjects as they are written about, rather than in the abstract. The Decimal Classification Division submits proposals for amendments and extensions to the DC Editorial Policy Committee for consideration. Sections of the scheme which are to receive complete revision (or phoenixing as it was known until the present edition) are decided upon by the publishers, OCLC and the Editorial Policy Committee, and these completely revised parts may be published as part of a new edition, as was Music in the 20th edition, or as separates, as for example Data Processing which was published initially as a separate schedule, subsequently incorporated into the next new edition. These are subjects where change and expansion have been dramatic or where developments have led to changes in the way in which a topic is viewed. When sections to be phoenixed are revised the policy of integrity of numbers is ignored. Early warnings of suggested major changes are announced in *Decimal Classification, Annotations, Notes and Decisions*, known more briefly as DC&. This periodical publication also explains the decisions taken by the Decimal Classification Division and serves as a forum for users' problems, questions and points of view.

Current evaluation of the Decimal Classification

DC has a long history, a sound administration and a great number of adherents. Theoretically it may not be as sound as modern classificationists might wish, having evolved from practical considerations and many of its features having being devised in response to problems rather than designed in anticipation of them. However, that development may well be attributed to the fact that DC was in many ways a trail-blazer and modern theory has learnt much from the problems encountered and the solutions implemented by DC – and indeed from its omissions and errors. The slowness with which revision takes place is one point upon which DC has often been criticized. To level the balance one must bear in mind that the users of DC, often large public library services, are naturally somewhat loath to undertake regular major revision with all the concomitant practical problems and considerations involved. Indeed there are those who are highly critical of the quantity of revision and reclassification already involved. Sanford Berman[7] charges the publishers with a commercial desire to sell new editions rather than concern for the improvement of the scheme as the motivation for frequent new editions and the Library Association Dewey Decimal Committee is concerned that the proposed 21st edition scheduled for publication in 1996 is following too swiftly on the heels of the 20th in 1989.[8] Certainly at a cost of £200 per copy the financial implications alone are not insignificant. The result may well be libraries not adopting new editions and unwilling to implement changes and improvements, an undesirable situation for the libraries or for DC.

DC remains for many the most acceptable general scheme. Its use is growing internationally and it has many excellent qualities such as the hospitality of its notation via the device of decimal division; the quality of instruction and guidance provided throughout the schedules and the manual; the concern of the administration to respond to users' interests and requirements; its history which has demonstrated DC's adaptive qualities and the ensured continuation of the scheme; the growing acknowledgement in DC of the need to cater for differing approaches to culture and religion; the universality and simplicity of the notation; and the extensive use which is made of DC in bibliographic sources and the availability of DC classmarks in centralized cataloguing records. DC is now available in electronic form – the *Electronic Dewey* – where the scheme's structure allows the classifier to track hierarchical relationships. Numbers are linked to a maximum of five LCSH headings and the searcher can enter a keyword and main class and be directed to the classmarks, related classmarks and the corresponding LCSH terms. The approach may be via keywords, phrases or classmarks and online help, of a limited kind, is available. As a working tool the *Electronic Dewey* is still at an early stage and we should expect to see improvements and developments as it is monitored in practice. Future developments are likely to include the implementation of methods of establishing authority control both of vocabulary and of the choice of classmark. Future editions of the *Electronic Dewey* should also provide a dictionary of definitions and scope notes to guide the classifier.

It has been suggested that electronic access to schedules will lessen the sudden and drastic impact of new editions and hence render revision a less demanding but more continuous process and a more attractive proposition for libraries. *Electronic Dewey* schedules will be published annually, complete with updates, thus offering the potential for a more gradual process of revision. In print editions have not appeared so frequently. A more orderly process of revision which ensures mature and thorough consideration of the whole and is based upon a philosophic or consensus classificatory vision might be deemed desirable, if utopian. The likelihood is that DC will proceed in a more workmanlike and pragmatic manner to change where change is necessary and demanded. In the 21st edition, we can expect to see the 350s, *public administration*, completely revised and the present bias towards the USA in the class to be removed; *education*, too, will be updated to ensure that present educational practice is better represented in, for example, removing the present over-emphasis of religious and single-sex schools. Interestingly, the new edition will see the introduction of the use of facet indicators, reflecting the increasing importance of synthesis in the scheme overall.

Criticisms of DC have largely taken the form of attacks upon its theoretical principles and the fact that its use is not based upon the clear analysis of subjects into definite categories. The main class order has been criticized for faults such as the separation of language and literature. Bliss described the main class order as unphilosophic and impractical. However, one must acknowledge equally the impracticability of such major changes as the correction of main class order at this advanced stage of DC's evolution. Criticisms have also been made by D. J. Foskett, for example, of the rigidity of the scheme's framework and in particular the straitjacket of the decimal process, providing as it does a restricted base for subjects at each stage of division. Charles Martel, the Chief Cataloguer of the Library of Congress, said of DC when the Library of Congress was considering the choice of a classification scheme, that it was a 'system bound up in and made to fit the notation, and not the notation to fit the classification'.[9]

And what of DC's plans for the long-term future? The overriding concern, judging by DC's research agenda, would seem to be to ensure that DC is at the leading edge in the interaction between classification and technology, whether this is via the exploitation and maximization of the effectiveness of the *Electronic Dewey*, or via the development of the use of DC in OPACs and electronic databases and systems, such as the Internet. Other areas of interest centre upon the desire to apply general classificatory principles to other tools of information retrieval, such as thesauri, and to make DC easier to use and to apply, via the improvement of the Index and of the instructions throughout the schedules.

There are now close links between OCLC, the Dewey Policy Committee and the Library of Congress, via its DC Division, and these should be built upon to maximize the effectiveness of the systems for which each is responsible. However, it is likely that two major factors – the accessibility and universality of DC's notation or language and the scheme's administrative support and extensive use in libraries – will ensure DC's continuing influential position in general classification.

2. THE LIBRARY OF CONGRESS CLASSIFICATION (LC)

The Library of Congress was set up in 1800 to provide a reference collection for the government of the United States in Washington. By 1870, ensuring that copyright deposit was strictly adhered to, the then librarian Ainsworth Rand Spofford was supervising the enormous growth of the collection and its metamorphosis into a true national rather than governmental library.

As the collection grew to almost a million books, with annual accessions of approximately 100,000 items, the space which had been allocated in the Capitol for the library, basically a series of rooms, and even corridors which were latterly pressed into use, was no longer sufficient. In 1897 it was moved to its new and handsome home – which, it was felt, ought to be a showpiece, representative of the culture of the American people, the Thomas Jefferson Building. Until that date material had been arranged according to the system devised by Thomas Jefferson, whose personal collection had formed a major constituent of the library's stock. The Jeffersonian system consisted of 44 main classes and their subdivisions, within which a system of fixed locations operated to determine the shelf locations of individual works. However, in the decades prior to the move even that arrangement had broken down and any consistency in arrangement had disappeared. With the physical removal of the library came the opportunity to instigate a variety of changes, not least the opportunity to investigate and adopt a more helpful and flexible arrangement. It might have been expected that an existing scheme would have been chosen and indeed three were considered: the Dewey Decimal Classification, Charles Cutter's Expansive Classification and Otto Hartwig's *Halle Schema*. It is interesting to speculate upon the developments which might have arisen had DC been chosen, but DC was rejected, largely because Melvil Dewey was, as ever, reluctant to see control of the scheme fall into other hands and to allow the Library of Congress to modify and alter the scheme to suit its own requirements. The *Halle Schema* was felt to be inappropriate because of its bias towards German scholarship and tradition and Cutter's Expansive Classification became almost by default the base upon which what was largely a new and independent classification would be developed.

Even at the level of the main classes, there were considerable changes to Cutter's scheme and from that point new schedules were developed. LC was created by individual teams working on each class and within these teams individuals would work independently on their own particular subject specialisms under the coordinating control of a subject editor. This is a feature which has continued to the present day and accounts for one of the unique aspects of LC, that is, that it should be considered essentially as a coordinated series of special classifications. Each major class is published separately and is virtually independent of the others, having, for example, its own form and geographic divisions and index, with a concomitant lack of unifying structural features. Classes are also published individually, have differing revision schedules and hence degrees of currency. It is also significant that the scheme has been created inductively, that is, to represent and cater for an existing collection and to try to predict and create space for that collection's future development and growth. At its inception LC was designed for the helpful arrangement of books rather than for the retrieval of possibly abstract subject concepts and it was designed specifically for use with the Library of Congress's collection – both of these factors have had an impact on LC's subsequent development and its value as a general classification scheme. Given that the Library of Congress's collection is an enormous one, no longer even limited to national publications, the coverage is indeed extensive and the detail available is adequate for many library situations, as is proven by the fact that it is used by a number of research libraries with very specialized collections. However, the scheme does not and cannot attempt to provide universal subject coverage, particularly for information retrieval at a more specific level than the book, and it is nonetheless a limiting factor that the contents of the schedules are fundamentally controlled by the contents of the Library of Congress's collection.

Despite the fact that the scheme was not initially intended to be adopted by other libraries, that is precisely what did happen fairly quickly upon its appearance and it is now used by a significant number of American and Canadian libraries, particularly in the academic sector where a survey conducted in 1975[10] established that over 62% of university libraries used LC. In the 1950s and 1960s there was a very significant trend towards the reclassification of US academic libraries from DC to LC and there were fears that the trend would be continued in the large public libraries. The situation has stabilized in recent decades and considering the costs of reclassification it is unlikely that large library services will undertake such shifts in large numbers in the future. Much of the LC's popularity can be attributed to its governmentally controlled and well supported administration, the speed with which works are classified, the coverage of monograph material largely corresponding to libraries' stock and the availability of LC classmarks on Library of Congress catalogue cards and LCMARC records. It is then the support of the scheme, rather than its potential for information retrieval or its inherent structural qualities, which has been the major contributor to LC's popularity. 'Any reasonably comprehensive classification system developed and maintained by the considerable means of a federally supported agency, that is, the Library of Congress, is the logical scheme for general library use.'[11] The logic of the argument is largely an economic and administrative one rather than one based upon a classificatory appraisal, although the argument is no less cogent for that. It is an argument which may have been overtaken by events as the DC classmarks are now developed by the Library of Congress and are equally available on LC records.

The scheme is arranged first into main classes and their subclasses, where appropriate, and schedules for these are produced in groupings:

Classes and Subclasses		Schedules published	
A	General, Polygraphy	A	General, Polygraphy
B–BJ	Philosophy, Psychology	B–BJ	Philosophy, Psychology
BL–BX	Religion	BL–BX	Religion
C–F	History	C	Auxiliary History
		D	History–Ancient/Eastern
		E–F	History – American
G–GE	Geography	G	Geography/Anthropology
GF–GN	Anthropology		
HA	Statistics	H	Social Sciences
HB–HJ	Economics		
HM–HX	Sociology		
J	Political Science	J	Political Science
K	Law	KD	Law – United Kingdom
		KF	Law – United States
L	Education	L	Education
M	Music	M	Music
N	Fine Arts	N	Fine Arts
P	Language and Literature	P–PA	Linguistics, Classical languages and literatures
		PB–PH	Modern European Languages
		PG	Russian
		PJ–PM	Other languages
		PN,PR,PS,PZ	English Literature
		PQ1	French Literature
		PQ2	Italian, Spanish, Portuguese Literature
		PT1	German Literature
		PT2	Dutch/Scandinavian Literatures
Q	Science	Q	Science
QA	Mathematics		
QB	Astronomy		
QC	Physics		
QD	Chemistry		
QE	Geology		
QH	Biology/cytology		
QK	Botany		
QL	Zoology		
QM	Human Anatomy		
QP	Physiology		
QR	Bacteriology/ Microbiology		
R	Medicine	R	Medicine

S	Agriculture	S	Agriculture
T	Technology	T	Technology
U	Military Science	U	Military Science
V	Naval Science	V	Naval Science
Z	Bibliography, Library Science	Z	Bibliography, Library Science

Each of the classes is further subdivided into its main divisions, for example in Class L, Education, we have:

L	Education (General)
LA	History of Education
LB	Theory and Practice of Education
LC	Special Aspects of Education
LD–LC	Individual Institutions
	LD United States
	LE America (Non-US)
	LF Europe
	LG Asia, Africa, Oceania
LH	College and School Magazines and Papers
LJ	Student Fraternities and Societies, United States
LT	Textbooks

This is the limit to the use of letters in the marking of classes and divisions; notation is further expanded by the addition of numbers used arithmetically. Gaps have been left in the allocation of letters to allow for insertions. This use of letters has clear advantages as a directional aid, providing a simple and easily retained symbol for the major sections of knowledge. It is very useful to be able to direct users to Photography at TR or Commerce at HF. There is a certain unevenness in the allocation of notational space to subjects and so some resultant unevenness in the significance of subjects at this level. One therefore finds fairly disparate levels of subject being represented at the two letter stage, such as:

QA Mathematics	LH College and School magazines
(32 pages)	(1 page)

This disparity in allocation may in part be attributed to the focus of the Library of Congress itself and of course to early perceptions of the state of knowledge.

Each of the divisions has available to it the notation 1–9999 for further enumeration of subjects and these are read arithmetically with gaps left for expansion

HV 6254	Offences against the government (general)
HV 6273	National general works
HV 6275	Treason
HV 6278	Assassination of rulers. Regicide.

Where necessary, that is where the available unallocated space has been used, decimal extension is employed to allow further detail, as has inevitably proved necessary with the unforeseeable expansion of certain subjects. For example, under suicide only the notation from HV6543 to HV6548 was originally available; in modern times it has been necessary to specify suicide amongst special classes of persons and the classmark (HV6545) has been decimally subdivided:

HV 6545	Suicide 1801–
HV 6545.2	Aged
HV 6545.3	Children
HV 6545.4	Gays etc.

For each published schedule there may be tables of subdivisions provided, applicable to all of the class, usually just before the index and these may be for form, geographic areas, chronological periods, special subjects, for authors (only found in Class B, Philosophy and Class P, Literature) or for combinations of one or more of the foregoing tables. The particular tables provided relate specifically to the particular needs of the class, so that for example in Class L, there are tables which provide notation which can be added to American institutions, British institutions and others as directed. If one is dealing with the University of London, one finds from the schedules that the notational space from LF400–419 has been allocated and one is directed to use Table II from the Table of Subdivisions. From there one can devise the notation for the early history of the University of London by using 12 from the Table, giving a classmark of LB412. This is the only example of synthesis in the schedule for Education.

The fairly straightforward process of classification is complicated by the use of Cutter numbers to provide notation for a variety of reasons throughout the schedules. Cutter numbers are basically a means of providing an alphabetical arrangement on the shelf, but translating that into a notational device or set of symbols. This is most commonly used to allow for the arrangement by author for books all of which are on the same subject, in which case the Cutter number has no subject significance. In LC Cutter numbers are used in a variety of other situations. They are used to alphabetize a particular subject in the schedules, for example, at 'manual training in elementary education' one is directed to alphabetize particular examples of manual training by using Cutter numbers for the subject term. Another example of this use of alphabetical order for end-topics within a group appears in Criminology at HV8079, where it is possible to specify the investigation and detection of special crimes by assigning Cutter numbers, achieving a final shelf order:

HV 8079.A7	Arson
HV 8079.A74	Assassination
HV 8079.A97	Automobile theft

HV 8079.B62	Bombing
HV 8079.B8	Burglary etc.

Here then the Cutter number is being used to provide an alphabetic subject arrangement. However, this is a clear example of a subject where a more helpful arrangement might be possible. The separation of related materials by alphabetization is significant, where 'robbery' comes much later in the sequence than 'burglary' and where 'homicide' is separated from 'assassination' by 'drunk driving' and 'fraud', among others.

Cutter numbers are similarly used at times to provide form, period, place and topic divisions throughout the schedules. The situation is further complicated if one wishes to add a book number to the classmark in which case a further Cutter Number is added to signify authorship and a number to distinguish the edition of the work when the work is a subsequent edition and consisting of the date of the edition. For example, a second edition of the above work by Anderson would generate the Cutter Number A53 and if published in 1975 the numbers 1975 would be added resulting in a final shelfmark of LB1599.K6A53 1975.

The subsequent classmark can be broken down into its constituent elements thus:

L	Education	Class
LB	Theory and practice	Division
LB1559	Types of manual training	Subdivision
LB1599.K6	Knife work	Cutter No.
LB1599.K6A53	Author Anderson	Author Cutter No.
LB1599.K6A53 1975	Subsequent edition	Ed Date

Cutter Numbers are also used to specify place names and wherever the instruction 'By region or country, A–Z' is found then a Cutter number is devised for the name of the region or country, providing an alphabetical arrangement by place name. For example in a simplified form one might subarrange:

Abyssinia	A2
Afghanistan	A3
Algeria	A4
Argentina	A6 etc.

The frequency of recourse to Cutter numbers in LC, except when there is no sound and logical subject arrangement possible, would suggest that the attempt to determine and provide a helpful arrangement is being abnegated. The alphabetic arrangement of places is likely to be somewhat arbitrary in practice and may not reflect the most common or likely approach by users. The very frequent use of alphabetical order by topic has on the other hand been highly praised by Metcalfe[12] and it must be acknowledged that a truly systematic arrangement is often very difficult to achieve, the ethos of the arrangement can be very subjective, questionable and, in any event, totally lacking in significance to the user. But there are many examples in LC where a more helpful arrangement could have been devised and where typical approaches to the material might be envisaged. The example above from criminology is a group of subjects where the material is classified by the investigators of crime themselves and where their own methods of dealing with types of crime might have been built upon. Equally crimes are classified by type at other points in the schedules. Inconsistency of this sort may be confusing for the user. However, there are other groups of topics where to rank or classify is not likely to aid the user and an open and accepted policy of alphabetical subarrangement in such instances might be the most helpful and easily understandable option. Other classification schemes may be said to err on the side of a too frantic attempt to achieve significant order at all times, even when none is possible.

LC is fundamentally and irrevocably an enumerative scheme, with perhaps the least synthesis of all the general schemes. It does not employ notational synthesis through the use of common form or geographical divisions or their equivalents, nor does it make extensive use of the 'divide like' concept which would allow use elsewhere of notation from one point in the schedules where this is appropriate. In the capital punishment example already alluded to, such a device might have been economically used. Instead, in LC a list of subdivisions is given every time such a list is needed. This necessitates much repetition and bulking of the schedules but such avoidance of the provision of standard listings has advantages and disadvantages; advantages chiefly reside in the fact that each class has its own specially created and hence particularly appropriate form, geographic, period and topical tables, which reflect the true needs of the class and will only contain such material as is likely to be used. The provision of individual tables for disciplines also ensures that elaborate instructions and methodologies do not need to be incorporated into the text of the schedules. Use of tables can be kept as simple as possible and can take account of the particular notational needs of each class or section of a class. It might however be seen as a disadvantage that there is no dedicated, mnemonic and retrievable chunk of notation applied uniquely to recurring concepts as there is in DC. The repetition of tables also means that classifiers have no standard of practice upon which to rely and in certain classes the common tables, for example in History, are extensive and elaborate and, despite their provision, additional special tables have to be provided within the text of the schedules at certain points. Number building does exist in LC but in a very limited way and the degree of synthesis available varies from one class to another. Even where the same material is repeated in tables in different parts of the schedule the notation allocated to subjects may differ dramatically and therefore present no mnemonic aid to the classifier. In some instances the tables provided list a number of options as far as notation is concerned and choice depends upon the notational needs of the number you are adding to, for example in Education there is a table of possible additions to American institutions and 4 alternative numbers are listed for each:

I	II	III	IV	
x17	0	0	0	Charter and founding
x173	0.3	0.3	0.3	Heraldry
x199	5.8	6.5	6.5	Policy and organization
x2d	9	10	11	Requirements for admission
LD 3914		Nichols School, Buffalo, NY (Use Table IV)		
LD 4100–4119		Notre Dame University, Ind. (Use Table II)		

LC's notation, from its inception, has been a mixture of capital letters and Arabic numerals which, as we have seen, may be followed by the Cutter number, another mixture of numbers and letters. When the classification was first being designed Spofford was adamant that numerals should be ordinal rather than decimal, with immediate implications for the hospitality of the scheme. Only by leaving empty blocks of notation could unforeseen future subjects be accommodated in their appropriate place. Inevitably expansion exceeded space availability and decimal extension had to be introduced, thus causing further complications in establishing filing order. LC classmarks are not expressive of subject content and make no attempt to display the hierarchy of subjects. They therefore do not provide a symbolic language where the notation can be said to reflect the subject content but rather provide simply a locationary device. The result is that the notation conveys no sense of the structure of the scheme and the hierarchy or relationship of subjects is often difficult to discern from the schedules. Equally the lack of detailed summaries or breakdowns of classes in the schedules makes it difficult to find one's way around the subjects without recourse to the Indexes.

Another common criticism of LC's notation, that is, its length, may be unjustified. Certainly it is possible to cite examples of inordinately long classmarks, but these tend to occur when minute detail is being specified and may in fact illustrate a great strength of the scheme: the availability of enormous detail in certain parts of the schedules. These are variable, it has to be said, but certain disciplines are dealt with almost exhaustively and it is difficult to imagine classes such as Sociology, Economics or Political Science being unable to specify sufficient detail. A good example of this occurs in Criminology again, where one is provided with a list of methods of early capital punishment which includes 'beheading', 'boiling in oil', 'breaking on the wheel', etc. However, oddly, modern methods of capital punishment are not differentiated in the same manner and there is simply a general number.

There is no single index to the Library of Congress Classification. Each separately published part of the schedules has its own index and these can in themselves be fairly extensive; the Index to H–HJ Economics is 85 pages long and contains over six thousand entries. The indexes are relative, bringing together aspects of a topic which are scattered throughout the schedules, but within that discipline, so that for example if one were looking for material on the role of parents, one would find that the Index to the Sociology Class schedule, HM–HX would contain:

Parent and child	HQ755.85
Parental rights	HV9086
Parents	HQ755.7+
of handicapped children	HQ759.913
Parents, Adolescent *see* Adolescent parents	

However the Index to Class L, Education would also produce:

Parent participation	LB1140.35.P37
Parent–Teacher associations	LC230+
Parents, education by	LC40

while the Index to H–HJ, Economics has:

Parental leave	HD6065+

To an extent the schedules themselves compensate for this scattering of topics across disciplinary boundaries by providing see also references, such as:

HQ755.85   Relationship between parent and child
                 Cf. BF723.P25, Psychological aspects

There have been attempts at the cumulation of these separate indexes, one produced by the Canadian Library Association, the other compiled by Nancy B. Olson and consisting of 15 volumes. A useful publication[13] which appeared in 1992 was the first edition of a manual to guide classifiers in the use of the LC scheme. Covering general principles as well as particularly thorny areas such as filing rules, alternative class numbers and so on, this is long overdue and should be a boon to all classifiers. It is astonishing that the scheme should have survived for so long without such an official guide, although *Immroth's guide to the Library of Congress Classification*[14] has long provided an unofficial one.

Current evaluation of the Library of Congress Classification

One of the great strengths of LC lies in the fact that classificationist and classifier are the same person. The scheme is therefore a superb example of a pragmatically developed system of proven success and value to the many libraries who use it and one which is well supported administratively. It provides minute detail in specification and a more scholarly approach in many disciplines than the more populist DC. Although enumerative, and unashamedly so, it may therefore serve the needs of the academic sector more satisfactorily than any other popular general scheme at the moment.

In comparison with CC or UDC, indeed all of the other schemes discussed here, it does lack a sound theoretical base, principles consistently applied and a logical structure, but many of its supporters and users would argue that it is more important that it be a workable system rather than an exemplar of classificatory principle and textbook theory. However, there are practical weaknesses too. The lack of consistency and of an overall application of principles in its development means that it is a difficult scheme to describe and to apply. The schedules themselves lack guidance or instruction for classifiers – a fault recently remedied by the provision of an official guide – and general rules cannot be applied or learned. It is unlikely that there will be any overall rationalization of techniques as this would require major revision of the whole scheme; this is particularly so given the fragmentary nature of publication.

This lack of a logical structure has been seen by some commentators as a strength in that such lack of rigidity may, in fact, allow greater ease of adaptation when the structure of knowledge changes. This is a comforting but apathetic and unhelpful argument. Certainly some classification schemes can be accused of procrustean rigidity in allowing structure to dominate the natural shape of the literature which is produced. But when might we assume that we know enough of the structure of knowledge to devise a means of conveying that structure via classification? Acknowledging that no structure or schema of knowledge will ever be perfect enough to cope with the unpredictable future, accepting that knowledge is never complete, we can still attempt to provide the best map of knowledge as it exists at present.

One problem for users relates to the fact that LC does not provide any mechanism to allow flexibility in depth of classification. There is no simple method of truncation, allowing the user to choose between broad and close classification, which can be a very useful feature for public and school libraries. For some parts of the scheme abridged editions are available, for example for music, and there have also been produced abridged editions for children's collections.

LC is the least international of the major general classification schemes. In its coverage it predominantly reflects a national collection; there is a distinct bias towards the social structure, history, law and cultural concerns of the United States. The notation is complex and not truly comprehensible internationally. In particular, the use of Cutter Numbers, which has a linguistic dimension, is not likely to be consistently applied internationally. There is little likelihood that LC will ever be used extensively outside the United States.

The process of automating LC is encountering a number of problems, largely relating to faults in the scheme which have already been identified in this chapter. These stem often from the scheme's lack of a sound and universal theoretical base. They include: the fact that LC is not a single unified entity, that it has inconsistencies and anomalies in the ways in which it is constructed and in the terminology used to explain its use; the complexity of the system of *see reference* notes throughout the schedules; the existence of no single unified and internally consistent index; and the fact that the notation is not expressive of hierarchy and that no automatic process of truncation of numbers can be developed – although even schemes which are expressive must be so consistently if this approach is to be developed without hiccoughs. Great attention is being paid at present – by researchers like Rebecca Guenther, Mary Micco, Karen Markey and Diane Vizine-Goetz – to the way in which LC can be implemented via the *USMARC Format for Classification Data,* in order to provide an automatic schedule, and, given its great use and popularity, LC is unlikely to leave this field clear for its competitors.

In conclusion, despite LC's lack of theory, it remains in practice an effective method of classification, perhaps particularly for the classifier. It is practical and easily used. It is up to date and constantly revised in the sense that classmarks are created almost concurrently with the literature as it is produced. It is likely that the coverage will be detailed enough for the largest academic libraries and that the scholarship of the treatment of subjects will remain one of LC's great strengths. Its use is unlikely to decline; having made such a major shift those libraries which have adopted LC would not relish the major upheaval of another reclassification and in operation LC has much, as we have seen, to recommend it. It is the helpfulness of the final order, its logic and consistency of approach that remain the most evident faults of the scheme. Helpful order may not be the most significant feature of the scheme for the Library of Congress, where much of the stock is effectively on closed access, but for many libraries its importance is paramount. The lack of helpful order is mirrored in the utility of the classmark for subject retrieval and it is in this area that LC may be asked to prove itself in the future.

3. THE UNIVERSAL DECIMAL CLASSIFICATION (UDC)

Of the three most popular general classification schemes UDC is the one aimed specifically at retrieval of information by subject rather than at the achievement of a helpful shelf arrangement. It is also the most synthetic and plans are afoot which may mean that the synthetic elements of UDC are developed considerably in future.

UDC was designed as a practical classification scheme, by Paul Otlet and Henri La Fontaine, to provide a subject arrangement for a vast card catalogue of bibliographies covering all literature published throughout the world. The impetus for the scheme derived from an attempt to contribute towards universal bibliographic control and the origins of the scheme necessitated that minute specification of detail and infinite expansiveness should both be possible. UDC is chiefly a bibliographic scheme, that is designed for the indexing and description of the contents of documents, rather than for the physical arrangement of a collection. It is therefore based on and aimed at the organization of and retrieval of information from all kinds of literature and in particular the provision of the detail necessary to handle pamphlet, report and periodical literature, wherein analysis could be carried to an almost extreme fineness. These features have remained integral to both the development of UDC and to its field of greatest impact in the classification of special libraries, documentation centres and information bureaux, where it may be found in use for shelf arrangement and in the arrangement of the classified catalogue. A range of abstracting and indexing services, particularly in the fields of science and technology, either arrange entries in their classified sequence in UDC order or carry UDC numbers on the entries. The scheme is also used to classify United Kingdom Atomic Energy Reports and the publications of certain technical organizations.

Despite its use in such a variety of applications and, ironically, in view of the early commitment to the attainment of universal bibliographic control, UDC has not made significant advances towards this goal. Indeed it has been seen as a major disincentive to expanding use of the scheme that UDC classmarks are not provided on MARC records and that the scheme is not used by any of the major national bibliographic agencies.

UDC was initially conceived as an expansion of the basic structure of DC, which would exploit the internationally comprehensible qualities of DC's notation. Permission for this use of DC was granted on the condition that the first 1 000 classes and divisions would remain identical. It has been argued that this adoption of the DC main classes and divisions has meant that UDC is built upon an unsound scientific base, with the implication that this has limited the potential value of UDC particularly in terms of main class order. However, from that original common ground, the two schemes have developed in very different ways and considerable differences now exist between the main divisions of the two schemes even at a basic three or four digit level.

DC as a whole was taken and examined by a number of subject specialists, each of whom reshaped and completed their schedule according to the necessities of their specialities. In the process the scheme altered in nature. While they are both documentary classifications, DC is intended chiefly for arranging and guiding the library; UDC is chiefly bibliographic, for the detailed indexing and description of documents. In addition to expanding upon the enumeration of subjects, UDC developed considerable synthetic qualities. In the *Introduction to the International Medium Edition* of 1985, UDC acknowledges itself to be a 'hybrid'[15] of the enumerative approach in the Main Tables, where the primary notation for subjects is listed, and of the analytico-synthetic elements which are available via the use of the Auxiliary Tables. As we are told in the *Introduction*, 'UDC has evolved from a project to develop an enumerative into a faceted classification'. We will later examine the synthetic aspects of UDC, but let us look first at the basic structure of its schedules, as the major divisions are enumerated in UDC's Main Tables. At the first stage of division the universe of knowledge is arranged thus:

0   Generalities
    Science and knowledge

	Organization
	Information
1	Philosophy
	Psychology
2	Religion
	Theology
3	Social Sciences
	Law
	Government
4	(Vacant)
5	Mathematics
	Natural Sciences
6	Applied Sciences
	Medicine
	Technology
7	Arts
	Recreation
	Leisure
	Sport
8	Language
	Linguistics
	Literature
9	Geography
	Biography
	History

This is an arrangement very little changed from DC, apart from the bringing together of language and literature in 8. Again in the same manner as DC, notation is decimal and expresses the subject's rank in the hierarchy of subjects. The classes have, however, developed quite independently and the extent of detail provided is much greater in UDC than in the equivalent DC classes. In addition, main class order is not of major significance as the UDC is infrequently seen in its entirety to classify large collections. If we consider an earlier example, domestic architecture, from DC we may recall that there was a limited differentiation of types of housing. In UDC we find:

728.1	Housing and dwellings
.2	Multi-family dwellings
.22	Blocks of flats
.222	Tenement blocks
.224	Smaller blocks
.3	Single family dwellings
.31	Terraced houses
.34	Semi-detached houses

.37   Detached houses

.38   Bungalows

Locating subjects in the Main Schedules in UDC differs very little from the process in DC, it is really in the extent of the availability of synthetic devices to add to that basic number that UDC forges ahead of its progenitor. There are two types of synthetic device in UDC. The first is to allow for the construction of compound numbers to specify interrelated subjects, which it would be impossible to foresee and uneconomic to list exhaustively. The nature of the relationship between the two subjects can also be expressed to a limited extent by the use of various notational symbols. These relational indicators form part of what are termed the 'common auxiliary signs'. The plus sign '+' is used to link the notation representing two subjects from the main tables, where those subjects are treated equally within a document; for example 622+629 is the combination for Mining and Metallurgy. The stroke '/' is used when a document covers a range of topics which are consecutive in the UDC schedules; for example 511/514 would indicate that the work deals with arithmetic, algebra and geometry. A colon ':' shows that there is a relationship between two subjects, but does not specify the nature of the relationship nor the relative importance of the two subjects as treated in the document classified; for example, agricultural employment would be 63:331.5. This reflects the fundamental aim of the scheme which is to satisfy user needs for information retrieval rather than to devise an optimum shelf arrangement. However the double colon '::' may be used to fix the order of the component numbers in a compound subject, although it is suggested by UDC that this feature will be chiefly useful in electronic files. Square brackets '[]' are used as an algebraic grouping device, a feature often essential with compound subjects in order to express the correct connotation; for example, the gardens and stately homes of Scotland would be expressed as [712+728.8](411) to indicate that both the gardens and the stately homes are Scottish and not only the stately homes as would be the interpretation of 712+728.8(411). When using the plus sign, square brackets and the colon the order of elements is flexible and the order may be chosen to reflect most closely a library's interests or both may be used in the classified catalogue, bibliographies and indexes, ensuring that no matter which component of a compound subject is chosen the user will locate relevant items. It is the citation order of the subject elements that determines the overall notation and thus the shelf location. However, each notational element can be brought to the front in the catalogue, index or bibliography.

The second synthetic feature of UDC is the separate listing, as tables of auxiliary numbers of concepts common to many if not all subjects. The *Independent Auxiliary Tables* of language, form, place, race and time, can be used with any UDC number or alone. *The Dependent Auxiliary Tables*, of point of view, materials and persons, must be used with a UDC number from the Main Tables.

Symbols are used to introduce or enclose the notation from the Auxiliary

Tables. The equals sign '=' is used before the notation for language. The form and geographic subdivisions are enclosed in parentheses. Thus 53(05) is a dictionary of physics, while 385(4) denotes European railways. The treatment of notation from the Race Subdivision combines the two approaches as it is enclosed within parentheses and introduced by the equals sign, (=942) for example would stand for the Mongolian peoples. Inverted commas '" "' as the time symbol are used to indicate the period covered by a work. It is possible to specify very precisely to the year, day, hour and even second if desired, thus "1982.12.25.10.15.03" would be three seconds after quarter past ten on Christmas morning 1982. The auxiliary table for time also includes concepts such as sunrise, wartime and leisure time. The symbols point nought, nought '.00' are used as a facet indicator to introduce notation from the point of view table, which provides a range of useful ideas; for example .001.4 is used to classify a work on a topic which is at the testing or experimental stage.

In addition to these Common Auxiliaries which may be used with any UDC number, there are under various divisions of the schedules Special Auxiliaries. These are specialized subdivisions which are listed within the schedules and may only be used within that subject area as they are likely to have significance only within that context. These may be introduced by a hyphen '-' or point nought '.0' and are enumerated as appropriate in the schedules. The apostrophe is used for a similar purpose but only in the schedules for chemistry and chemical technology. UDC also allows fairly extensive use of a 'subdivide as' instruction, which allows one to use the detail of provision in one part of the schedule to build notation in other parts when instructed. This instruction '≃' provides a very powerful synthetic tool.

A listing of these facet indicators, with a brief description of their role may be useful:

Symbols used in UDC	Role
=	Language
(0...)	Form
(1/9)	Place
(=...)	Nationality
"..."	Period
+	Combination of discretely notated subjects
/	Combination of topics identifiable as a range of notated subjects
:	Combination of notation implying relationships between subjects
::	As above but not reversible
.00	Point of view
– 03	Materials
– 05	Persons

$$\left. \begin{array}{l} -1\,/-9 \\ .01\,/.09 \\ \text{'1 /'9} \end{array} \right\}$$ Special tables provided in
the schedules

A great range of auxiliaries then exist in UDC and there is great scope, via the use of these, for the expression of compound and complex subjects. Their variety can, however, be somewhat bewildering for the user.

This synthetic apparatus of UDC may well be developed beyond all present recognition. A Task Force, considering the future development of the system, recommended in 1986 that the scheme should be restructured in order to be as effective as possible in electronic systems, both now and in the foreseeable future. Changes to the scheme internally and to its overall philosophy may therefore be on the way. Those most closely identified with the scheme seem confident that internal changes to the system which would render it more fully effective in the online environment are on the way and while such changes might take a variety of forms, some more far-reaching than others, one suggestion is particularly intriguing. Nancy Williamson[16] describes one possible scenario which such a restructuring might take and which is 'theoretically and intellectually sound as well as useful'. This scenario involves the mapping of the 'UDC classes and subclasses onto the facet structure of an acceptable existing system'. The existing system which has been identified for this purpose is the second edition of the Bliss Bibliographic Classification (BC2), which we shall examine in full detail later in this chapter. Suffice it to say at this point that it is considered by Williamson to be a well structured, logical and well explained faceted scheme which, given that it is a general classification, is capable of providing the bones for a restructured UDC. This project is at present at a very early stage: indeed as yet it is but a proposal. Problems are already evident in the disparity between the two systems – UDC and BC – both in theory and in methodology. Such a restructuring would also involve great upheaval and reclassification for the present users of the scheme. The benefits, however, are potentially very great, to say nothing of the potential for the future of such a meld of faceted principle and minute specification, and it is to be hoped that the proposal will be considered in a positive manner and not, as with so many good ideas, be constrained by pragmatic considerations and the caution of users.

Revision and administration of the Universal Decimal Classification

UDC is at present at a very volatile point in its history and therefore it is worth paying particular attention to the issues raised by the changes taking place and the likely future strategic developments. In the last manual Arthur Maltby[17] stated 'that UDC might be said to have the best revision policy of all'. Much has changed in recent years and it is worth spending some time considering this point.

Since its first publication in 1905, UDC has been owned and administered by the International Federation for Documentation (the FID) who approved and controlled the revision process via a fairly complicated and slow, but continuous, careful and well-vetted, consultative committee structure. Individual and widely disparate national bodies were responsible for the actual publication of schedules (the British Standards Institution produced the English language schedules, other national bodies might be non-profit-seeking organizations, while one was a commercial publisher) and, although international development was thus necessarily uneven, the scheme is available in various manifestations in 22 languages. Editions can be full, medium (30%) or abridged (10%) and schedule publication has tended to be slow; the full edition in English is still incomplete, although begun in 1936. One attempt to standardize schedule publication internationally involved the decision to publish three International Medium Editions in English, French and German. A major disadvantage of this decision, however, was that the English edition, although published in 1985, could show no development from the German edition which had been completed in 1977, despite the major progress which had taken place in certain subject fields over that period. The result overall of this publication methodology was an editorial function which had little cohesion and even less centralized control and maximization of resources.

In the 1980s, however, major new strategic developments took place. In 1986, based upon the recommendations of the Gilchrist Report, a new and more streamlined committee structure was implemented to bring in expertise from the 'more commercial areas of the information industry',[18] which set up under the supervision of the UDC Management Board (UMB) five Co-ordinating Revision Committees (CRCs), consisting of subject specialists, whose role was to develop the schedules for specific subject fields in line with sound classificatory principles. This new structure was intended to speed and give coherence to the previously fragmented, complex and committee-dominated revision process, while ensuring a still carefully considered, but more systematic and consistent development of the scheme, linking subject expertise and classificatory expertise in an effective manner.

In 1986 the Task Force for UDC System Development was set up, under the direction of Ia McIlwaine, to rationalize further the strategic development of UDC and to advise on its future direction. The Task Force reported to the FID in March 1990 and made several recommendations as to the way ahead for UDC, including the creation of a 'standard version' in machine-readable format at the medium level. A new 'Code of Practice' for revision was also drawn up to standardize the process. Administrative developments have continued apace. At the end of 1991 responsibility for and control of the UDC passed from the FID to the *UDC Consortium*, a professional consortium of six commercial publishers who – it is hoped – will fund and manage the scheme in a more stable and economically effective manner, capitalizing on the UDC resource and guaranteeing its commercial future. The FID remains one member of the consortium, as does the British Standards Institution, while the other four members are organizations from Spain, the Netherlands, Belgium and Japan. This decision was taken in order to ensure investment in the future development of UDC, particularly if its technological potential was to be realized, although in its announcement of the new administration,[19] the FID was to assure existing users that their interests would be maintained. Of equal significance has been the recent revelation, in 1993, that an editor-in-chief would be appointed in order to ensure a single vision and to achieve direction which combines commercial and intellectual goals. The first appointee will be Ia McIlwaine who has been long associated with UDC.

Although revision will now be under the control of this new body, it was clear from this announcement that UDC will continue to rely on voluntary effort – of librarians, documentalists and organizations such as the UKAEA, who use the scheme – as the labour force for its development and revision, although there has been a limited use of contracted expertise in recent years and this may continue. This reliance on users, in response to their own needs, generating and bringing forth revision has resulted in an uneven development of the schedules, which are particularly strong where most heavily used and where it has been in the users' interests to assist and speed the process.

One major recent development, now complete, is the production of a version in electronic form. This is the English Medium Edition of 1985, although it incorporates all additions and corrections since that date in order to ensure that it is as current as possible. This online database will not equate with the full schedules but will comprise approximately 60,000 entries. It is not envisaged that the full schedules will be converted to the electronic standard format in the immediate future, a decision which may well disappoint many of the special library users who require the level of detail the full schedules provide. However the advantages of this file are very considerable and include access to a standard version and accepted classmark; immediate access to revisions as soon as they are agreed; the potential to link or exploit the file in the production of other automated systems; and speedier publication of printed versions. (See Section 3 for further discussion.) Already the British Standards Institution is planning a new medium edition and others are likely to follow. The Master Reference File, which is at present being created in the Hague under the aegis of the Technical Advisory Committee, will be an authority file. The electronic UDC is accompanied by two guides, a manual explaining how to use the file for the classification of materials, and which will expand upon the introduction to the existing International Medium Edition, and a guide to the ways in which the file can be put to use, for example in online public access catalogues.

It is too early to comment on the effect of all of these changes but UDC has had a good record and a revision apparatus which has proven to work in the past. If indeed the new developments, as intended, do achieve greater universality, greater currency of schedules and a continuing responsiveness to user needs, then it is likely that UDC's revision policy will continue to be an effective and well considered one.

Current evaluation of the Universal Decimal Classification

As has already been noted, UDC is the most synthetic of the three popular general classification schemes. However UDC was not originally designed as a totally synthetic scheme and it is not, therefore, based upon as sound synthetic principles as is CC; synthesis has been grafted on to a basically enumerative structure and the result is a somewhat uneven and unpredictable mixture of enumerative and faceted devices. Systematic mnemonics are used more consistently in UDC than in DC via the auxiliary tables, for example Scotland is always (411) and that piece of notation is used to represent no other concept; similarly the twentieth century is invariably "19". This has two benefits; the easy recall of commonly used numbers by the classifier; and the ability to recognize pieces of notation, either by the human user of the scheme or by an automated system.

In order to allow the scheme to be used by individual libraries and bibliographic services in the manner which most closely reflects their particular interests, the classifier can exercise discretion in the choice of citation order, either where more than one of the Common Tables is used (time and place are for example interchangeable) or where a compound subject is being specified. While ensuring that the best interests of a particular user group are being met in individual instances, this feature does, however, lead to extreme variations in usage and to a situation where there is clearly no universally accepted standard notation for subjects. This lack of a specified and fixed citation order means that the principle of inversion is not rigidly applied, which in turn means that the achievement of a standardized and consistently helpful order is impossible.

Although used internationally – UDC in various forms is available in 22 languages – there still exists in the scheme a Western bias, inherited though it may be from DC. This is particularly evident in the Religion class, which is still heavily dominated by Christianity, but is also present in the treatment of political ideologies and cultural variations. Users of the scheme come from all over the world; the peak of its popularity is found in certain European countries and in Russia where it has been used extensively. Equally UDC has been most popular in special libraries and information services and has not attained as high a profile in the public and academic library sector. This may be related to the fact that the full schedules have in places approximately ten times as many entries as the corresponding DC schedules and, where one is operating in a specialized subject area and the schedule for that area has been fully developed, UDC is therefore a more attractive option, particularly for subject retrieval.

A related advantage of UDC lies in its independence of any one tongue. It is therefore possible to use UDC classmarks as a complement to post-coordinate indexing language techniques, to represent subject concepts, to act as a thesaurofacet or to display hierarchical structures. It was thought at one time that automation held great promise for UDC in the sense that UDC was felt by many to be the most suitable of the general schemes for retrieval of information in electronic files. There remain problems, however, particularly in relation to the breakdown of the hierarchical structure of the scheme as represented notationally and in the automatic interpretation of the significance of symbols. In addition, while the advantages of enumerative classifications in retrieval – that for each distinct subject there is an identifiable and unique classmark – and the advantages of faceted classifications – the elements of a subject can be individually combined allowing for Boolean combination – are both recognized, the mixture of both enumeration and synthesis in UDC may create difficulties. However, in a report on a project to develop a thesaurus from a revised, more synthetic demography class, the authors Wiesthuis and Bliedung[20] state that 'even a UDC class with enumerative subclasses can be connected with a thesaurus through the notations. Connecting a post-coordinated thesaurus with the existing UDC may be a way to make UDC more suitable for the online age without drastic structural revisions to the existing UDC.' This is a subject which will be further considered in Part Three, Information Technology and Classification. Equally, the work of Williamson and McIlwaine which has built upon this concept, in the development of a strategy to reconstruct UDC upon the faceted base of the Bliss Bibliographic Classification (BC2), responds directly to the criticism of UDC that it is a hybrid, neither fully synthetic nor enumerative. Such a development is an enormously exciting prospect for students of classification.

Due to the reliance on voluntary revision effort, development of the scheme has been piecemeal; that position may change with the implementation of the new organizational structure. UDC also tends to have been applied in a fairly inconsistent manner; not all users have employed the full detail available, nor have they availed themselves of the full apparatus of the methodologically confusing mixture of symbols and tables. There is, however, a growing convergence towards harmonization of UDC at the international level and a recognition on the part of the UDC administration that standardization is essential, both in schedule publication and revision, and in use of the scheme, in order that the scheme should combine wide appeal with consistency. The publication of the 'Master Edition' at the medium edition level, with the potential for expansion of full schedules in subject areas where it is felt that greater detail is needed, is likely to aid this process considerably. This will help to ensure standardization with the provision of sufficient detail to cope with the needs of the majority of collections.

At the moment UDC is at a dynamic and fluid point in its history where, organizational change having already been implemented, the ethos and future development of the scheme are being examined. The future for UDC is likely to include: attempts to render the scheme more attractive and effective for online retrieval of information; the provision of a sounder classificatory base; the identification and targeting more specifically of present users; and the development of strategies to encourage new users to adopt the scheme.

4. THE COLON CLASSIFICATION (CC)

S. R. Ranganathan had special links with the authors of the previous editions of this manual, Berwick Sayers having been his teacher and Arthur Maltby being, through their correspondence, one of the many to receive encouragement from him. Certain fundamental aims underlie all Ranganathan's texts on classification as well as CC itself. His basic aim was to provide a unique language and theory for classification. In so doing, he expressed his zeal for a helpful filiatory – Ranganathan's word for filing – order; the desire to express fully in a classmark the specific subject of each item and then to individualize it by means of a full call number; and the idea that the individual classifier should be given the opportunity to anticipate revision in the scheme by inbuilt guidelines on coping with new subjects as thrown forth by a turbulent world of knowledge. CC abounds with ideas and features. It has changed quite rapidly from edition to edition because of the insistence on accuracy of subject specification and on keeping pace with the introduction of new compound or complex subjects – and also because of the sheer intellectual fertility, inventiveness and investigatory zeal of its creator. The introduction of new and radical theories has been a common occurrence in CC, such as the development of PMEST as a citation order.

Most subjects can be seen as compounds. They draw their elements from the facets of a single subject field with, perhaps, the addition of common elements for space and time. CC enumerates broad conventional subject areas and then within each lists elements which can be combined as necessary. Citation order is controlled by means of a facet formula, for Ranganathan argued that all elements relate to one or another of five fundamental concepts: Personality, Matter, Energy, Space and Time. In citation the categories present are represented in this order, often written as PMEST. Each of the facets is introduced by punctuation marks, serving as facet indicators, which identify the notation and the facet to which it belongs. Thus, in CC, a comma heralds Personality. Matter is prefixed by a semicolon and energy by a colon (originally the only punctuation used and hence the name of the scheme). Space is introduced by a full stop and Time by the apostrophe. Time and Space are self-explanatory facets but the others are more abstruse and require some clarification. The Energy facet is used to represent processes, activities or operations which consume mental or physical effort. Matter, used comparatively rarely until the seventh edition, covers materials. Personality is best expressed as the core or root element found in most specific subjects.

Before providing examples, an observation may be made. Although relatively casual about main class order which he felt need only be 'reasonably tolerable', Ranganathan worked tremendously hard to secure detailed, consistent, high quality sequences within classes. His formula, although far removed from the ideas of Cutter and Bliss, has its own distinctive philosophical overtones, as does much of his writing in the field of librarianship and information science. Thus, when we find in the major work of one nineteenth century philosopher that the world is an infinitely powerful blind will (energy) and that as perceived by our personalities it represents itself as matter within the confines of time and space, we might ponder about Ranganathan's sources – especially when we consider that this is the Western philosopher closest to certain aspects of Hindu and Buddhist teaching.[21] Ranganathan expresses his ideas with fervour and an almost messianic conviction, in often vivid and figurative language, and this combination, with the sound and logical basis of many of the ideas themselves, help to explain both his stature and the influence of many of his theories. In a quantitative analysis of the biographical treatment of librarians, Ranganathan stands head and shoulders above the others, with only Melvil Dewey a not very close second.

Three questions may also be asked about the facet formula – and briefly answered. Do PMEST categories cover all concepts? It would seem not in the light of further research. What if we have difficulty in deciding, say, what is Personality(P) and what is Matter(M)? In practice, the classificationist always decides this for us within CC. Is PMEST always the best citation order? Not necessarily. Ranganathan's own probings in the light of such questions led to the introduction into CC of Rounds and Levels of facets, which allowed for facets to appear more than once and in different orders according to the requirements of the particular class. If, in the analysis of a highly specific and developed subject, Personality(P) is required twice before the introduction of Energy(E), this is said to constitute a second level of Personality. On the other hand, a second manifestation of Personality(P) after the Energy(E) facet would constitute a beginning of a new Round of the formula. Energy(E) is the pivotal category in this respect. Little wonder then that it has retained the use of the punctuation symbol that gave the scheme its name! But these ideas are best illustrated and examined by means of examples.

Example A
(from Class X Economics)

Subject	Economics in the USA
Verbal concept analysis	Economics/USA
Facets present	Space only (since economics is a main class)
Classmark	X.73
Comment	A simple example

Example B
(from Class S Psychology)

Subject	The anxieties of the old
Verbal concept analysis	The aged/anxieties
Facets present	Personality(P) and Matter(M)
Classmark	S,38;56[22]
Comment	In earlier editions anxieties would indubitably

have been assigned to the Energy(E) facet.

Example C
(from Class Y Sociology)

Subject	Prevention of poverty
Verbal concept analysis	Poverty/prevention
Facets present	Matter(M) and Energy(E)
Classmark	Y;435:5
Comment	'Poverty' used to be in Energy(E). Like the first example this one shows that (P) is not always present.

Example D
(from Class 2 Library Science)

Subject	Administration of manuscript collections in British academic libraries today
Verbal concept analysis	Academic libraries/manuscripts/administration/Britain/1990s
Facets present	(P)(M)(E)(S)(T)
Classmark	2,3;12:8.56'N6
Comment	A rare example of all five facets being present.

Example E
(from Class V Political Science)

Subject	The work of the British Prime Minister
Verbal concept analysis	British Politics/Prime Minister
Facets present	Personality twice – hence two levels of Personality. (P1)(P2)
Classmark	V,56,21
Comment	An example of successive levels of Personality.

Example F
(from Class L Medicine)

Subject	X-ray therapy of tuberculosis of the lungs
Verbal concept analysis	Lungs/tuberculosis/therapeutics/X-rays
Facets present	(P)(M)(E)(2P)
Classmark	L,45;421:6253

It will be noted that what constitutes (P), (M) and (E) varies according to the 'raw material' of each class. It has also varied from edition to edition. The distinction between Rounds and Levels is really simply to enable us to cope with certain specific items, fortunately few, which offer more than one manifestation of a particular facet, and at the same time to preserve the most helpful citation order.

We should see from these examples that numerous other themes can be specified in a highly flexible manner, for example:

Academic library administration   2,3:8
Therapeutics   L:6
Poverty in the 19th century   Y;434'M

We must also realize that there is insistence on good order through strict control of citation order and through the application of the principle of inversion, by which facets file in the opposite order to that in which they are cited. As we recall, the principle of inversion is achieved by the filing value Ranganathan has assigned to the facet indicators, rather than by the symbols in the notation. Thus, it is possible to take any main class, say X, as an example and supposing every possible grouping of an application of PMEST is found, the filing order would begin:

X(T)
X(S)
X(S) (T)
X(E)
X(E) (S)
X(E) (S) (T)

and so on until all combinations were filed.

The list would, of course, be extended to add (M) and (P). In practice, not all combinations will occur. The eventual outcome is to concentrate grouping in (P) with a little scattering in (M), rather more under (E), still more under (S) and a great deal under (T). Our brief example shows the collocation under (E) having priority over that in (S) and (T).

The Colon Classification abounds with vigorous ideas, but only two more will be touched upon. A distinction was made earlier between compound and complex subjects as defined by Ranganathan. Facet analysis is linking elements of a compound. Complex subjects are rarer and are specified by means of phase analysis. This enables CC not only to cater for, but to differentiate between the nature of complex relations in themes like 'the influence of philosophers on German literature' or 'management performance indicators: a manual for educators', where concepts are combined from across disciplinary boundaries. The other interesting idea is one whereby the revision process of the scheme can be assisted through the individual classifier having the power to anticipate the number of a new subject, which does not yet appear in the schedules. This bold and perhaps over-ambitious notion (described earlier as seminal mnemonics) links numbers to certain themes – for example, money is associated with the number 6, women are linked to the number 5 – and the classifier can then predict the number which is likely to be assigned to a new subject in subsequent editions. The process is complicated by the fact that several concepts, which it is claimed are philosophically linked, are associated with each digit. The technique is indicative of the drive for effective innovation in CC.

Current evaluation of the Colon Classification

Some see CC as difficult to grasp. This is a problem which is more apparent than real, although scant justice can be done to its wealth of features in a review as brief as the above. It provides not only a remarkable degree of precision in specification but also control of the required order, all delivered in a unified and cohesive package. The notation offers interpolation to a marvellous degree. By listing essentially elements from which compounds can be made, the schedules are kept slim. It is as unfair to criticize its Eastern bias as it would be to criticize the Western bias of, say, LC. Weaknesses do exist and they include: over-dependence on one man's energies and ideas; awkward notations (it is difficult to distinguish between colon, semi-colon, comma and full stop); and the rapid changes effected from edition to edition. It has been said that while Ranganathan's work on cataloguing represented sound sense and an eye to user needs, his work on CC was over-ambitious. True or otherwise, it simply reflected his determination not to deviate from searching out optimum standards. His debt to UDC is evident, but although it has features which CC does not, Ranganathan was right to say that it did not 'go the whole hog' in redesigning the basis for classification, since it grafted synthesis onto the enumerative DC base. The CC scheme would seem in a sense to be in competition with UDC rather than LC or DC in that its application to order on shelves raises issues of simplicity of notation. Ranganathan's belief that a single scheme could serve various purposes is well-known. His analogy of an elephant's trunk which can deal with large and small packages with equal facility scarcely holds good, however, since the multi-purpose system cannot do all things with due economy. The obvious legacy of CC is seen in modern faceted systems and in much classificatory research. Less obvious is the challenge posed to other systems: there have been changes in DC and UDC over the years which surely owe something to Ranganathan, whether or not these are acknowledged. As for learning to use CC to the full the secret is essentially the idea, implicit throughout, which emerges perhaps most clearly in the seminal mnemonics – one must learn to think like Ranganathan, to be 'spiritually attuned'! (If that seems unacceptable, we might ponder how much computer hardware and software demand that we obey their rules and processes inexorably in all matters.) It has also been the present authors' experience that many of the alleged difficulties associated with classification using CC are in practice found to be negligible and that students, for example, often take to the scheme very quickly and experience fewer problems than in working with the, at times, methodologically confusing DC.

On a global scale of use and interest, CC is used by a few, greatly admired by some, totally neglected by many. Not everyone is convinced of the value of faceted classification in any context. Yet the idea of concept analysis is akin to what all individual classifiers do, or should do, when they apply any system and those disinterested in CC might bear in mind that some study of it (or similar analysis) is, at the very least, valuable training in ascertaining what a specific subject is and the sequence in which its constituent elements should be cited. In India the work of developing CC goes on, it is used in a variety of libraries and it is studied in detail at every level of library science education.[23] However, questions are being raised even there. M. P. Satija, writing in 1989 in a practical introduction to the seventh edition, seems to have lost faith somewhat, expressing the opinion that this new edition has moved away from the needs of practising librarians and of the profession. CC has no formal editorial board and little professional input into the way in which it develops. Without such interaction it may lose its niche in the marketplace, despite its many excellent qualities.

Ranganathan really sought precision akin to computer analysis in a pre-computing age. The other general schemes are investigating their own suitability for assisting the process of automated information retrieval and yet this is an area where research with CC has not been carried out, despite the fact that many of its features would lend themselves to the exploitation of the electronic medium.

Despite some reservations that arise because it may carry too great a burden by seeking to accomplish a variety of tasks which have competing priorities, we wish the Colon Classification well. It may, nevertheless, be expected that it will slowly – very slowly in its own country where it still rouses fairly violent partisan emotions either pro or anti – fade away, leaving behind something valuable although intangible: a profound direct and indirect present and future influence on information retrieval systems, including computerized systems, which use classificatory ideas to any significant degree.

5. THE BIBLIOGRAPHIC CLASSIFICATION

H. E. Bliss laid the foundations of his work in two large tomes. These seek to establish the credentials for the classification which was to come and also recognize that reconstruction must be preceded by some demolition. *The organisation of knowledge and the system of the sciences*[24] (1929) concerns the structure of knowledge, showing his considerable debt to the ideas of the scientists and philosophers. *The organisation of knowledge in libraries*[25] published in 1933 discusses the principles of bibliographic classification, notation and what he saw as the faults of existing systems. His thoughts can be traced back at least as far as 1910 and yet BC (or BC1 as we should now call it, as there is a considerably revised BC2) was not completed until 1953.

Use and revision of BC

In the lifetime of Bliss and soon after, there was some interest generally in the BC and it was adopted as a scholarly scheme by about a hundred libraries, some of these being new services able to make a fresh start with impunity. The majority of these users are British libraries using the full BC. The publisher, H. W. Wilson, provided a revision bulletin and in the late 1960s two enthusiasts, Stott and Freeman, produced an abridgement for use in school libraries (referred to as the

ABC, Abridged Bibliographic Classification), which accounts for the majority of other users of the scheme, a maximum of 30 school libraries. If it were to serve the library and information world of the future, however, the longer term position had to be secured. Accordingly, a Bliss Classification Association was set up in 1967, and a particularly keen enthusiast, Jack Mills, initiated plans for a second edition of the scheme, to be known as BC2. This revision was based upon the retention of the much admired order of the main classes, but with the key concept of thorough-going facet analysis within each main class added to those features which had been considered essential in BC1.

Four or five of these desirable features must be considered. First, we have the concept of consensus; the scientific and educational consensus as Bliss called it. This is simply a way of acknowledging that an effective classification should be based upon the way in which specialists expect their knowledge to be organized and the way in which subjects are taught in colleges and universities. Bliss thought that the classificationist could find and act upon this consensus within each subject field. He also contended that the consensus is relatively stable and tends to become more so as subjects and disciplines become traditionally fixed. Critics have disputed whether there is such a clear-cut consensus, whether it is indeed durable, and to what extent Bliss found it. Nevertheless BC1 produced a useful and scholarly order within many classes. This was helped by a second principle, that of collocation and subordination. Collocation merely means the bringing together of groupings which have strong relationships into close proximity in the final order: one example is seen in Bliss collocating some (but not all) pure sciences with their appropriate application as in the bringing together of the human sciences, human biology, anthropology, health and medicine. Subordination means, of course, the careful placing of each specific theme in due subordinate position to the appropriate general subject. However, Bliss also used the term subordination in a more specialized sense, in his development of the idea of gradation by speciality. This concept reflects the influence on Bliss of the great French writer and classificationist, Auguste Comte, who had developed a system in the nineteenth century. The idea of gradation by speciality suggests that although a number of topics may be equal in rank, some are in a sense more specialized in that they draw on the findings of others, being therefore dependent upon these other subjects. Such dependent subjects should follow, rather than precede, the subjects on which they depend.

The result has been a much admired order of classes in BC given in the following table:

BC outline structure

2	Generalia	I	Psychology
3	Phenomena multidisciplinary topics	J	Education
6	Universe of knowledge	K	Society
7	Information Science	LA	Area studies

A	Philosophy and logic	LB	Geography
AM	Mathematics	LC	Travel
AY	Natural sciences	LD	History
B	Physics	P	Religion
C	Chemistry	Q	Social welfare
D	Astronomy	R	Politics
DH	Earth sciences	S	Law
E	Biological science	T	Economics &
GY	Ecology		management
H	Human sciences and studies	U/V	Technology &
HA	Human biology & anthropology		useful arts
HH	Health and medicine	W	Fine arts
		X	Philology

Bliss knew that no one order could ever satisfy everyone and a third memorable feature of BC1 is the provision of alternative locations – where they were sanctioned he felt by scholarly authority – which he built into the scheme. He thus provides two or more locations for certain subjects: one would be chosen and the other or others left blank. For instance, economic history can be subordinated to General History, or can go instead under Economics. Likewise in BCl, Bliss preferred Religion to be at Class P, where its association with History, Ethics and Social Work are stressed by contiguity, but he provided an alternative alongside Metaphysics in Class A, where Religion schedules could be developed as they are in Class P. This provision of alternative locations is a bold feature and one which reflects one of the major headaches for the classificationist and the classifier. It has been subjected to some invalid criticism. The real problem is that the various institutions applying any general system would want to exercise their distinctive individual right to determine what legitimate alternative locations should be.

The other principles of Bliss which warrant mention concern his insistence on brief notation and his choice of letters with this end in mind; and his provision for what in this manual is called synthesis, but what Dewey called *number building* and Bliss called *composite specification*. Bliss provided various schedules in BC1 for this; some were of general application, others for specialized use only. Some of these schedules were grafted on late in the development of BC1 and, not unnaturally with their quest for classification in great detail when such detail is required, they frequently sit rather uneasily alongside the idea of brief notation. The basic notation gives short and distinctive classmarks, with some scope for literal mnemonics, although Bliss was careful not to disturb the chosen order to create these. The full BC1 notation, that is if and when the extensions offered in the schedules of composite specifications are in evidence, is rather cumbersome to say the least.

However, our main purpose here is to examine the developments of the essential BC1 features wrought in the classes so far published of BC2. To date, these have been mainly in the social sciences, including education, but religion and ethics, health sciences – which is a particularly huge class – and economics/management have also appeared. The most recent class to appear has been Class J, Education, revised by D. J. Foskett and J. Foskett. The quest for helpful order within each main discipline has been revolutionized by rigorous facet analysis, using a standard citation order whenever possible. This provides predictability and should aid the integration of classification into a total information retrieval strategy for, by examining the citation order, we can readily see which associations have been displayed via the classification and just what the inevitable *distributed relatives* are. There are more alternative locations than before, systematic schedules for recurring themes, such as Form of Presentation and Geographical Area, have been improved and some recasting of the Generalia Class (the only class denoted by numerals and called by Bliss the *anterior numeral classes*). This has enabled the treatment of phenomena, allowing for the classification of the thematic work which deals with all aspects of 'coal' or 'water' in all of its possible contexts and so complements the more usual case in which they would belong in the context of one particular discipline. The whole enterprise is pervaded by the theories of Ranganathan and those who continue to probe the possibilities of faceted classification, notably the Classification Research Group in Britain.

A basic feature, not nearly as daunting as it may sound, is the promotion of retroactive synthesis by means of an inverted schedule. As examples should make clear, this merely means that the major facet in any class comes last in that class, so that when qualified by earlier facets, the notation becomes a retroactive one, which will indicate the appearance of a new facet in the classmark by a reversion to an earlier letter of the alphabet. The principle is well explained in the scheme itself and in other writings; the latter incidentally are mostly by Jack Mills,[26] although there is an independent monograph on BC1 and BC2[27] with valuable comment, although it was produced at a surprisingly early stage in the development of BC2.

It should always be borne in mind that detailed classification is optional in BC. Some examples may serve to illustrate the character and potential of BC2. The verbal concept analysis, crucial to all classifying, forms a vital part of these. For any theme with more than one facet, concepts must be identified, then put into BC citation order before the notational chain of linkage can be applied. Incidentally notational gaps may be made after each facet, as shown here, or after every three symbols. Either method, consistently applied, is permissible.

Example A
(From Class K Society)

Subject	Depressed areas and the problems of local handicapped people
Verbal concept analysis	The handicapped; depressed areas

Notational chain	KOBL Handicapped; KANV depressed region
Classmark	KOBL ANV
Comment	A simple example showing retroactive notation in operation

Example B

(From Class P Religion and Ethics)

Subject	Pentecostal hymns
Verbal concept analysis	Pentecostal Church; hymnology
Notational chain	PUXPE The Pentecostal Church
	PDXL hymnology
Classmark	PUXPE DXL (or expressed alternatively PUX PED XL)

BC: Current evaluation

In any critical scrutiny there are both features to praise and causes for regret. On the credit side, strenuous efforts have been made to incorporate the best original BC principles and to provide, within the shell of the original, a fully faceted and predictable modern system. There is ample advice in the schedules and elsewhere on applying the scheme, the Bliss Classification Association in Britain remains active, and Tony Curwen edits a lively *BC Bulletin*. There has been a little new uptake of BC by specialist organizations with interests in the areas covered by the publishing programme thus far. On the debit side, users have been lost to the scheme over the years because of revision delays, through institutional mergers into larger library units, and on account of the appeal to economy for libraries from participation in centralized cataloguing services which provide ready-made LC or DC classmarks. The geographical spread of users must be disappointing for the BCA. Also BC provides detail which many users might not need. Mills would argue that this detail is optional, but one pays for it in buying each class and the cost of buying the whole scheme, when or if it is ever finished, could well prove prohibitive. Like Bliss earlier, Mills might feel that crude sequences and blatant inefficiencies can be perceived within the older schemes, where others would see inefficiencies, of one sort or another, in BC2. While the enthusiasm and energy of Jack Mills and close associates deserves admiration, it has to be said that in many practical matters there has been projected an unfortunate impression of *other-worldliness*.

Work on this comprehensive revision began at the start of the 1970s and Mills once firmly believed that it would definitely be completed before the end of that decade: yet more than twenty years later the work is less than half done. It could be argued that this relates solely to lack of resources or that the information profession should have found financial support for a system so much in the vanguard in embracing modern classificatory principles. Yet, whatever is now argued, the actuality is there to see. The fact is that the scale of the enterprise was really quite enormous. It might have been better to have produced a broad classification as a revised BC (in harmony with the 1967 School's abridgement) and then to have worked on compatible depth classification schedules purely for those subject areas where demand clearly existed. As it is, the pattern of a predominantly one-person scheme, taking far too long to complete, looks all too sadly like a repetition of the problems encountered in BC1. Moreover, many BC1 users have been exasperated, not only by delays, but also by the extent of change demanded from the BC they had known and applied. BC2 represents as good a place as any to study the role and potential of classification in general, as well as faceted classification in particular. One might, however, query whether Bliss, a very conservative person, would altogether have approved of the BC of today. The most sceptical could argue that he might not even recognize it.

Finally, the future does hold the promise of interesting developments. The suggestion that a major restructuring of UDC should use as its base the BC2 faceted structure is an exciting one. It also indicates the high esteem in which BC is held and the many excellent qualities it displays, particularly its structure, rigid adherence to and observance of faceted principles, inherent logic and the clarity with which it is explained. These are important considerations and may suggest a role for BC in the future which could not have been predicted.

GENERAL SCHEMES – CURRENT DEVELOPMENTS

Although Fremont Rider's *International Classification* was the last fully developed general classification to appear and we might have expected no major schemes to appear suddenly, in 1992 Robert M. Losee[28] proposed a new scheme based upon the binary Gray Code which could classify documents automatically, 'without human intervention'. The system uses similarity techniques and measures in a quantitative fashion – such as the measure of expected mutual information – in order to analyse and provide a physical placing for documents. Losee distinguishes between the essential and desirable requirements of a classification system. The essentials he sees as: objectivity in classification; a scheme should be capable of dealing with all subjects comprehensively and in detail; it should provide a linear filing structure; and it should achieve an order which displays *increasing dissimilarity* as documents are increasingly separated from each other on the shelf. Less essential features are considered to be that the system should: be easy to use and search; be capable of being automated; be consistent with an existing popular system; include guidance and explanation of its implementation; and be hospitable to new subjects.

In its removal of the human classifier and its application of automatic classification theory (which will be fully discussed in Part Three) this is an interesting experiment – it suggests possibly the major thrust of forthcoming research and development. Perhaps, too, classificatory research will be less dominated in the future by the great figures – the individual personalities – who have loomed over it Titan-like to date. As M. P. Satija,[29] a disciple of Ranganathan, colourfully expressed it:

> Making or revising a general scheme of classification is far too heavy a load to be placed on one man's shoulders. Only an angel could dare to tread alone on this perilously zig-zag path strewn with thorns and obstacles. Inevitably rebukes always overwhelm the possible rewards in this one of the most difficult library tasks.

It remains to be seen how well the computer will cope with such a hazardous and thankless task. We should also emphasize, however, that Losee's system is at a very early stage in its career at present – an outline proposal – and has still to wrestle with all of the problems of implementation on the large scale and in practice. It suggests, however, that the field of general classification is not as fixed and immutable as we might at one time have imagined.

ISSUES FOR CONSIDERATION

1. 'The supposition that for a changing world this ever developing problem of the subject approach . . . was solved by an undergraduate in 1873 . . . has been an illusory assurance.' (Bliss) Will DC ever lose ground substantially? What, if anything, could replace it?

2. Have the problems with which UDC and CC wrestle been largely superseded, as concerns which might be solved by classification schemes, by the possibilities of the computerized retrieval methods?

3. Alan Gilchrist[30] poses an interesting question when he comments on the existence of the major general schemes:

> UDC was an improvement on DDC; and Bliss 2 is an improvement on both. Yet it is clear that DDC is used more widely than UDC which, in turn, is used more widely than Bliss 2; and this suggests that any new scheme, even if it is better than Bliss 2, is unlikely to be widely adopted . . . Clearly, DDC is useful as carried by MARC, but equally clearly it does not go far enough for many users. Conversely, the UDC is not useful for the users of MARC tapes but is widely used by others; while Bliss is struggling to gain a foothold. Is it inconceivable to think of some fruitful collaboration between these three schemes?

Is it indeed inconceivable? Clearly there are factors which militate against such a collaboration, not least the commercial imperative, while users too might have something to say about the form such a collaboration might take. How likely is such cooperation and how might it be implemented in practice?

4. Is it almost axiomatic that a specialized collection needs, for information management requirements, a specialized classification and retrieval system? This last point leads us nicely onto our next chapter where we will examine the nature, features and some particular examples of special schemes.

NOTES

1. Richardson, E. C., *Classification, theoretical and practical.* New York: Charles Scribner's Sons, 1901.
2. Clark, J. W., *The care of books: an essay on the development of libraries and their fittings from the earliest times to the end of the eighteenth century.* 2nd Edn. Cambridge: Cambridge University Press, 1901, p. 5.
3. Eco, Umberto, *The name of the rose.* Cambridge: Secker and Warburg, 1983.
4. Cited in Newman, L. M., *Leibnitz and the German library scene.* London: Library Association, 1966.
5. *Dewey Decimal Classification and relative index.* 20th Edn. Albany, NY: Forest Press, 1989.
6. Sweeney, Russell, An overview of the international use of the Dewey Decimal Classification. In *Dewey: an international perspective, workshop on the Dewey Decimal Classification and DDC 20.* London: Saur, 1991.
7. Berman, Sanford, DDC 20: the scam continues. *Library Journal,* 114 (15), 15th September 1989, pp. 45–49.
8. Sweeney, Russell, Library Association Dewey Decimal Committee. *Catalogue & Index,* 101–102, Autumn/Winter, 1991, p. 1.
9. Lamontagne, Leo E., *American library classification with special reference to the Library of Congress.* Hamden: Shoe String Press, 1961, p. 224.
10. Comaromi, John P., Michael, Mary Ellen and Bloom, Janet, *A survey of the use of the Dewey Decimal Classification in the United States and Canada.* Albany, NY: Forrest Press, 1975.
11. Tauber, Maurice F. and Feinberg, Hilda, The Dewey Decimal and Library of Congress Classifications: an overview. *Drexel Library Quarterly,* 10, Oct 1974, pp. 56–74.
12. Metcalfe, J., *Subject classifying and indexing of libraries and literature.* Sydney: Angus and Robertson, 1959.
13. *Subject cataloging manual classification,* prepared by the Office for Subject Cataloging Policy, Library of Congress. Washington: Cataloging Distribution Service, Library of Congress, 1992.
14. Chan, Lois Mai, *Immroth's guide to the Library of Congress Classification.* 4th Edn., Englewood, CO: Libraries Unlimited, 1990.
15. British Standards Institution, *Universal Decimal Classification.* (BS1000M:1985) London: British Standards Institution, 1985.
16. Williamson, Nancy J., Restructuring UDC: problems and possibilities. In *Classification research for knowledge representation and organisation: proceedings of the 5th International Conference on Classification Research, Toronto, Canada, June 24–28, 1991,* edited by Nancy J. Williamson and Michelle Hudon. Amsterdam: Elsevier, 1992.
17. Maltby, Arthur, *Sayers' manual of classification for librarians.* 5th Edn. London: Deutsch, 1978.
18. Gilchrist, Alan, UDC: the 1990's and beyond. In *Classification research for knowledge representation and organisation: proceedings of the 5th International Conference on Classification Research, Toronto, Canada, June 24–28, 1991,* edited by Nancy J. Williamson and Michelle Hudon. Amsterdam: Elsevier, 1992.
19. New deal for UDC. *FID News Bulletin,* 41 (11), 1991, p. 3.
20. Wiesthuis, G. A. and Bliedung, S. Thesaurification of UDC: a preliminary report. *In* The UDC: essays for a new decade, edited by Alan Gilchrist and David Strachan. London: ASLIB, 1990.
21. See, for example, the exposition of these ideas in Magee, B., *The philosophy of Schopenhauer.* Oxford: Clarendon, 1983.
22. Note that the comma is not normally displayed between the main class notation and the notation for Personality. This is in accord with Ranganathan's Canon of Reticence; if something is obvious it is not needed.
23. Satija, M. P., Use of Colon Classification. *International Classification,* 13(2), 1986, pp. 88–92.
24. Bliss, H. E., *The organisation of knowledge and the system of the sciences.* New York: H. W. Wilson, 1929.
25. Bliss, H. E., *The organisation of knowledge in libraries.* New York: H. W. Wilson, 1933.
26. Mills, Jack, The Bibliographic Classification. In *Classification in the 70's: a second look,* edited by Arthur Maltby. London: Bingley, 1976.

27. Maltby, Arthur and Gill, Lindy. *The case for Bliss: modern classification practice and principles in the context of the Bibliographic Classification.* London: Clive Bingley, 1979.
28. Losee, R. M., A Gray Code based ordering for documents on shelves: classification for browsing and retrieval. *Journal of the American Society for Information Science*, 43 (4), 1992, pp. 312–322.
29. Satija, M. J., *Colon Classification: 7th edition: a practical introduction.* New Delhi: Ess Ess Publications, 1989.
30. Gilchrist, Alan, UDC: the 1990's and beyond. In *Classification research for knowledge representation and organisation: proceedings of the 5th International Conference on Classification Research, Toronto, Canada, June 14–28, 1991,* edited by Nancy J. Williamson and Michelle Hudon. Amsterdam: Elsevier, 1992.

4 Special classification schemes and alternatives

Having considered systems which attempt to cater for all of knowledge, we shall now look at schemes which take a narrower view, focusing their attention in some way. The field of special classification is more vital than that of general classification in that a greater number and variety of interesting projects have been and are being developed. A special scheme is a smaller entity, both easier to envisage and to carry through.

A special classification scheme is a system with a narrower focus. Basically, special schemes attempt to do one of three things: they either attempt to provide a classification for a narrower subject, a discipline of study or an area of professional practice; or they provide a scheme which is aimed at a particular user group; or they cater for a form of material which requires special treatment.

Special classifications are particularly useful and often deliberately created for use in special libraries; they clearly have no value in general public or academic libraries for the arrangement of the major part of the collection. However, they may sometimes be of use in part of such a larger unit where the library has perhaps a very special section or an extended collection in a specific subject area, such as book printing and production in an art school library or in the Shakespeare collection in Birmingham. The local studies collection is another instance, for which large general libraries, both academic and public, have often had to create their own special scheme, in this case to allow for special local emphases in, perhaps, industries of significance and, more commonly, to cater for a greater specification of detail of place than any general scheme could afford to provide.

It is argued by Alan Bunch[1] that a community information collection too has very specialized needs which may not be met by the general schemes. For a small collection he details the Cambridgeshire Libraries' community information arrangement, which consists of 21 categories, with, as can be seen below, exceedingly mnemonic notation:

Ben	Benefits	Gov	Government
Bus	Business	Hea	Health
Car	Careers	Hou	Housing
Com	Community	Law	Legal rights

Con	Consumer	Mon	Money
CR	Community relations	SC	Senior citizens
Dis	Disability	Tra	Transport
Edu	Education	Ump	Unemployment
Emp	Employment	Wom	Women
Env	Environment	You	Youth
Fam	Family		

This is an unsophisticated but user-friendly scheme. But it illustrates the lack of helpful collocation of such a simple alphabetic arrangement of classes, separating disability and health – however memorable and easily retained it might be. It also illustrates the range of topics which would be gathered together by such a community information arrangement, topics which would inevitably be scattered by the disciplinary approach in a general scheme, where Law and the Environment and Business would be likely to be found in widely separated classes. The very basic categories, which have been identified in this scheme, can be added to and then further subdivided as necessary.

The limitations of the general schemes we have just examined are most noticeable in the special library, where the materials in a collection may be very strictly limited to only a small part of the schedules of a general system and yet where the general system's detail is not nearly great enough to satisfy the needs of the collection in those subject areas that are represented. There is an enormous range and variety of type of special library, covering all subject fields from atomic energy to botany to recipes. Most have as their function the provision of a service to a group of people in a specific industry sector, such as chemical and pharmaceutical, or a profession, perhaps architects or accountants, or it may be a group who share a similar interest or life experience, such as the library of an animal rights group or a collection serving a local women's association.

The main factor affecting the special library's selection of a scheme is that their collection will be limited in some way, usually in its subject content but sometimes by form in, for example, a library for the blind. In these circumstances, there is a dual purpose to the development or adoption of a special scheme; the desire for economy in not subscribing to a system which will provide vast areas of unused material and the wish fully to exploit and reflect the nature of the special library's own collection. It is the particular emphasis on the special subject field which is unlikely to be reflected by the general scheme. Although UDC, in its attempt to provide for the greater need for detail required in documentation work, may therefore provide for sufficient specification in the particular area of interest, it will still suffer from the first problem for special libraries in that all other subject areas are dealt with in excessive, even gratuitous, detail. To an extent this problem may be solved by provision of fascicule, when sections of schemes are published separately and may be purchased by libraries who only require a part of the coverage. UDC is, however, the most frequently used general scheme in special libraries and there are advantages to its use, not least its continuing and assured maintenance and development; an assurance which is often sadly lacking with special classification schemes. Another argument sometimes posited in favour of the use of a general scheme in the special library is that it prevents the special library user from taking too blinkered a view of the universe of knowledge.

What is most commonly needed in a special library is a detailed classification for the major subject of interest and a broader treatment for all of the rest of knowledge. In a special library in the oil industry, for example, the chief focus will obviously be upon petroleum engineering and the related technologies, as represented in the collection. The likely interest in construction engineering will not be enormous, but there will be a need for materials on construction of specific types of vessel and platform. There may, thus, even be differences of emphasis, interpretation and use of the other disciplines, depending upon the attitudes of the users of the special library. Construction engineering will be considered almost entirely in such a situation from the point of view of the industry itself, as will environmental science and personnel management. Yet the general scheme in its justifiable desire for neutrality of treatment can never afford to reflect such a bias.

General classifications are often unwieldy in use in special libraries, because even if they do provide sufficient detail, the resultant shelfmark or notation is likely to be excessively lengthy. The base will have to accommodate subjects which may never be used. The general scheme may also suffer because of its size as revision and updating is notoriously slow and each of the special subject areas has to compete with all of the other classes in the race for revision. The special library is going to suffer more in these circumstances than the general, as their collection will reflect more quickly the full range of new subject coverage.

The other situation in which a special scheme has advantages is when a library has special users with their own identifiable needs, as in the school library. In addition to the abridged versions of general schemes which have been produced, such as the *Abridged Bibliographic Classification* mentioned above, there are also a number of special schemes, two of which, *The Cheltenham Classification* and *Early stages*, will be examined in some detail later. The needs of a special group of users can often best be met by a scheme's flexibility in not prescriptively determining citation order. This is a common feature of special schemes, such as the *London Classification of Business Studies* and allows for the collocation of subjects on the shelf to be chosen to reflect the commonest approaches made by the users. Special systems also exist to deal with particular physical forms of material, which require an unusual arrangement or are likely to be approached in a different manner by users. The *Slide classification scheme*, for example, was created by Wendell and Tansey[2] in order to provide the most effective form of access to pictorial representations, whatever their disciplinary subject content.

There are several options available to the special librarian, then, in organizing and accessing stock from the collection:

1. Use of a general classification, with all of the attendant problems discussed above.

2. Adaptation or extension of a general classification scheme, often a difficult task, which may create problems as the collection grows in size and complexity. This solution too does not reflect the perspective or bias of the special library's users, but simply means that the class of most significance to the library can be expanded upon. Problems may ensue if, in the course of time, the division is revised and updated in the general scheme; having chosen to go one's own way, it is very difficult for the library to go back and take advantage of such changes and the consequent improvements which may have been made.

3. Use of an existing special scheme designed to cater for an appropriately restricted subject coverage or for a specific type of library. Clearly this solution is only possible where such a system exists, covers the subject area effectively, is available to the library in purchased form and, preferably, where the scheme is likely to be updated and revised on a regular basis. Often there are no guarantees of such future development when an excellent special scheme appears, particularly since such schemes are frequently the work of enthusiastic and dedicated individuals.

4. The development or creation of a special scheme by the library itself. This option, as with adaptation, is accompanied by dangers and these, along with the manner of creation of such a scheme will be examined later in the chapter.

5. The rejection of classification in the library. Materials may be arranged by some other principle and subject access provided by a subject index or via an automated database of records. Again we will return to this option later when we consider the use of post-coordinate techniques as an alternative to classification.

THE PRINCIPLES OF SPECIAL SCHEMES

There are a large number of special schemes in existence. Some are very limited in usage, perhaps developed by an individual and used in only one library; others have become popular among a number of libraries. There are schemes which have been created by librarians or curators of a collection, devised by an organization to provide access to or to arrange its documentation, and those which have been invented to organize bibliographies. Interested non-professional enthusiasts have developed their own, just as Jefferson did in the scheme which was first adopted and developed by the Library of Congress. The following are a select sample, with brief descriptions, of some of the schemes which exist, illustrating the range of subjects covered and purposes:

- *Social Services Libraries' Classification Scheme* – This is a fairly straight-forward treatment of a restricted subject area.
- *Moys' Classification scheme for law books* – created by Elizabeth Moys for Butterworths who publish a very wide range of materials in the field of law, including the LEXIS databases of legal information.
- *ICONCLASS: iconographic classification system* – here we have a scheme designed for the accessing and retrieval of pictorial images rather than documents.
- *Hitlist: a classification scheme and thesaurus for housing information* – published by Sheffield City Council. The existence of this scheme reflects an awareness of a subject poorly treated which as a topic would likely be scattered amongst a number of disciplines, such as architecture, social services and so on.
- *CI SfB* – a faceted scheme for use in the organization of all kinds of documentation relating to construction projects.
- *Thesaurofacet* – a combined faceted classification and thesaurus, produced by English Electric (see Chapter 5 for a fuller discussion).
- *Thesaurus of play terms: a thesaurus with an associated classification relating to all aspects of children's play* – an interesting and unusual subject for classification.
- *Classification scheme for railway company archives* – here a special role for the information is clearly envisaged and again the special needs of documentation and archival material are indicated.
- *Scheme of classification for careers-related information* – published by the Institute of Careers Officers, an organization which evidently felt that their subject area had special requirements. In professional practice subjects often display a quite different relation to each other from that which is found in their academic study.
- *Classification scheme for adult education* – published by the Institute of Educational Librarians, we have here not only a restricted subject area but also a level of treatment within that subject.
- *A slide classification system for the organization and automatic indexing of interdisciplinary collections of slides and pictures* – this scheme deals with all subject areas and is therefore general in subject but special in its treatment of those subjects as they are found in a specific form.
- *Historical collections classification scheme for small museums* – produced by the Museums Association of Australia, this provides restricted subject coverage further restricted to a particular size of collection.

Some of the most interesting of these schemes will be discussed in more detail later in the chapter; the list, however, illustrates the range of scope, subject coverage and emphasis which may prevail.

There are no guarantees that a subject will have been catered for in the form of the existence of a special scheme; the appearance of such schemes is quite arbitrary and often dependent on the chance enthusiasm of an individual. The proportion of schemes which combine the functions of classification with that of a thesaurus is significant. The special classification scheme must start from a very clear perspective of the role it is going to play within the library. The first question we must ask ourselves is *why*; why is the scheme being created? Will it be used for shelf arrangement or for subject retrieval? Why are existing schemes not catering sufficiently for the particular demands of the subject? Do users have particular needs which are not being met? Does more detail have to be provided? If so, are there aspects of the subject in which such detail is especially desirable?

A full understanding of the needs of the likely users of the scheme is essential; of their most typical approaches to information and of their attitudes to their discipline. Equally the scheme should be based very firmly on literary warrant, that is, a firm knowledge of the kinds of document with which the classification will have to cope. Many special schemes of excellence have thus been developed for use with a comprehensive collection, such as the *FIAF classification* for film and television which is published by the International Federation of Film Archives, or they may have been created for the arrangement of an extensive bibliographic tool such as the *Inspec classification* created for the subject arrangement of bibliographic records in *Science abstracts*. In both instances, these build very effectively upon such an awareness of the literature of the subject. It is also important that the scheme is based upon sound classificatory principles, although as Gilchrist[3] has noted 'successful schemes have been devised without conscious recourse to classification theory'.

While special classification schemes may be either enumerative or faceted in nature, the latter approach is the more common. A significant number of excellent special schemes are based upon synthetic principles, such as the construction industry's *CI SfB* – an early faceted scheme with a sound and continuing development programme – and, in many ways, it is in the field of special classification that such principles have been most enthusiastically seized upon.

SOME EXAMPLES OF SPECIAL SCHEMES

The most effective way of discussing special classification, given the variety and idiosyncratic nature of many of the schemes in existence and the consequent impossibility of stating general principles which may equally apply to all, is for us simply to examine in a little more detail some examples which illustrate the range of approach that has been taken.

THE LONDON CLASSIFICATION OF BUSINESS STUDIES[4]

The first edition of this scheme, by Vernon and Lang, was published by The London Graduate School of Business Studies in 1970, having been tested in the School's library for a number of years. In 1973 a programme of revision by a small working party was established to produce a second edition which would allow updating of the scheme and the expansion of certain classes. Unfortunately, despite the expressed hope in the Introduction to the second edition (LCBS2), which was published in 1979, no further significant revision or new edition has as yet appeared. Based upon the basis of literary warrant, the scheme has also drawn extensively upon the expertise of a large number of practitioners as well as utilizing some sections of BC2. From this wealth of expertise it emerges combining classificatory theory with pragmatic effectiveness. In 1979, at the time of publication of the second edition, there were 76 known users of the scheme, ranging from a graduate school of business administration in Tel Aviv to institutes of management, banks and industrial companies. The wide geographic spread was particularly noteworthy and encouraging for the creators of the scheme.

LCBS was the second business studies classification to appear; its only predecessor, the *Harvard Classification of Business Studies* (1960), is an enumerative scheme, while LCBS was designed upon analytico-synthetic principles. It consists of a number of classes, the notation for the foci of which may be combined to specify compound subjects. The scheme itself does not dictate the facet citation order, leaving that decision to individual libraries and classifiers with a reminder to record decisions for future consistency. Clearly this flexibility is designed not to discourage users by too dogmatic and restrictive an approach; this means, however, that there is no assurance of standardization in usage of the scheme. LCBS does, however, suggest a preferred order of citation, which may be adopted in order to avoid inconsistency.

The schedules for the classes provide an abundance of detail and these have the added advantage of forming a thesaurus, which can be used in compilation of a subject index in support of the shelf order. There are three main categories, each of which contains a number of classes and a set of auxiliary schedules:

Management Responsibility		*Environmental Studies*	
A	Management	J	Economics
AY	Administrative Management	JZ	Transport
AZ	The Enterprise	K	Industries
B	Marketing	L	Behavioural Sciences
BZ	Physical Distribution	M	Communication
C	Production	N	Education
D	Research and Development	P	Law
E	Finance and Accounting	Q	Political Science
F	Personnel	R	Philosophy, Science &
G	Industrial Relations		Technology

Analytical Techniques		*Auxiliary Schedules*	
S	Management Science	1	People and Occupations
T	Operational Research	2	Products and Services
U	Statistics	3/4	Standard Subjects
V	Mathematics	5	Geographical Divisions
W	Computer Science	6	Time
X	O & M and Work Study	7	Form
Y	Library & Information Science		

As can be seen, only certain subjects are included – the editors being very conscious of the need to avoid the temptation of becoming over general – and other disciplines which in any general scheme would have their own place in the arrangement, such as mathematics, are dealt with as though a subdivision of business studies. This is of value to the majority of users, as this is how they will view the material required, but one can see how a distorted view of the universe might be promulgated in a user who is thus encouraged in his or her vision of mathematical science as a subsidiary aid to business management.

As we see from the above outline, the notation is comprehensible and conveys order reasonably well as it is chiefly alphabetic, although standard subdivision tables use numbers. It is not consistently expressive of hierarchy and facets are joined simply and in all instances by a slash '/', which although it fails to identify the nature of the facet to follow, does ensure simplicity for users.

Examples
1. Trade unions in the oil industry.
Trade unions	GC
Oil industry	KTC
Classmark	**GC/KTC**
2. Labour relations in England in the motor industry.
Industrial relations	GA
Motor industry	KHB
England	5111
Classmark	**GA/KHB 5111**
3. The use of sampling techniques in market research.
Market research	BD
Sampling	UD
Classmark	**BD/UD**

The schedules are very well supported by an able and informative introduction by K. G. B. Bakewell, who revised the scheme for its second edition, and by the helpful and prolific notes throughout. Overall this scheme has a very important contribution to make in the burgeoning field of business studies. It has developed a solid phalanx of users and these should be encouraged to remain loyal to the system. It will be a matter for regret if LCBS is not maintained and supported by a programme of ongoing revision.

INSPEC CLASSIFICATION[5]

INSPEC is a classically simple, enumerative scheme, which provides enormous detail in specification within four broad classes:

Section A   Physics
Section B   Electrical engineering and electronics
Section C   Computers and control
Section D   Information Technology

These classes represent the published sections of the *Science Abstracts* and the scheme's main function is to provide for the physical arrangement of these abstracts in the classified sequence of the publication, rather than for shelf arrangement. In the Introduction to the published schedules, attention is also drawn to the use of the classification as an aid to subject retrieval online from an electronic database of records. The use of the scheme is largely seen, then, as an aid to subject retrieval whether from a printed source or from an electronic database. The user interested in neutron physics turns first to the subject index, where they find the classmark **A2820** and, then, consulting the schedules, find attention directed to related subjects and notes indicating the extent of use of that classmark.

A2820   *Neutron physics*
(see also A2540 Nucleon induced reactions and scattering)
1977–. 1973–76 use A4610; before, use A1243.

The final note in this entry indicates what will be retrieved by use of the notation, when the notation is combined with a date of publication as part of a search. This latter feature is necessitated by the fact that as INSPEC has grown it has proved necessary to allow for ever-greater specification of detail in order to cope with the way in which the literature has become ever more minutely focused. However, older material has not been reclassified as it would in most library collections, understandably enough, given the many millions of records available via INSPEC online. Such a reclassification would be a mammoth task and could not be applied retrospectively to a printed index, the value of which is precisely as a retrospective resource. In information retrieval too, especially in such a rapidly changing field, searchers are often interested in material of a specific age, most commonly recent material, and therefore it is not unhelpful to combine the classmark with a time-span, as one must do here.

The chief advantages of INSPEC are its provision of enormous detail and special subject concepts such as the mass ranges peculiar to Physics, and the quasi-hierarchical structure of its notation. The latter allows for the effective use of truncation in an electronic environment, when, for example, one can identify all records which have a classmark beginning **A28**, knowing that they will all be concerned with nuclear engineering and nuclear power.

THE CI SFB SYSTEM: FOR USE IN PROJECT INFORMATION AND RELATED GENERAL INFORMATION[6]

The CI SfB began life in 1966 when the Swedish SfB system was described by B. Agard Evans and Egil Nicklin and recommended as a tool for classification and filing in the building world. Initially it was suggested that it be used in conjunction with UDC for the arrangement of libraries, but since then the system has developed considerably with the addition of new tables. CI Sfb evolved under the aegis of the SfB Bureau and the International Council for Building Research Studies and Documentation (CIB) and its original intention was to provide a means of coordinating the control and handling of project information. It has therefore a different emphasis from the other special schemes which we have examined.

The system has to be able to handle, describe and identify the subject content of a range of different types of document and different information sources. We are not limited to published documents of the traditional kind, although these must be dealt with by the system. Rather, it caters for the full range of sources: conventionally published materials, such as books and journal articles; non-conventional publications such as reports literature, briefings and translations; trade literature, such as product catalogues and pamphlets; illustrative materials, such as drawings and specifications; official information, including legislation, regulations, codes of practice and standards; and management or project control information, like contracts, budgets and communications between the various parties involved in any project. CI SfB was designed as a system which would allow the cross-referencing of such a collection of disparate materials, where someone working on any project could identify useful material on, for example, drainage systems from any source whether general or specific to this project or perhaps consider solutions from other projects. The sources would include materials which were exclusive to an individual building organization as well as conventionally and freely available information. CI Sfb is therefore a more complete, if very specialized, approach than those we have so far considered, which might find favour in other types of organization with the development of *management information systems* and *executive information systems*, which have the aim of bringing together relevant information whatever the source both internal and external to the organization.

The principles underlying the development of the system were that: it should be internationally applicable, providing unambiguous and internationally comprehensible codes for concepts; it should ensure standardization of concept description; it should be flexible and built upon faceted ideas; it should provide the most helpful order of concepts; and it should provide a useful mechanism for the sorting and retrieval of information in an automated system. Three major facets are identified in the system:

Table 1	Table 2	Table 3
Elements	Construction	Resources
e.g. external walls	e.g. wiring	e.g. cable

CI Sfb takes a fully faceted approach with the combination of notation for individual facets, the use of facet indicators such as brackets and the ability to develop and build further facets as required. It has a continuing development programme under the coordinating control of the SfB Development Group with responsibility for publication devolving on individual national agencies – the most recent reprint appearing in 1992 – and it has a body of devoted users internationally. It is likely to continue to build upon the sound work which has been achieved to date.

MOYS' CLASSIFICATION SCHEME FOR LAW BOOKS[7]

It is refreshing to come upon a classification so unabashed about its focus upon books as to name these in its title. The first edition of this scheme appeared in 1968, with a second edition in 1982. It is the work of a single author Elizabeth Moys who has also produced a *Manual of law librarianship* and, as such, it is an example of the excellent work which can be accomplished by a dedicated and knowledgeable individual. The field of law is a complex subject area with many very special characteristics, such as the significance of jurisdiction, in its classification. Documents often have to be classified as a piece of legislation, interpretation, discussion or case study. The concept of division into primary and secondary materials must, therefore, be acknowledged in the classification of law. The scheme has, as a consequence of its creator's special understanding of the literature and its users, proven to be very popular.

One might have expected that law, as an ancient and revered subject of study, would by now have developed a classification system reflecting its significance, but it is rather sad to note that, in her *Introduction* to the second edition, Elizabeth Moys declares that consultations were mainly with 'law teachers and law librarians (practitioners being unenthusiastic on the subject of legal classification)'.[8]

Moys' system has several interesting features, the most unusual of which is the provision of two class marks for each subject listed in the schedules. This has been done largely in acknowledgement of the fact that often general libraries want and need the extra detail and features of a special scheme and Moys therefore utilizes a notation which will allow libraries using the two most popular general schemes, DC and LC, to fit the scheme into their existing arrangement at the appropriate class, **340** for DC and **K** for LC, without affecting the use of all of the other classes. Even in a special library such an approach may have advantages in that the library may, therefore, choose to employ the rest of LC or DC for other subjects as treated, thus allocating them a more representative place in the universe of knowledge than would be achieved by their subordination as an aspect of law. However, Moys does offer the use of a subdivision **KZ** for other subjects for special libraries who prefer a more economical approach and do not wish to purchase the complete editions of LC or DC.

For each subject as found in the schedules, then, there are two classmarks provided:

LC		DC
KE	Ancient and Medieval Law	343
	BYZANTINE LAW	
251	General works	.5
255	Collections	.51
256	Basilica	.52

so that for the subject of general works on Byzantine Law, there are two options **KE251** or **343.5**.

The approach is fundamentally enumerative with respect to jurisdiction, with all the common law jurisdictions grouped together with the individual countries, such as Scotland or the United States or the Channel Islands, being specified by the application of notation from a special Table. The basic order of classes is therefore:

General and non-national legal systems (including international, religious and
    ancient)
Modern national legal systems
    Common Law
    Treatises
    Other modern legal systems
Non-legal subjects

Beyond this basic enumeration, synthesis is utilized fairly extensively via such tables as the one described above and others which specify elements, for example, the legislative nature of materials and the subjects of law.

At all times, there is indicated in this scheme an awareness and understanding of the use to which the classification will be put. Since the second edition, revision has continued and amendments and additions are published in the *Journal of Law Librarianship*.

FIAF CLASSIFICATION SCHEME FOR LITERATURE ON FILM AND TELEVISION[9]

This scheme was originally devised by Michael Moulds and the first edition appeared in 1980. It immediately became popular in the documentation collections of the members of the *Fédération Internationale des Archives du Film* and, as a consequence of its wide appeal, an international editorial committee was set up with members from Britain, Holland, Denmark, Australia and Sweden to supervise the production of a second edition, which eventually appeared in 1992. There has been then an implicit acknowledgement of the value of Moulds' initial work and an affirmation of the likely continuation of the FIAF classification.

As in all special schemes, the main divisions of the subject have been chosen to reflect the major concerns of the subject area with which users will be primarily concerned. In this instance, we have a set of categories, peculiar to film and television:

(0)	Reference material	FT5	Education, research
FT0	Generalities	FT6	Aesthetics, theory,
FT1	Corporate bodies		criticism
FT2	Industry economics, production	FT7	History, genres, specific films/programmes
FT3	Distribution, exhibition, transmission	FT8	Biography
		FT9	Miscellanies, varia,
FT4	Society and cinema/TV		special collections

This is a flexible and very detailed system. Primarily enumerative in structure, it also allows for some synthesis via the provision of *Auxiliary Tables* for Form, Persons and Technical terms. In addition, at various points in the schedules there is provision for the further specification of subject using the UDC Systematic Tables. For example, if one were classifying the photography of crowds one would turn to the photography section of the schedule at FT23, a subdivision of which FT231 allows for the specification of photography of particular subjects. Here the classifier is instructed to divide further by UDC, that is, to go to the UDC tables for the number for the particular subject 'crowds' which is [301.182]. This notation can then be added to the original notation to provide a final classmark for photography of crowds of **FT231 [301.182]**.

The extent of the detail which can be specified is very great and is evidently considered necessary as is witnessed in the popularity of the scheme. The emphasis on archiving and documentation in its application would, of course, render such a level of detail necessary. There is, however, a degree of flexibility available to users of the scheme who do not feel the need to utilize the full extent of the detail and they may, for example, choose not to apply the division by tables. The specification possible is impressive and potentially very valuable as can be seen from the following examples taken from the index:

Gag comedies	732.2
Gags: acting	227.14
Gambling in fiction films/plays	748.1
Games in fiction film/plays	739
Games: merchandising	336.3

| Games shows | 759.5 |
| Gamma control: signal processing | 237.72 |

The use of alphabetic subdivision, at various points throughout the schedules, is a very common feature and is well justified here, where often the arrangement will be by titles of films or of people. For example, in the *Genres and specific films* class, there are various points at which such a listing is encouraged. At 757 specific characters as the subject of films or plays are listed alphabetically (e.g. FT757JAM is given for 'James Bond in films or plays') and we are told that a reference or added entry (in a catalogue) may be made from the genre number 734.5 for 'Espionage' or 'Agents'. This would involve a certain degree of scattering of material and one would expect to find material on the James Bond films at both numbers. A degree of further scattering is evident in a perusal of the schedules as there might also be material in works on spies as an occupational group in films at FT757-05[355.4]; while at 79GOL one would find works which dealt with *Goldfinger* as a film alone. The index to a collection would, of course, address this problem of scatter, but it is interesting to note the appearance of the phenomenon, evident both in general and special classifications.

The notation can and does become fairly complex, largely in its filing order of elements such as dashes and brackets. One interesting feature of the scheme is the emphasis on its use in the creation of parallel sequences of works by the material in which they are manifested. The prefix FT is used for Film and Television but other sequences or collections could use other prefixes such as M for mass media and R for radio. Thus it would be possible to separate the various media within a single collection or if one were dealing with a single sequence collection and did not wish to distinguish the media concerned one could simply omit the prefix. Equally the prefix could be used as a non-filing element, purely for identification of media as subject, although this might lead to some confusion on the part of the user.

THE CHELTENHAM CLASSIFICATION: A LIBRARY CLASSIFICATION FOR SCHOOLS[10]

This is a very old special scheme. Originally published in 1937, the second edition appeared in 1958 and had at that time been in use in the Cheltenham Ladies' College for 50 years. Designed specifically to meet the needs of school libraries, the system was adopted by a number of school librarians, although it does possess some notable idiosyncrasies, perhaps due to the time and setting of its creation. It is a broad, enumerative scheme which attempts to provide an arrangement 'on similar lines to those on which subjects are taught'. This principle produces a main class outline quite different from that of the general schemes:

Main Classes

A   Theology

B	Philosophy
C	Sociology
D	History
E	Language and Literature
	General
	English
F	French Language and Literature
G	German Language and Literature
	Other Teutonic Languages
H	Italian Language and Literature
	Other Romance Languages
J	Spanish and Portuguese Languages
K	Classics (Greek and Latin)
L	Eastern European Languages and Literature
M	Science
P	Geology and Geography
R	Applied Science. Technology
S	Fine Arts
W	Junior Library
Y	Fiction Library
Z	Generalia. Library Science

The emphasis on languages is probably the most notable feature of this outline, reflecting as it does the emphasis placed upon these in the curriculum. The separation of history from geography, but its collocation with sociology, again is reflective of the organization of teaching in schools. The scheme in outline sits not unnaturally with the curriculum even today, although the lack of attention to mathematics is perhaps disappointing and there are obvious omissions, such as computer science. The influence of a certain type of school and something of a bias towards young ladies is also evident in the schedules. The sports section, which includes a division for 'Shooting, Fishing and Big Game Hunting' but fails to mention such inappropriate sports as basketball, would perhaps not best represent the literature or the interests of the pupils in a modern state secondary school run on co-educational principles. There are also some fairly sexist observations to be found in the Introduction, where we are told, for example, that 'Food and Food Values may go under either Domestic Economy or Chemical Technology. (Boys and Girls schools would probably differ here.)'

There are two interesting classes: the Junior Library and the Fiction Library. The former, an attempt to provide an even broader and simpler treatment for younger pupils in just 14 classes; it provides some unique categories, such as 'Legends', 'Folk and Fairy Tales' and 'Animal Stories' and eschews disciplinary titles, such as geography, in favour of the more approachable and appealing descriptors 'Travel and Adventure'. The Fiction Library is rather far removed from

Language and Literature and exists to cater for what are described as non-standard authors, presumably those who are not part of the curriculum and who might therefore be deemed popular and light. The scheme does suggest that this division may be ignored and that literature and fiction may be classified together, thus restating the perennial dilemma of literature (serious study) versus fiction (light amusement). Fiction, as a class, consists of a fairly conventional series of genres such as 'Detective and Mystery Stories' and 'School Life'.

The notation is a mixed one which uses capital letters for the main classes, unusually Roman numerals for their chief divisions and Arabic numerals for the subdivisions of these. In such a broad treatment this complexity would seem scarcely necessary.

It is worth examining a particular division to see the extent of specification which is thought to be desirable in a school library by the devisers of the system. Therefore, for biology we find in the schedules:

M	Science
VI	Biology
51	General
.1	History
.2	Biography
.3	Microscopy
52	Nature study
53	Evolution and heredity
54	Bacteriology
55	Pathology: general
56	*Blank*

The full classmark for 'Bacteriology' would, therefore, be **M.VI.54**.

Fegan and Cant, who revised the scheme for the second edition, state that, 'We have not let the scheme run away with us; that is we have not run the tables out to very minute subdivisions not likely to be needed in a school library', and, indeed, this is wise for, as with any special scheme, the detail should reflect the literature and its usage – despite the impulse to provide ever more detail.

EARLY STAGES LIBRARY CLASSIFICATION SCHEME AND INDEX[11]

This scheme, designed by the Grampian Region Schools Library Service, targets specifically the early primary years, Primary 1–3, in school libraries and is designed to cater for the needs of that user group. The essential characteristic of the user group which has been identified is that they may not be able to read, yet it is felt useful that the concept of subject arrangement should be introduced in the junior library. The Cheltenham Scheme too has a Junior Library section but there a larger segment of the primary school is clearly envisaged. *Early stages* has been used for a number of years in Grampian, in order to ensure consistency of approach across Grampian primary schools, and the present scheme represents a recent revision.

Having acknowledged that the primary problem is that of users who will not be able to translate and interpret notation, the scheme has opted for a colour-coding approach. This is simple and very effective. However, it is likely to be very unhelpful for the small, but significant, proportion of users who have difficulties in distinguishing colours. There is also no order to the significance in colour and the order of the categories will, therefore, have to be identified via guiding, not admittedly a huge problem. It is perhaps an oversight that the filing order of the colours was not ascertainable from the published schedule.

Subjects are analysed on a topical basis and the outline of the classes below illustrates the scheme in its general application:

Green	**Nature**	**Brown**	**Community**
A	General	A	General
AN	Animals	B	Human body, senses
AP	Pets, zoo	C	Clothing
B	Birds	F	Food
C	Country	HB	Houses, homes
E	Environment	HS	Health, safety
F	Farming/fishing	I	Industries
I	Insects	M	Myself
P	Plants, trees	P	People at work
R	Rivers, ponds	S	School
S	Seasons	T	Transport
SEA	Seashore	U	Underground, holes
		V	Villages, towns

Yellow – Places and Past		**Orange**	**Science**
A	General	A	General
C	Countries, places	C	Colour
H	History	E	Earth Sciences
P	Prehistoric life	H	Hot, cold
		M	Measuring, counting
		SH	Shape
		SP	Space, stars
		T	Time
		W	Water, weather

Blue	**Activities**	**Red**	**Language and Lore**
A	General	A	General
C	Crafts	B	Books, reading
F	Festivals, customs	D	Dictionaries, words
M	Music	F	Fairy tales, legends
S	Sport/entertainment	G	Ghosts, witches

P	Poetry, rhymes
R	Religion

Ironically, Religion appears last in this scheme and first in the Cheltenham Classification. The categories here identified are a good reflection of children's informational topics as they appear in the literature for this age group, as they are taught in primary schools and as they interest young readers. An unusual aspect of the scheme's treatment of works is that, although fiction and non-fiction are distinguished, a white sticker on the spine indicating fiction, both are analysed in precisely the same way for subject content and stand alongside one another on the library shelves. This is likely to be useful in that young children do not really distinguish the two and may be happy to find a book about aeroplanes or puppies, whether in fictional or factual form. Equally, a lot of picture books for young readers, although apparently fictional in treatment, are really using the mechanism of the story to get information across to the child; witness the many story books about the birth of a new brother or sister in a family, and works on difficult social situations, on separation and visits to hospital and the like. There is then a lesser distinction in the minds of writers and readers alike; it is, therefore, justifiable and ultimately more helpful to group fictional works in this way in such a library.

The scheme has a straightforward and attractively illustrated manual and index, which provide guidance on the implementation of the system and its relationship with the catalogue in the library. The schedules are simple enough in their published form to be given to slightly older children to explain the concepts of subject arrangement. While the end result is, inevitably, still a fairly broad arrangement of works on the shelves, it is one which will be easily understood by children and, hence, will satisfy the demands of practical utility. The junior library for the early stages is also likely to be sufficiently small not to test the fairly constrained limits of the system.

ICONCLASS: AN ICONOGRAPHIC CLASSIFICATION SYSTEM

To conclude this brief and select examination of special classification systems, it is interesting to note the parallels evident in one non-bibliographic classification system, Iconclass. This system was created in order to provide a means of identifying the content of works of Western art in terms of their subject content, themes and motifs, so that the records of the works themselves could be retrieved from electronic databases, as an alternative form of approach from retrieval purely by title or artist. The scheme would be applied to the photographic reproductions of such works rather than the works themselves. Such subject content differs significantly from the subject content of documents and we can imagine the difficulties associated with the correct subject analysis of, for example, a piece of abstract art where the image is not obviously representational and we may have to rely on statements of intent by the artist or the interpretation of art theoreticians. There is also the associated problem of differences in interpretation of artistic entities; the same difficulties would apply to the analysis of the subject content of one of Ezra Pound's poems. What is it about? Many volumes may have been devoted to the justification of interpretations of such works.

Iconclass tackles the problem, interestingly, in a reversal of the commonly accepted classificatory approach, not by an analysis of the materials, basing the system upon a principle related to that of literary warrant, but by taking the philosophic and abstract route of providing 'descriptions *not of actual works of art* but of subjects, themes and motifs *in abstractio* represented by codes'[12] (author's italics).

Originating in 1947 under the direction of Professor H. van de Waal, although not at that point envisaged as a tool for automated retrieval systems, Iconclass has been adopted as a useful mechanism in such an electronic environment. The scheme assigns notation to concepts in a way with which we are perfectly familiar as classifiers and provides great detail in specification of subjects, as these have been revealed in Western art. It is explicated in 18 volumes of classification, bibliography, index and users' manual; a magnum opus indeed, the classification schedules listing tens of thousands of subjects and vying in sheer extent with the major general bibliographic classification schemes. The bibliography (1973) is arranged in a classified sequence according to Iconclass and for each classmark a brief bibliographic record of all of the documentary literature which deals with art iconographically is listed. It is possible by consultation of the classmark for 'apples' in the sequence to locate the records for documents which discuss apples as a subject of art. Works which deal with Salome's dance could therefore be retrieved as a group or those which portray sunflowers or death. Iconclass has also been used as the system of arrangement in published collections of photographic reproductions of works of art.

As in any bibliographic classification, van de Waal identified the main classes into which any subject or theme would fit:

1   Religion and magic
2   Nature
3   Human being, man in general
4   Society, civilization, culture
5   Abstract ideas and concepts
6   History
7   Bible
8   Literature
9   Classical mythology and ancient history

There are some unusual divisions here, which we would take serious issue with if we were dealing with a bibliographic classification, such as the separation of Religion and the Bible and the interpolation between History and Ancient History of the Bible and Literature. The order of main classes would appear to be

131

somewhat arbitrary, although clearly reflecting the subjects as they are found. It is also refreshing and thought-provoking to find the open acknowledgement of *Abstract ideas and concepts*; this is a solution which in practice many a hard-pressed classifier would warmly welcome, when struggling with the topical treatment of ideas.

The notation is mixed, complex in its use of punctuation marks and expressive of hierarchy. The scheme employs the device of tables interpolated at various points in the schedules which may be applied to a particular group of subjects. There are also points in the scheme where notation is not employed and, for the representation of individual people, for example, names can be placed within the notational string enclosed in brackets.

While this system is not designed for the physical subject arrangement of materials – largely because it is uncommon for pictorial images to be arranged iconographically – but rather for the arrangement of a bibliography or subject/concept retrieval in an automated environment, it has experienced many of the problems common to any bibliographic classification and has turned to some of the same solutions. The enumerative listing of subjects, in main classes, supported for economy by tables of standard divisions where applicable, is a solution with no great novelty for those of us familiar with bibliographic classification.

We have, then, seen schemes created by individuals and schemes created by committee. We have seen local, parochial systems and ones which are truly international. Some are strictly enumerative, others enthusiastically synthetic. About the only point of agreement in principle is that there should be wholesale disagreement. It is, however, a healthy variety and one which bodes well for the future. Little is fixed and no doubt new schemes will appear quite different from those we have discussed here.

CREATING A SPECIAL SCHEME

What if there is no scheme which caters for our special needs though and we decide to go it alone? We might choose to embark upon the creation of our own special scheme. There are certain considerations which must be borne in mind before we rush into the not inconsiderable task of inventing a classification scheme, even if it is *only* a special scheme. The initial work of developing schedules may not in itself be onerous and, given that no appropriate available scheme exists, then such work may be deemed desirable if not unavoidable. However, the scheme must be developed according to principles best suited to the collection and the library must be alert to the need to continue to update and revise the scheme. One danger lies in the relegation of such a task to an individual in the library service, who may not bear in mind the need to establish and record the principles and the method of practice in both using and continuing to develop and expand the scheme. The establishment of policy, codes of practice and a manual of use of the scheme, for both classificationists and classifiers, are therefore essential.

Aids to the creation of a special scheme are available and anyone attempting such a task would, of course, be well advised to familiarize themselves with the principles of classification. There may also be guides which would be helpful in specific subject areas such as the booklet produced by the Northern Ireland Council for Voluntary Action, *Designing a community information system.*[13] Significant organizations of this kind may be able to provide help and guidance or refer you to other sources of assistance, perhaps suggesting libraries to contact in order to benefit from the experience of other practitioners.

There are several stages in the construction of a special classification scheme, which are detailed below.

Stage 1 – identification of concepts

The first stage in the process is to identify the subject terms used in the field to be covered. For this purpose it is best to work from the literature and from the literature of the kind with which the scheme will be used, that is, if only books are to be arranged then the terms should be chosen from books; if journal articles then these should be examined; if reports literature are to be included then they should form part of the base from which the system will be developed. The intention here is to build up a select base of terms, from which the subject area can be analysed into its component facets, and that that base should be built upon literary warrant.

A significant sample of pieces of literature should therefore be analysed into its discrete subject concepts. This sample should, as noted, reflect the kinds of documents which will be held in the collection and should also represent not just the most recent publications, but should reflect the subject as it has developed over a period of years, thus avoiding a slanted view of the significance of current issues and concerns. Where one has an existing developed collection to work from, then there is no difficulty in identifying materials; where a new collection is being developed then it may be necessary to work from subject bibliographies or indexing services.

If we take as our example a special collection of materials on the 'Cinema', then from the *British National Bibliography* we find the following random sample of documents which might form part of the collection:

Ninety years of cinema in the Malverns
Child of paradise: Marcel Carne and the golden age of French cinema
Biblical epics: sacred narrative in the Hollywood cinema
To free the cinema: Jonas Mekas and the New York underground
Hammer and horror: bad taste and popular British cinema

Cinema Arthuriana: essays on Arthurian film
Narrated films
Hidden cinema: British film censorship in action
Vampires and violets: lesbians in the cinema
Screening the male: exploring masculinities in Hollywood cinema
Cinema: great directors
Cinema of the blind

This highly selective listing already begins to reveal some of the aspects and concepts for which our scheme must cater. Clearly, a much larger sample must be assembled in order fully to investigate the nature of the subject.

The significant subject terms or concepts must be isolated from these documents and would in this instance produce:

ninety years
the Malverns
Marcel Carne
French
Biblical
epics
freedom
the Underground movement
  New York
Hammer – production company
horror
bad taste
British
popular cinema
Arthuriana
narrated films
censorship
lesbians
males
Hollywood
blind

Stage 2 – analysing concepts into facets

These concepts must then be analysed or arranged into the category or facet to which they most naturally belong. Some facets will be quite obvious and readily conceived, others may cause some mental turmoil. In the above example 'geographical area', 'time' and 'genre' are fairly easily spotted and would produce:

Geographical area
Britain

New York
Hollywood
France
the Malverns
Time
Ninety years
the golden age of French cinema (the exact time period of which should be identifiable with the work in hand)
Genre
Biblical
horror
Arthurian films

We might have been tempted to place epics under genre too, but that would not then reflect a single stage of division within the facet, as we can have Biblical epics or wartime epics. Another facet is emerging:

Extent/grade of film
epic
B film etc.

A facet which must be catered for are the types of personalities associated with the cinema. But here again we have some distinctions to make. We have the people who are involved in the making of films, the people about whom films are made and the people for whom films are made; each of these should ideally be distinguished as a separate facet, as they would not consist of the same groups or individuals:

Film makers: actors, directors, cinematographers etc.
directors
Marcel Carne
(This is potentially an enormous facet, as many works exist on significant individuals such as Eisenstein and Woody Allen.)
Film subjects
lesbians
males
(Again this facet may have to be extended as far as individual characters like James Bond or Napoleon in order to provide full specification.)
Audience
the blind

Three final categories have been identified in the list above:

Film styles
narrated films
Film movements
the Underground

Society and the cinema
  censorship
  freedom

Ten facets have thus far been identified from the very brief list gathered together, the list itself having failed totally to reveal one very significant facet 'film technologies'. We also have identified two rogue concepts *bad taste* and *popular*, qualitative ideas which do not form obviously or easily into a category but might form part of an *Aesthetics* facet. This number from such a small sample illustrates the difficulty in restricting facets in any classification which wishes to provide full specification of detail and, given that the random list from which we are working are all books, it also illustrates the complexities of treatment which are to be found even at that level of publication. Most schemes would not seek to cater for this level of detail. Each of these facets must then be fully extended, identifying and listing existing and potential foci as comprehensively as possible.

Stage 3 – arrangement of foci within facets

The equal foci or individual concepts, referred to as isolates, must be arranged in the most helpful order within each of the facets. Sometimes a logical order will present itself very obviously, at others there will be no evident reason for adopting one order over another. In the 'Film makers' facet, for example, there is nothing to tell us what the order *should* be, but there are some general principles which might be built upon in reaching that final order. On the general to specific principle, we might, for example, decide that those who have to do with the overall making of the film should come first. Producers who oversee every facet of film-making would therefore have priority in the sequence over editorial staff. Another principle which might be applied could be that of developmental or evolutionary sequence, that is, those who are concerned with smaller scale efforts in the production of the film come in the order in which that effort is made, so that pre-production casting would come before wardrobe, which would come before make-up. Or we may consider using what is termed canonical order, that is, an order which is traditional and generally acceptable to users of our scheme. In this case, for example, we might arrange our persons facet in the order which is generally given in the credits list at the end of a film. Also, the *Wall-Picture principle* which may be applied suggests that the relationship between subjects should be considered in determining order. How do these two concepts relate, which is the picture and which the wall? A picture cannot be hung without the wall to place it upon. An editor cannot cut a film unless that film has been shot. Therefore, the shooting comes before the editing. This principle is in many instances chronological, but may not always be so. If one were dealing with disease and preventative medicine, then one might argue that the prevention comes first – the disease may not appear at all – but the disease must have existed before prevention could be considered necessary.

However this sequence is arrived at, like groups of isolates should be identified and collocated, so that all photography and camera work are kept together, thus making the process of arriving at a logical order that much easier and ensuring that like subjects are grouped as part of that process. It is not helpful to stick rigidly to a chronological sequence when that would separate subjects which are related in other ways. Rather than create entirely new facets, where possible it is perfectly reasonable and more economic to base the commoner facets such as space and time upon those of existing schemes such as BC or UDC, although, obviously, if your own special scheme were ever to be published then it would be necessary to obtain permission from the publishers of the one from which you had borrowed.

Stage 4 – establishing the facet citation order

The question to be considered when establishing the first facet in our citation order is which of the facets is the most important in terms of ensuring that works dealing with any given focus within the facet should be collocated. The degree of collocation of works will decrease in facets placed lower in the facet formula or citation order. In order to establish this, it is necessary to examine each of the facets, establishing the priority of the significance of each. Are we most concerned with place? Do we want to gather together all material on the British cinema or are we more concerned with the genre, whether the film is a comedy or thriller? If we had a work on the directors of thrillers would we want it to file with works on directors of comedy or with works on actors in thrillers like Boris Karloff and Vincent Price? There are many such questions which have to be asked and they will eventually lead us to the preferred form of arrangement on the shelves. We should use as our guide the literature of the subject and also the preferences of the typical user of such a collection. How is the subject studied? How do people in the industry approach material? How do interested readers look for material? Clearly, the answers may vary depending on the organization which the library or collection will serve. One can of course avoid the issue by saying that the choice of facet formula is left to the classifiers, the library itself. The advantage of course is that it is possible to ensure that the optimum order is achieved for the particular environment in which the scheme will be used in practice.

Stage 5 – creating the schedules

The next step in the creation of a classification scheme is the recording or writing out of the schedules. The simplest method of applying the principle of inversion, at this stage, is to record the facets in reverse order, creating an inverted schedule. Then the notation can be simply applied in a logical filing sequence and the desired shelf order will be obtained when the facets are combined. Here decisions have to be made about what the notation will hope to achieve: whether it is to be expressive or simple; how facets will be introduced and so on. The arguments in favour of the various possibilities have already been rehearsed, in

Chapter 2, and will not be repeated here; the ease of approach of the notation may play a significant part in determining the users' response to the scheme.

The final stage, the importance of which should never be underestimated, is that of providing an index – catering for all of the relationships not revealed by the chosen citation order – to the schedules, together with instructions, either in an Introduction or Manual, as well as where necessary in the schedules, which will aid the classifier in the use of the scheme.

Stage 6 – testing and evaluating the scheme

It is all very well to develop a scheme according to the best principles, but before full implementation it is vital that the scheme be tested, initially in order to identify any problems. This can be done with a fairly small number of records, 100 is probably sufficient, in order to ensure that the principles have been applied correctly and to see what the final shelf order looks like. After all, this must be our basic concern. Even after implementation of the system, it must continue to be evaluated for effectiveness so that revisions and improvements can be carried out as necessary. Inevitably, as the collection and the literature grow, there will be expansions and developments which were not foreseen and it will be necessary to expand upon classes; your scheme must therefore be monitored constantly in the light of these new appearances.

ISSUES FOR CONSIDERATION

1. There are far more special schemes than general ones. This is, of course, perfectly natural given the relatively fixed nature of the universe of knowledge and the enormous task involved in developing new general schemes. In many ways we are therefore likely to see the most interesting developments taking place in the field of special classification. In what circumstances might we find ourselves in a position where we might become involved in the development of a new scheme? For what subjects or for which users do you feel a new scheme might be useful?

2. If you found yourself in such a position, that is, where you felt that the best solution for your particular library or collection would be to develop a new special classification, what would be the implications of such a decision? Draw up a list of the advantages and disadvantages of taking this step.

3. One of the most effective ways of learning about classification is to create a classification scheme of your own. Then, the principles have to be worked through very carefully and the practical effect of these principles becomes clear when you see the finished result as a physical arrangement. With a subject of your choice, work through the stages in the creation of such a scheme as outlined above and test them.

NOTES

1. Bunch, Alan, *The basics of community information work*. London: Library Association Publishing, 1993.
2. Wendell, W. S. and Tansey, L. C., *A slide classification system: for the organisation and automatic indexing of interdisciplinary collections of slides and pictures*. Los Angeles: UCLA, 1970.
3. Gilchrist, A., *The thesaurus in retrieval*. London: ASLIB, 1971, p. 3.
4. Vernon, K. D. C. and Lang, V., *The London classification of business studies*, revised by K. G. B. Bakewell and D. A. Cotton. London: ASLIB, 1979.
5. *INSPEC classification: a classification scheme for physics, electrotechnology, computers and control*. Stevenage: The Institution of Electrical Engineers, 1988.
6. *Construction indexing manual*: CI SfB, edited by Alan Ray Jones and David Clegg. London: RIBA Publications, 1976.
7. Moys. Elizabeth, *Moys' classification scheme for law books*. 2nd Edn. London: Butterworths, 1982.
8. Ibid., p. 1.
9. *FIAF classification scheme for literature on film and television*, edited by Michael Moulds and Karen Jones. London: International Federation of Film Archives, 1992.
10. Fegan, E. S. and Cant, M., *The Cheltenham Classification: a library classification for schools*. 2nd Edn. Cambridge: V. Heffer & Sons, 1958.
11. *Early Stages library classification scheme and index*. Aberdeen: Grampian Regional Council, Schools Library Service, 1992.
12. Couprie, L. D., Iconclass: an inconographic classification system. *Art Libraries Journal*, 8 (2), Summer 1983, pp. 32–49.
13. Northern Ireland Council for Voluntary Action, *Designing a community information system*. Belfast: NICVA, 1980.

5 Indexes, thesauri and classification

In this final section on the principles and systems of classification, we will conclude with a brief overview of the relationship between classification and other methods for accessing subject information. This discussion will help us to gauge the value of classification as one tool among a number in the retrieval of subject information.

POST-COORDINATE INDEXING AS AN ALTERNATIVE TO CLASSIFICATION IN THE SPECIAL LIBRARY

We have examined the contribution classification can make to special libraries via the use of general schemes, the use of special schemes and the creation of an in-house classification. Let us turn to our last alternative which is to eschew the use of classification altogether. One might decide that a subject arrangement on the shelves simply was not the most effective means of subject retrieval, either for part or for all of the collection. It may be felt, particularly in the special library, that the rigidity of a single linear preferred order on the shelves does not allow for the variety of approaches which might be made by users. Equally the emphasis in the collection on diverse types of documents, like reports and periodical articles, is, in the special library, likely to create physical difficulties in the provision of a manageable collection on the shelves. One response then is to reject the whole idea of formal classification and for the collection to use instead some method of arranging materials which does not represent or display subject groupings but merely locates the item for retrieval – sometimes referred to as the mark and park approach. In dismissing classification, so long as one provides some other effective method of subject retrieval, what one chiefly loses is the facility to browse in a physical linear sequence, whether in a physical collection of works or in a collection of records on the printed page.

If this route is taken, then it is, of course, essential that the library provide, in the place of classification, some other means of identifying documents upon a subject. That other means most commonly takes the form of some kind of post-coordinate index, which would allow the user to put together their subject in any order and allow for the location and retrieval of materials on that subject. For the user who is interested in the subject of writers of comedy, for example, items might be located variously whether these deal with television or cinema, whether they are writers of plays or of songs, and this despite the citation order employed in a classification scheme or even in the absence of such a scheme altogether.

Where a collection had deliberately and totally excluded the use of classification, the post-coordinate index would have fully to assume the role of collocation of subjects. More commonly such indexes are used to complement classification and therefore are often designed specifically not to gather together the material which has already been collocated on the shelves. There are a number of methods of post-coordinate indexing; in order to examine the role which they can play and the classificatory principles upon which they are built, some of these will be briefly examined here, principally to illustrate their adoption and adaptation of such principles.

Post-coordinate indexing systems usually analyse the subject matter of documents into single concepts and allow the user, at the search stage, to combine such single concepts, matching each with the documents in which they are discussed. Each single concept is equal in rank and there is, therefore, no need to consider which belongs to the most significant facet or for the users to concern themselves with citation order in any way. Let us imagine that we are searching for information on the manufacture of tents for polar expeditions. Here we have potentially four concepts, all of which might be of equal significance to our enquirer and the absence of any one of which from a document would render it worthless.

In consulting a classified sequence, we would have to decide whether to look in the section dealing with manufacture or that concerning polar expeditions. We should certainly have to scan through a number of items before we might find the document which deals with all four. In consulting a printed index we might consult first one term and be guided to another:

Manufacture
   see Tents, manufacture

At best we might be scanning again, this time among the multiple entries for a heading. With a post-coordinate system, however, we would select all of our terms and the system would tell us in which documents all of these were to be found. A post-coordinate system is built upon the same principles as faceted classification, as the concepts are isolated singly and then combined, but the idea is taken a stage further in that no citation order for these concepts needs to be identified, thus allowing total freedom for the user in the manner in which he or she specifies the sought after subject. At the stage of indexing documents, a new document is analysed into its component concepts and for each of these concepts a record is made of the fact that the document refers to it:

Document number – 179
Subjects – Tents, manufacture, polar, expeditions

The information is then recorded:

Subject Term	Document numbers
Tents	9, 16, 51, 68, 88, 89, 104, **179**, 221 etc.
Manufacture	4, 16, 13, 65, 72, **179**, 202 etc.
Polar	3, 77, **179**, 183, 199 etc.
Expeditions	53, **179**, 199 etc.

The combination of concepts is then carried out at the searching stage. As can be seen from the above we have a document, 199, which deals with polar expeditions, another, 16, which deals with the manufacture of tents, but only document number 179 deals with all four.

UNITERM INDEXING

The classic form of post-coordinate indexing technique, the Uniterm system of Mortimer Taube, appears to be a negation of all things classificatory. This theory is based upon the idea of using only single words as units which may be combined – the uniterms of the title of the system *Uniterm indexing* – in any way. It rejects classificatory principles in the sense that it removes any concept of control or any imposition of rules upon the terms or the way in which they are combined. However, there are difficulties in the implementation of uniterm indexing, largely in the nuances of meaning terms may possess, the application they may have in different circumstances and the effect upon meaning of the manner of association of terms. A valid uniterm might therefore have a quite different meaning in a variety of situations, as a quick consultation of any dictionary or thesaurus will tell us – to say nothing of the use of affective or figurative language. The 'women of the Bible' is quite different from the 'view of women in the Bible'; 'devolution' may mean something quite different in the political and the scientific setting; 'squirrel' and 'cage' are two individual terms which when combined together have a quite different meaning from that which one might suppose when considered separately. Uniterm indexes may be manual or automated in method. Two manual systems exist: the Uniterm card index, in which cards for individual concepts are retrieved and visually scanned in order to detect matching document numbers; and optical coincidence or peek-a-boo cards where holes in cards are used to represent document numbers and, when the two (or more) cards are aligned, the light shines through for documents which contain all the concepts.

A further distinction in the discussion of post-coordinate systems should be made, that between *term entry* and *item entry* systems. Term entry implies that an entry is made in the system for the term, that is, for the subject heading, the identifier, the descriptor. If we have an item on whisky consumption in Scotland, we would have entries for:

Whisky   114
Consumption   114
Scotland   114

the relevant identifying number for this item having been added to the entries for the three terms which appear. The peek-a-boo and uniterm systems we have just examined are examples of term entry.

Item entry systems make a record for the document or entity containing the information, and then allow multiple access to that item from any of the descriptors or terms which have been applied to it. The process is most simply illustrated in practice via a description of one method, the *edge-notched card* system, where for each item to be indexed a card is created with holes around its edges. At its simplest each hole represents a subject descriptor, a single concept, and when a term is present in an item the edge of the hole is notched. When a subject is sought, let us say Scotland, the pile of cards representing the documents in the collection is assembled, a needle is inserted at the appropriate hole and the cards which fall from the needle have notches and are therefore about Scotland. The process can be repeated on the Scottish cards, this time inserting the needle at the point representing whisky; those which fall will be about whisky and Scotland. This process can be repeated as frequently as there are sought after concepts and citation order, or the order in which the terms are sought has no significance.

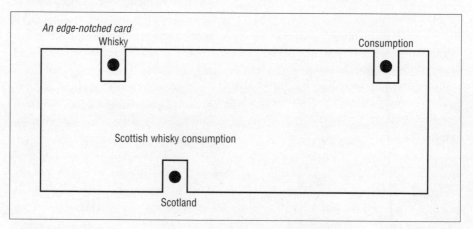

An edge-notched card

Whisky   Consumption

Scottish whisky consumption

Scotland

Clearly, there is a limit to the number of cards which can be searched simultaneously and to the number of concepts indicated around the edge of a card, although the above is a simplified example and in fact subjects treated can be multiplied by a variety of mechanisms.

Automated systems of indexing for online subject retrieval, from databases of records in electronic form, are built upon the same principle. They allow multiple access to a single document via their inverted file structure. From the record for each document subject headings are generated and the postings for each such heading are identified. No citation order need be applied when searching for composite or complex subjects. Therefore, it may be argued that the advantages and disadvantages of the Uniterm approach, as initially designed by Taube, are basically similar to those encountered with the use of keywords in Boolean combination in electronic databases and these will be discussed at greater length later in Part Three.

CLASSIFICATORY PRINCIPLES AND THEIR APPLICATION TO PRE-COORDINATE INDEX AND THESAURUS CONSTRUCTION

This has been necessarily a very brief examination of the principles of post-coordinate indexing. In the present work what is of greater interest to us is the way in which classificatory principles have been applied to their creation. Let us now consider these principles as they are found in traditional, pre-coordinate indexes in order to control and render more effective the process of subject retrieval. Pre-coordinate indexes, as has been noted elsewhere, replicate the problems associated with classification in general, by forming a fixed order of citation of elements, but they perform an additional function in that they will support the classification and should draw attention to the alternative locations of a topic in the various disciplines as found in the classification. Before considering pre-coordinate indexing methods we may begin by examining the way in which effectiveness can be measured in subject retrieval. Recall and precision are the two most commonly applied measures and it would be useful for us to pause and define these before considering further methods of indexing.

Recall and precision are attempts to calculate mathematically levels of success in the retrieval of information. Recall is the number of items which have been retrieved from a system or collection on a subject as a percentage of the total number of items in the system or collection which deal with that subject. Let us assume we have a user who is interested in cats and who searches our collection finding 15 items. This can be measured against the total number of works on cats, which in this instance we will assume to be 20. The recall rate here would be 15 as a percentage of 20, that is, a recall rate of 75 per cent. A success rate of 100 per cent in subject retrieval would be a situation where every item on the chosen subject was retrieved. However, one might locate every work on a subject in a collection but at the same time locate a large number of other works which were not relevant. Precision, therefore, measures the number of works retrieved that were relevant against the total number retrieved. If we stay with our earlier example, our searcher for information on cats might have found 15 books which dealt with cats, but at the same time might be presented with ten books on other subjects. This would reflect a level of precision of 60 per cent, where the number of relevant books, 15, is expressed as a percentage of the total number of books found, 25. Precision of 100 per cent would be reflected in a situation where all the items located were relevant to the user.

Very frequently, it is impossible to reconcile the two measures. In order to ensure 100% recall, it may be necessary to sift through large numbers of undesirable items. If one wants perfect precision then it may be impossible to ensure comprehensiveness. The requirements of the particular enquirer must also be borne in mind, for example whether or not full comprehensiveness is important. In any case, what we are concerned with is the way in which classificatory principles can be applied in order to enhance recall and precision in indexing systems. As far as recall is concerned, classification is all about ensuring that all materials on a specific topic are collocated and, in its attempt to avoid the vagaries of terminology via the assigning of codes to concepts, then classification will aid recall. Recall largely depends upon the depth and accuracy of indexing. If a topic is being sought then it may be scattered amongst a variety of disciplines. This can be overcome by the synthetic approach, where the concept as it is represented by a focus in a facet will have been assigned a unique code: that code can subsequently be identified wherever it appears in a piece of notation.

Classification also acknowledges the concept of hierarchy, where one is guided via the notation to more general or specific works within which aspects of the subject of interest might be discussed. The idea of more general and more specific terms being linked in an index is therefore a useful one, which has been utilized both in *chain indexing* and for subject headings assignation in indexes for works such as the *Current Technology Index*. In the Library of Congress subject headings (LCSH) we are instructed on the creation of references to be made from a subject to related and subordinate topics. For example:

Accounting
  see also Auditing
    Inventories etc.

There is no provision for the link from subordinate to more general topics. The intention is that headings in such an index should be *specific entries*, that is, they should correspond precisely to the subject content of the document. Entries are therefore not made under broader concepts, nor are cross-references made to broader concepts. Such links can be most useful in guiding the user, particularly the uninitiated, as, for example, when an enquirer is searching for information on acupuncture and some of the most valuable material may be found in works on holistic medicine. Certain indexes adopt this approach and would provide links thus:

Acupuncture
  see also Holistic medicine

CHAIN INDEXING

One indexing method, which explores this approach extensively, is *chain indexing*, a system designed by Ranganathan, where for each item included in a collection a series of entries are made in a subject index corresponding to the several stages of division in the classificatory process. In the example above the process of classifying acupuncture would have revealed several stages:

Medicine	610
Therapeutics	615.5
Specific therapies	615.8
Other therapies	615.89
Acupuncture	615.892

At each stage one would consider the significance of the concept introduced as the verbal equivalent of the last digit. Some of the above have no subject meaning, such as 'Other therapies', which would therefore be ignored in constructing the index. Synonyms would be sought for all of the terms, which it was felt should be included in the index and the result would be a number of entries, eventually filed alphabetically:

Acupuncture: Therapeutics: Medicine	615.892
Acupuncture: Holistic medicine: Medicine	615.892
Therapeutics: Medicine	615.5
Holistic medicine: Medicine	615.5
Alternative medicine: Medicine	615.5 *(synonymous term)*

The searcher who has sought acupuncture as his or her point of entry to the index would, therefore, be guided by the form of the entry to holistic medicine as a broader class. Chain indexing is a pre-coordinate system and may fail to reveal subjects as specified by a searcher. If we take the example of English poetry, a chain index based upon Dewey would contain the following entries:

Poetry: English Literature	821
Verse: English Literature	821 *(synonymous term)*
English Literature	820
Literature	800

The problem here largely arises due to the fact that the searcher is more likely to look for 'English Poetry' than 'Poetry: English Literature'. Chain, however only offers one single co-extensive entry, that is, only one entry which displays the full range of concepts. The next indexing system we will examine was a response to this problem, an attempt to provide for all possible pre-coordinate approaches on the index.

SLIC (SELECTIVE LISTING IN COMBINATION) INDEXING

SLIC indexing identifies all the possible subject combinations in a document and produces as headings or entries a selection of these, eliminating those already found in a larger grouping, which will form part of a list or index locating documents on that subject. If we have a document on the subject of the welding of aluminium cans, then we may find that our classification scheme has grouped all information on cans together on the shelves, but that information on their welding is subordinate, as is the material, aluminium. If the enquirer seeks to locate material on the welding of other kinds of aluminium objects then the search becomes a very scattered one and the advantages of browsing the classified shelves are almost non-existent. With a SLIC index, if we assume a document exists in the library on the welding of aluminium cans, then for that document a number of entries will have been created in the index. The subject will have been analysed into its component elements and combined in the variety of ways possible for its specification. We have here three concepts – aluminium, welding and cans – and they might be combined by the enquirer in any one of a number of ways:

Potential entries A–Z index
Aluminium
Aluminium: welding
Aluminium cans
Aluminium cans: welding
Aluminium: welding: cans
Cans
Cans: aluminium
Cans: aluminium: welding
Cans: welding
Cans: welding: aluminium
Welding
Welding: aluminium
Welding: aluminium: cans
Welding: cans
Welding: cans: aluminium

This is, potentially, a very unwieldy number of entries to create for a single document in an index, although as the index grows such entries need only be made once, standing for all of the documents on that subject, and of course there are likely to be a large number of documents for a subject such as 'welding'. The problems multiply exponentially as the number of concepts represented in a document grows: where we have five concepts there would be 120 entries if these were permuted as we have shown above. What pre-coordinate indexing techniques seek to do is to limit the numbers of entries which need to be made for each document by applying rules. The first rule might be that all collocation achieved on the shelves should be avoided in the index. Thus the general to special entries above would be removed, that is, all, for example, of the entries for cans apart from the general one. Also removed would be those entries which are repetitive and unrevealing, such as 'Welding: aluminium' and 'welding: aluminium cans'. Finally, SLIC is designed as an index of combinations rather than permutations in preferred order, that is alphabetical A/Z order, so that composites can easily be found by the user. In such an index a citation order is needed and it may be alphabetical or it might be some subject significant citation order such as we are familiar with in classification. There is then no need for an entry such as 'welding aluminium' for this is not in alphabetical order and the user would know not to expect it. The final entries in the SLIC index would therefore be:

SLIC A–Z index
Aluminium: cans: welding
Aluminium: welding
Cans: welding
Welding

producing a much more economical index and supporting the classification on the shelves, by bringing together aspects of aluminium.

The SLIC index is a form of index which can very readily be generated by a computer. Formulae can be applied to limit the nature and the form of terms which can be combined.

PRECIS AND COMPASS

Another system, *Precis* (the *Pre*served *C*ontext *I*ndexing *S*ystem), can also be automatically generated and again is a system designed to delimit the number of entries necessary and to cater for the preferred approach of the user. Precis was designed by Derek Austin and was used for some years to generate the subject headings which appeared in BNB. The idea of Precis is that whichever term a user employs to approach his or her subject, when the index is consulted he or she will find that term accompanied by a kind of precis or summary of the context in which the term has been dealt with by the author of the document located. The layout of the heading indicates the relationship of the terms used:

LEAD (sought term)   Qualifier (the wider context)
    Display (narrower context)

Acupuncture   Holistic medicine
    Pain relief

Classificatory principles are very much in evidence here, in that the specific entry is being shown in its hierarchical relation to the other elements in the subject of the documents. Precis also necessitates the concept analysis of documents in a manner very familiar to the classifier. It is not, however, linked to any single classification as chain indexing is in practice. Role operators are used to indicate meaning by the interpolation of semantic links such as 'of' into strings which would otherwise be capable of misinterpretation. Precis replaced the chain index which had been in use for BNB: Precis, itself, was then to be usurped in 1990. The latest system in use by the British Library is Compass (the *Com*puter *A*ided *S*ubject *S*ystem), which is basically a simpler and less labour-intensive method of creating an index. The resultant entries produce a simplified subject description, which was all that was felt necessary for subject searching. Compass retains some of Precis' special features, such as role operators, and allows for the meaningful access to the records available in BNB.

TITLE INDEXING

Title indexes using techniques such as KWIC (Keyword in Context) automatically generate entries from the titles of documents. These are useful for allowing economy of effort and can be effective when they deal with descriptive article titles, but often non-descriptive titles have to be enhanced by the addition of extra subject terms or unsought terms may have to be suppressed and so the process becomes less of a mechanical one. It is, however, a relatively speedy and largely non-intellectual process. The terms used are also likely to represent current usage and terminology, although there will be no consistency overall and all synonyms will have to be sought individually by the searcher.

CITATION INDEXING

Citation indexes, again automatically generated, provide an alternative to the subject analysis of documents for information retrieval. Instead they bring together documents by linking citations or references. If work **A** has cited work **S** then citation indexes assume that there is a subject relationship between documents **A** and **S**. On consulting a citation index under the author of a known relevant work, one can identify all of the other documents which have cited that work and which are therefore, it is assumed, likely to have developed the subject of the original work. This is an interesting approach and research has shown that citation indexes will reveal relevant subject information not revealed by conventional indexes. They are particularly useful in a subject search where a key author or paper has been identified. Again no intellectual effort is involved in their compilation, but they depend upon their central thesis that subject relationship is central to citation and there are many instances in which this may not be the case.

Such systems differ from those developed for use in online subject access, as they were intended for the computer generation of printed indexes and, therefore, because of the physical format in which they were to appear, necessarily had to limit the number of entries to be made. We will return to all such forms of automated index in Part Three, for a closer examination of their practical application.

CONTROL DEVICES IN INDEXING

Two forms of control which may be applied in indexes are *role indicators* and *linking devices*. Role indicators in a sense classify a concept by showing the purpose or role for which the term is used. This is particularly necessary when dealing with terms which have a wide variety of different applications such as 'therapy', where the process may be found serving different functions such as the clinical, the social, the educational or the occupational. It may also be necessary to distinguish a concept at different stages of its evolution, for example, as a raw material or as an end product of manufacture. Here it is necessary that the index display the role or function of a term, rather than simply qualify the meaning of a term. For example:

Polarization (charge separation)
Polarization (spin alignment)
Polarization (waves)

Linking devices show the nature of the association between a subject term and another term or terms to which it is related. The concept of the 'effect of therapy on drug addiction' is quite different from 'the treatment of addiction by drug therapy' and an index could use linking devices to convey the difference in approach, a difference conveyed in natural language by semantic construction. Linking devices seek to prevent *false drops*, that is the retrieval of information which is irrelevant although all of the terms sought are present. For example, if we were looking for information on 'the teaching of computer studies to accounting students', we might retrieve information on 'the teaching of accounts to computer science students'. A linking device can explain the nature of the relationship between the terms. The idea of *semantic factoring*, used at Western Reserve University, builds upon this idea by limiting vocabulary to a number of basic semantic units. Concepts are then assembled by the linking of these units in a manner similar to that of synthetic classification. Such devices as these may add to the precision of retrieval but they can also preclude total recall by putting obstacles in the way of a quite legitimate and simple approach. They may also confuse users of a system.

Weighting is another control device, central to classificatory principles, which may be applied to indexing. The whole business of classification is about weighting in determining the citation order of a document, deciding in which discipline a work may fall, deciding what is the main classmark for a work and the creation of added classmark entries in the classified sequence of a classified catalogue. In all of these operations we are determining where the chief emphasis of the document lies. We might have a work which deals with more than one subject in an unequal fashion, where, for example, financial management is dealt with chiefly in the private company sector but where a useful section deals with public sector organizations. Here, an entry which would guide those interested in financial management in the public sector would be useful, but it may be helpful to indicate the weight of the treatment in some quantifiable manner, that is, whether the term is the major subject of the work or whether it is dealt with incidentally. For example, in Medline, an item which deals comparatively with a drug treatment of insomnia and behavioural therapy produces the following list of index terms, where the major descriptors are identified by an asterisk:

*Behaviour therapy
*Insomnia therapy
*Triazolam – therapeutic use
Adult
Combined modality therapy
Placebos
Treatment outcome

Anyone interested in the use of placebos for insomniacs would thus locate this item, but be alerted to the fact that placebos had only been identified as a minor descriptor for this particular work. It is therefore possible to filter a set of retrieved references and to determine the likely significance of each to a particular enquiry.

THESAURI CONSTRUCTION

Automation has resulted in an ever increasing need for authoritative and standardized vocabularies. Thesauri are an attempt to provide guidance on the terms which should be used both in indexing an item and in its retrieval from an indexing system. They control the natural language of the enquirer and attempt to overcome the complexities of semantic expression and the existence of synonyms, homonyms, differences in spelling, word forms and so on, by conveying to the searcher for information the terms used by the indexer to describe that concept. Thesauri construction has much in common with classification and we have already noted the frequency with which the two are developed in tandem. A thesaurus, like a classification scheme, imposes order on a subject and displays the structure and relationships within that subject. It normally shows the scope of each term and the context in which it is to be applied. It will also direct users to the preferred terms and provide references from those which are not to be used. The *Thesaurus of Engineering and Scientific Terms* provides 'a list of engineering and related scientific terms and their relationships for use as a vocabulary reference in indexing and retrieving technical information.[1] It directs users from unused terms to the preferred:

Excavating machinery
  Use Excavating equipment

and then displays synonymous terms which have not been used, related terms, broader terms and narrower terms;

Evaporative cooling
BT   Cooling
NT   Film cooling
RT   Cooling systems
     Cooling towers

Such structuring, as we have seen, is enormously helpful in enabling the searcher to move up and down hierarchies where necessary, but we should of course remember that in classification any one specific term may belong to more than one hierarchy. Scope notes will give guidance on the interpretation and coverage of the term by the use of the abbreviation (UF), signifying the concepts the heading has been used for:

Fixed investment
UF   Capital investment
     Capital plant equipment

It also adds explanation or advice notes at times, for instance:

Biological detection
  Detection of objects or personnel by
  observation of their biological effects;
  excludes biological agent detection.

Some thesauri also provide classmarks for use in subject retrieval and therefore fully combine both approaches. Subject Headings for Engineering (SHE), produced by the publishers of the *Engineering Index* and *Compendex*, its electronic equivalent, provides a list of headings, with scope notes and their classmarks. Note that these headings may take the form of a multi-word phrase:

Computer integrated manufacturing   723
  (Beginning 01/87. May also be used
  as a general sub-heading)

and may utilize inverted word order:

Final control devices, electric   704, 732

Pre-coordination is evident in these phrases and inversions, as it is in the choice of entry form in any multiple term combination. The thesaurus also provides a list of general subheadings, such as 'manufacturers' or 'properties' which can be used with any heading, in a manner similar to the use of tables or auxiliaries in a classification scheme. Here, too, the concept of pre-coordination is being applied in that these concepts are deemed as less significant and therefore secondary in the search for information. Were one interested in manufacturers of automobiles, then the thesaurus determines that the subject term which should be sought is 'automobiles' and then the sub-heading 'manufacturers'. Such choices are made all the time in indexes, as they are in classification, and the important factor is that the choices are acknowledged and evident to the user and that the reference structure of the index supports and guides the user to the options available.

In thesauri, then, there has been a move away from the purely alphabetical specific single heading approach to the use of some systematic clustering of concepts. We have also seen the combination of classification and thesaurus and these developments are probably best exemplified in the *Thesaurofacet* which grew out of the English Electric Company's faceted classification for engineering. Associated chiefly with Jean Aitchison, the work is a faceted classification with a fully structured thesaurus as an index. It offers a tool which can be used in pre-coordinate and post-coordinate indexing. The searcher can find from the thesaurus the classmark for their subject and then proceed to the classified sequence where the hierarchy of the subject will be revealed. Alternatively, the searcher may approach the index for a specific subject and will there be assisted by the pattern of broader, narrower and related headings to which they are guided. The index does not reproduce but complements the associations made in the classified sequence and, therefore, to reveal all material of potential value both should be consulted. There are built-in links between the classification and the thesaurus and this is an added advantage of such dual purpose tools. Such systems attempt to provide both for shelf arrangement and for subject retrieval and the principles of classification are, in many ways, in such schemes applied to indexing method and vice versa. This is a healthy process.

Classification has other miscellaneous uses in the field of indexing. A formal classification can guide the compiler of an index or thesaurus to the terms to be used, and can assist in the formation of references by displaying the hierarchical structure of the subject. Classification also transcends the language barrier. Indexing systems and classifications are both attempts to provide vocabularies for a subject, whether that vocabulary is represented as a term or as a piece of notation, and as such they attempt to control the freedom and unpredictability of natural language. Some testing of the success of controlled language in comparison with a natural language (i.e. in the language of the documents themselves) approach has been carried out and, while the results of these are not conclusive, they are interesting in that they suggest that the natural language approach is slightly more successful. Certainly the natural language approach can produce relevant and apt results, that is, a good match between the users' perception of their subject and the manner in which it has been dealt with by the author. This is perhaps predictable given that both author and user have described it in the same terms and might be said to be on the same wavelength. However, the natural language approach will have taken no account of the synonyms, the homographs and the semantic relationships between concepts, which help to ensure high recall and precision. In a recent online search of the *Library and Information Science Abstracts*, the enquirer was looking for information on any surveys of the effectiveness of public library reference services which had been carried out. Searching was carried out using the controlled subject headings field and the chosen terms found there were utilized and yet known items were not revealed. It was only when a search was carried out in natural language, free text, that is, using all of the fields available in the record rather than just the index entries and using the phrase *unobtrusive testing* that the desired items were located. Both approaches were therefore necessary to ensure full recall. This is not to say that the controlled language approach has no value. Circumstances may affect success, such as the size of the subject area, the extent to which terms will be predictable and the consistency and accuracy with which indexing has been applied. The argument largely relates to the automated environment and will be further discussed in Part Three. Any of us with experience of using electronic databases would wholly concur with the view that all of the available tools should be exploited to the full and a combination of natural and control language techniques is often necessary to reveal all of the items on a subject and, therefore, to ensure anything like total recall. Searchers must be made aware of the techniques available for the retrieval of information, understand what they have to offer and their limitations in order to become aware of the existence of material which may be of value to them. Search strategy planning and execution should acknowledge the role of various techniques and respond interactively to the results displayed. What exacerbates the situation in the electronic environment is the invisibility of the environment in which we are searching. When we play hide and seek we can see at a glance the physical possibilities – there's a couch in the corner or long curtains which may conceal a body. On the shelves and in a printed index, we have similar ways of physically orientating ourselves. When searching a database it is useful to see these variant techniques as levels of exploration, which may overlap or may display unique caches of treasure.

ISSUES FOR CONSIDERATION

1. The debate between the natural and controlled language approach continues, whether about the use of prescribed descriptors or classmarks. It is useful to compare attitudes to bibliographic retrieval with the attitudes which prevail in other situations where classification is used to enhance specification and retrieval. If we look at finger-printing or blood grouping a quite different atmosphere prevails. Why is the argument still so pertinent in the field of

bibliographic classification?

2. Some see post-coordinate indexing as the negation of classification. Review what you see as the potential, or lack of potential, for the use of classificatory principles within it.

3. Looking ahead to Part Three, is this idea of the invisibility of information in an online environment significant? What effect might it have upon the searcher?

4. Much of this chapter has been about language: about the control of terms; about indicating relationship; about expressing syntactic concepts. To what extent can classification be said to transcend language and, conversely, in which respects might it be said still to be tied to human means of expression?

NOTES

1. *Thesaurus of engineering and scientific terms.* New York: Engineers Joint Council, 1969.

Part Two
The management and application of classification

6 The functions of classification in the library

Classification has a number of functions, some of which have already been referred to, in more or less detail, in earlier chapters. Here, we would like to pause and consider carefully these functions in order to determine the precise role of classification in the running of a library or the management of a collection, before going on to an examination of the implementation of classification in practice.

SHELF ORDER

In the eyes of the majority of librarians, the first and most important function of classification is to assist in the provision of a subject arrangement of materials in physical storage, largely books or documents on the shelf, but equally it might be for reports in pamphlet boxes or microfiche in a cabinet. Classification thus provides a physical and linear subject arrangement in order to facilitate the library user's ability to browse among the materials in the collection. Although browsing may be more effective amongst books than amongst pamphlets, this is largely due to the physical format of the book. The manner in which information is provided on the spine is an acknowledgement on the part of the publishers of the likelihood and delight of the book reader in browsing. Browsing is an activity which may be casual or directed. We might be looking for anything which will amuse or while away the hours or we may be actively seeking a work which will help us, for example, to combat shyness; whatever the approach taken by the user, none of the other tools devised by the librarian will ever completely negate the value of guided browsing in a subject sequence. The serendipity of coming upon something absolutely but unpredictably right, and the individuality of user needs for a particular authorial stance – we want a book about shyness but one which is sympathetic and reassuring, not one which counsels us as to how we might become assertive – mean that browsing will always have a potential value. Equally, the manner in which the human mind connects and links across disciplinary boundaries and the variety of ways in which people may seek information reinforce the value of browsing as an information gathering process, allowing for the individual and personal response to what is available; we have decided that we are shy but a book on the pleasures of joining the local rose lovers' association might lead us into other means of dealing with the problem.

Browsing is the preferred and first approach to information by the majority of library users. In most cases there will be some object in mind, when searching along the shelves. It might be a vague desire or a highly formulated one. Inevitably library tools have been designed with the more highly formulated approach in mind in a way which has not been emulated in the book shop, where a less sure knowledge of what is wanted on the part of the customer is assumed. Let us pause to ponder the users' needs briefly in order to clarify the role of shelf order in the library.

Most of us have in our time used this method of locating material but often in a very uninformed style; we should recall our days as novice library users, relying on our knowledge of where to locate material in a library without even the most basic understanding of classificatory principles and the way in which materials have been organized on the shelves. We knew that the books on pet care were in the third bay from the end of the ground floor of the library, on the bottom two shelves – and very awkward to reach they were too. We did not know why they were there; we did not know the number which had been assigned to them. We might have been aware that the dog books – let us imagine that this was what was of interest to us on this occasion – were very close to the books on cats and hamsters and goldfish; but that was the extent of our awareness as users. It was only when we approached the collection with a new subject of interest, that we might have had to seek advice or guidance, from library staff or from library catalogues. This seemingly casual and unsystematic technique is certainly a very common and invaluable method of coping with a library collection, particularly in a frequently used library, providing often the fastest form of access to information and bypassing any other library tool. The majority of users, knowing roughly where to go, are perfectly happy to operate on this principle and the classification schemes' internal features have in many instances been designed to facilitate this approach. There are, however, distinct disadvantages and the success of the method is dependent upon an effective means of guiding users around the physical sequence via signs, shelf labels and possibly maps of the sequence. The structure of the classification scheme should highlight and illuminate the sequence and may be used as a pointer or an arrow directing the seeker after information through the labyrinth of the shelves, particularly if the notation employed is a hierarchical or expressive one.

The awareness among librarians that such an unsystematic approach is in practice preferred by the majority of users – particularly in the public library environment – has led to the criticism of formal classification and of its too close or detailed application. It is enough, it is argued, to provide broad groupings and good signposts to the shelf arrangement, via some system such as *reader interest arrangement*. What this argument fails to acknowledge is the fact that, whether or not the user understands the intricacies of the system, if it is an excellently thought out and clearly associative form of subject arrangement, then it will support the subject search invisibly. The user does not need to understand the scheme in order to gain from its benefits.

PARALLEL CLASSIFICATION OR SEQUENCES

A complicating factor with any classification in practice is that inevitably the collection is not composed of one single sequence, where all materials are collocated with like subjects. There are a variety of situations in which separate sequences are likely to be necessary; these are often treated as entirely separate sections in a collection. Parallel classification is the term which is used to describe the situation in which the order of the classification scheme is adhered to, but with a single or several separate parallel sequences. A library operating on five sites would, for example, have at least five parallel sequences. Broken order occurs when the classification scheme is altered or deviated from or ignored for materials in the library, and its impact will be examined in more detail below. Let us first consider the parallel arrangement of items. There are some fairly common situations in which these appear:

Main lending sequence In the majority of collections, the lending stock will comprise the largest proportion of the library's stock. There are odd exceptions, as in for example the special library whose collection consists largely of standards for consultation not loan. Largely the lending stock will be the norm and it is items which in some way deviate from that norm which will require separate treatment in a separate section or sequence.

Reference materials These are held separately because they must be seen by the user as a kind of material which will be used in a different way from the normal stock, that is, consulted for a short period in the library. By their nature they will also answer different needs and queries and are designed to provide data and basic facts rather than to be used for extended reading. Depending upon the size of the collection, the size of a reference collection will vary. In some instances, as has been noted above, a whole library collection may be available for reference purposes only. In some universities, for example, undergraduate consultation collections have been set up as separate entities. The reference library is usually arranged upon the basis of the same classification as the rest of the library, although it may have some sections where special treatment is necessary, such as official publications which might be arranged by document number and accessed via special indexes and catalogues.

Short loan/heavy demand collections These are largely a feature of academic libraries, when frequently used material may be kept apart from the main lending stock, because it is subject to special loan conditions. It is very common for these not to be arranged in a subject manner, but simply as an alphabetic sequence (by author); lists will be provided to alert users to the contents of the short loan collection or academic staff will direct students to their use. In public libraries very popular material may have special loan arrangements but this is unlikely to form a separate sequence, because of the unpredictability of demand and the possibly short duration of the period during which demand will be high.

Oversize materials   Most libraries operate on the principle that it is uneconomic to house all stock on shelves which have been designed to accommodate oversize material and therefore tall or wide books have to be housed in a separate sequence. These are usually arranged to mirror the classified sequence, and may consist either of a single enormous oversize collection, or a large number of small sequences perhaps at the bottom of the corresponding bay of normal stock. There are advantages to both approaches: with a single sequence there is only one place to look for material; with several sequences these will be more conveniently adjacent to related material of normal size and are less likely to be overlooked by the library browser. However, in both instances such a separation will mean that oversize stock is likely to be less well exploited than the materials in the major body of the collection. In a library where oversize stock comprises a very large proportion of the stock – of art books let us say – then it may ultimately be more economic and more effective in the exploitation of resources to house normal and oversize stock together.

Large print works   These tend to be housed separately not because of their physical qualities but because of the needs of their users. The users of large print materials are likely to be exclusively interested in such materials and it is in their interests to have all material which they will be able to use collocated in one place. To house them separately serves the client and is an unchallengeable argument in favour of such an approach. Again, their arrangement is likely to mirror that of the main sequence.

Reserve stock   Infrequently used material, just like frequently used material, demands special treatment in most libraries. No librarian wants to fill his or her shelves with large quantities of items that will not appeal to the majority of users. Older material may be less used but still have value as a historical resource or for extended research on the development of a subject; it is therefore withdrawn from the main lending sequence and relegated to a reserve position in the ranks – usually in basement stacks or in some other remote and inhospitable region. Such reserve stock may or may not be held in a classified sequence; this is largely dependent upon whether the material is open to the public or not. If it is not then it will only be available via the catalogue and is therefore more conveniently arranged upon some other principle by which the item may be identified, such as accession number.

Special media   Items which take a different form from the majority of the collection may be housed in a parallel sequence. Most commonly, the main lending collection comprises average sized books and anything which cannot be easily shelved with such books will be separately housed. Pamphlet collections are quite common, as are report sections. Certain media, such as video, microfiche, tapes, computer programs, films and collections of visual images such as photographs, prints and so on, will require specially designed systems of storage. Some library collections will be particularly rich in such materials, as, for example, in a collection of ephemera. Whether or not these are arranged in a parallel classified sequence largely depends on the physical convenience of browsing among the items and what approach we expect to be made by the enquirer. It is very difficult on a purely physical level to browse through a collection of microfiche and, if such were attempted, the arrangement would have to incorporate special features to assist the process, such as identifying labels which could be scanned from above. In a collection of photographic reproductions likely to be sought frequently by subject – where a common and typical approach would be 'I want a picture of a cat' – the subject approach must be catered for. However, in most cases this approach would be satisfied by some form of indexing – such as the ICONCLASS system described in Chapter 4 – rather than a classified arrangement of the photographs themselves.

The existence of such examples of parallel employment of a scheme does not invalidate the principles of classification. The principles are still being adhered to and the potential for the user to exploit subject arrangement in the quest for information still exists, but in a number of sequences rather than in a single one. What is important is that the user should be alerted to the nature of the various sequences and should be encouraged to explore each of them.

BROKEN ORDER

Broken order, as distinct from parallel classification, occurs when the classification is changed, simplified, deviated from or ignored. In some of the examples given above this may happen, but there other situations in which broken order is the rule, rather than the exception. Broken order can be observed whenever the normal classificatory sequence is disturbed, whether it is for long-term or short-term purposes, for example, a display of recently acquired titles. Sometimes broken order is used to improve upon the classified sequence, as when a library chooses to bring together Language and Literature, ignoring the main class order of DC. It is very rare to find a library which follows the main class sequence rigidly in its layout of the shelves and stock. A small branch library with a single square room in which to house the stock may be able to do so; but as we have seen in most libraries of any size they will have to accommodate materials in a number of different rooms, floors and even buildings. This will often result in the main sequence being broken.

Most libraries will wish to ensure that the most frequently consulted stock is most readily and immediately available to their users. In a public library this will often mean that the first material encountered will be the fiction collection – which we will discuss further later – a sequence that is unlikely to be classified at all. The other materials in the collection may or may not follow the logical sequence of the notation. In a library much used by the present author, the main lending stock is arranged on two floors. On the first and most accessible floor, the available classified sections are those relating to leisure hobbies and interests, such as gardening and photography (the 700s in DC which is the scheme employed) and biography, another great favourite of the British reading public (900 in DC); on the second floor we find the rest, such as psychology (150), literature (as distinct from fiction) at 800 and so on. The internal logic of the main class order is therefore broken. However, the aim is to satisfy the majority of customers and to promote the use of the most attractive and popular materials, in much the same way as Marks and Spencers arrange their stock to please the busy customer. Nor do such breaks in main class order affect the user's ability to browse within sections.

The division of a library into departments, again primarily to meet user requirements, may also result in broken order or repeated parallel classified sequences. In a large public library, it is common to find several such departments:

Main lending department   As we have seen, there may be instances of broken order herein.

Reference department   Usually the reference department has a parallel classification.

Children's department/junior library   Often the junior library uses a modified or simplified version of the classification in use elsewhere in the library. This will be a smaller collection, comparatively, and the need for detail will be correspondingly less. There will be instances of broken order in this collection too. Displays are particularly important in encouraging children to respond positively to library materials. There is also likely to be a large picture book section in the junior library and it may be felt that any form of classification is pointless with such works.

Local studies collection   As has already been noted in an earlier chapter, the local studies collection will have differing needs from the rest of the collection. The emphasis on the geographic locality is going to mean that an extension to the geographic tables will be essential whatever scheme is employed in the library. Extensions and adaptations, and even completely new schemes, are found commonly here. Also the emphasis on a range of different media, such as photographs and tapes of oral history, will mean that the storage and arrangement of the collection will be further complicated. Special indexes and collections within the collection are likely to develop, for example many local studies libraries maintain special collections of cuttings and create indexes to local newspapers and journals. These are unlikely to be arranged in a subject manner compatible with the main library collection.

Records/video departments   This form of material represents a special type of subject with its own inherent logic as far as arrangement is concerned, more akin to the way in which fiction is conventionally arranged. Here, within broad categories of musical styles, such as 'Country and Western' and 'classical', the most common approach is by musician/recording artist/group and that is the approach which will normally be taken. Often no arrangement is imposed beyond broad categorization and an index alerts the user to the collection's holdings by a particular artist.

Business/commercial/technical departments   These may describe themselves in a variety of ways, but their chief aim is to collect and house in one place material which will be of value to local business and commerce in the furtherance of their interests. Often such collections use the classification scheme adopted in the rest of the library, but it is not uncommon to find that whole sections have been taken out of the main lending stock and are to be found in the business department. Management theory, marketing, taxation and accounting practice may be found exclusively here. Equally, all of the company information – including a wide range of reference material such as directories – in the library's collection will be most usefully held here. Some libraries choose to combine business and technical information in such a department and there one would locate the standard and patent information, materials which have their own form of arrangement, dictated by their publishers.

Journals   Journals are very seldom classified in libraries for shelf arrangement. This is largely because the journals themselves treat fairly broad subject areas, for example the *New Scientist*, although there are many more specialized examples to be found. However, generally speaking, we do not expect users to browse through journals in search of information, or, if they do, to do so by identifying a likely journal title and to scan the pages of that journal, for example, *Local Studies Librarian*. Other mechanisms are necessary to retrieve information from journals and bibliographic tools, such as *abstracting and indexing services*, designed to facilitate access to the subject contents of journals, have long been a feature of libraries. Such tools are now increasingly available in CD ROM format and are proving popular and attractive. The most economic and effective means of the physical arrangement of journals on shelves has therefore been simply an alphabetic one by journal title; the enquirer having identified the title, volume, part and pages via another bibliographic source, they can quickly locate a particular volume and number in such a sequence.

These are likely to be the major departments in a large public library; in the academic library we may find the additional complication of its division on subject lines, so that there is, for example, a *medical library*, an *arts library*, and a *law library* all under the aegis of one university library, each with their own inherent breaks in the classification and their replications of and amendments to the chosen scheme.

Broken order also occurs, perhaps more perniciously, when the classification scheme is altered or improved upon by the library. The temptation to improve, to tinker with a scheme, should always be regarded with caution. It is tempting but can lead to serious practical problems, when perhaps the improver has left the library service or when a library wishes to take advantage of standardized classmarks, such as are available on machine readable catalogue (MARC) records.

A more drastic example of broken order is when the classification scheme is ignored completely and materials are arranged upon some other principle, usually alphabetical by some feature. Perhaps the two most common and familiar examples are ones which have just been mentioned in relation to public libraries: the fiction collection and biographical works. We will return to fiction, which deserves special consideration, in the next chapter. Most public libraries ignore their classification scheme in dealing with biography. The typical approach is for the biographical element to be treated as of secondary importance – that is, the option preferred in LC and DC – and to treat the subject as the primary facet. A biography of a physicist would therefore be analysed as 'physics – biography' and shelved with works on physics. While this is acceptable in the academic environment where it is normally physicists who will seek a biography of a physi-cist and in large research libraries, in the public library, apart from the very large public library with many departments, it is not usually the field of interest of the subject of biography which is of interest to readers but the personality and identity of the individual. Most readers are going to look, therefore, for people – for individuals by name – and are consequently best served by a simple alphabetic arrangement by the name of the subject of the biography within a single biographical section. The form – 'biography' and its subject or biographee – is therefore treated as the primary facet. However, where this system fails is that we have no easy mechanism by which to deal with collective biographies of more than one person, when we may have to revert to the classified arrangement. It is also not uncommon to find that libraries are inconsistent in their treatment of biography; they may in fact classify some biography with the subject so that film stars are collocated with works on the cinema and football players in the sports section, while there is still a general biography section containing politicians and writers and even the odd film star and football player. This is very unhelpful to the reader of biographies and it is not particularly helpful for the football enthusiast. Whatever system is employed, it must be done with consistency and with guidance for the user.

Broken order, as we have noted, also takes place when displays of material are formed, often on a temporary basis and usually for a very sound reason: the promotion of stock and the alerting of users to the existence of information. Displays often seek to highlight and bring together material from across disciplinary boundaries, in much the same way as the relative index and, therefore, play their part in illuminating the classified arrangement.

USE OF MORE THAN ONE SCHEME IN THE COLLECTION

Less commonly, we may find that a library service has used different schemes in different sections or departments of the service. The business collection might be arranged by the London Classification of Business Studies, while the rest is arranged by UDC, for example. The local studies collection might have its own scheme created in-house. A broad reader arrangement might be used for the main lending stock. The majority of libraries recognize the effectiveness of using a single standardized scheme throughout, in familiarizing users with the subject arrangement.

Essentially, then, we find that in practice shelf order is enormously complicated in its execution, by the range of responses which may have been adopted in order to maximize access to a full collection. All of the above might be found in a single library service: several parallel sequences; many instances of broken order; and more than one scheme in use. When such is the case, the library must be vigilant to the potential confusion to the users and must take every opportunity to forestall it and guide the user to the options which are available.

CLASSIFIED CATALOGUES

The catalogue is an essential tool in any library. It allows the user to find out exactly what the collection contains, not limited to the stock which is available and evident on the shelves. Often the shelves only represent a fraction of the stock in a collection. Much will be on loan. Material may have been withdrawn for a period; it might have been relegated to reserve, as an infrequently consulted item, or be being rebound or repaired in some way. There is also the problem of the classification having been split into separate sequences, such as reference and oversize. The catalogue overcomes all such problems and reveals the full collection to the enquirer. It is therefore a valuable support to the subject arrangement of the material on the shelves.

Catalogues normally allow for several types of approach:

Author approach   Very commonly the user comes armed with a name or names and wants to know what the library has by that particular author. The catalogue must show each book in the collection by that author.

Title approach   The user may know the title of a work or works they wish to

167

consult. The catalogue must show each edition of a title in the collection.

Subject approach The user has a subject and they want to know what the collection contains on that subject. The catalogue must show each item in the collection on that subject. It is the latter that we are of course concerned with here, but it is also important to see how the various approaches fit together into a whole catalogue.

Catalogues are composed of two basic elements:

Author/title catalogue It is usual in catalogues for these two functions to be combined in one alphabetical sequence. The searcher consults the sequence and finds under the heading for their author a list of the works contained in the library. Author/title catalogues commonly provide entries not just for the main authors and titles of a work, but also for additional authors, editors, translators, series titles, variant titles and so on. There will also be a system of references guiding the user from alternative forms of headings; from, for example, pseudonyms to the real name of the author.

Subject catalogues These may be of two types, the *classified* or the *dictionary catalogue*.

Some critics have argued that the subject approach in the catalogue is unnecessary, as the enquirer will either come armed with personal knowledge of their subject or may consult bibliographies in order to discover what exists on the subject. The problem with reliance on bibliographies, however, is precisely that their contents are not limited to the contents of any one or even several collections and, while they will certainly show what exists on a subject, they will not guide the user of a particular library or collection. Certainly bibliographies are essential in a full subject search, where the enquirer will not want to be limited by the arbitrary nature of a single collection and will have the time, patience and motivation to wait until items can be sought from other collections on inter-library loan. In many cases the enquirer will not have such a comprehensive and long-term goal in mind and will be better satisfied by being guided to what is immediately available in the collection at hand. We should perhaps bear in mind Ranganathan's fifth law of library science, *save the time of the reader*. The greatest and most telling criticism to be made of the subject catalogue is one which can be levelled at any type of catalogue and, to an even greater extent, bibliographies – that is, that very few library users make any use at all of such secondary sources. They are, have always been and, unfortunately, are likely to continue to be reluctant to approach catalogues and bibliographies. There may have been a slight improvement with the advent of OPACs and it is true that the public library user is more reluctant than his or her equivalent in the academic and special library; for the majority of users this is still a serious problem. Such a reluctance reinforces the importance of sound shelf order as the chief and, in many cases, only method of subject retrieval used by the enquirer in the library.

It is with the classified catalogue – which exploits classificatory techniques to aid subject retrieval – that we are most concerned here; it is, however, useful to compare the way it functions *vis-à-vis* the dictionary catalogue – which ignores classification. The classified catalogue consists of a classified sequence, in the filing order of the notation employed, of all of the classmarks at which items are located in the collection. For each classmark a list of the works classified at that number is provided. The classification employed is that used for the shelf arrangement of the materials in the collection, unless of course the library does not use classification on the shelves, but arranges material by some other means, such as accession number.

The following imaginary examples are for a library which has a collection classified using DC.

Entries in a classified catalogue

738.15 Mas
Mason, Sheila. Painting on porcelain / by Sheila Mason. – London: Batsford, 1992. – 166p: ill; 26cm.
　ISBN 0713433362　　Central 1 copy
　　　　　　　　　　　Suburbia 1 copy
738.15 Zan
Zanardi, Nicoletta. Guide to decorating ceramics / by Nicoletta Zanardi. – Newton Abbott: David & Charles, 1989. – 114p: ill: 24cm.
　ISBN 0715385399　　Sea Side 1 copy

Ref 738.2094 Gui
A guide to European pottery / edited by Sean Cushion. – London: Constable, 1989. – 1004p: ill (some col.); 35cm.
　ISBN 0850973546　　Central 1 copy

OS 738.37 Osw
Oswald, Adrian. English brown stoneware / by Adrian Oswald. – London: Faber, 1982. – 220p: col. ill; 36cm.
　ISBN 0571119050　　East End 1 copy

As can be seen from the examples given above, the classified catalogue presents a sequence, mirroring that of the classified materials on the shelf, which will bring together items on a subject, in this instance porcelain, pottery and ceramics. It is comparatively easy for an enquirer to browse among such a list and from the records to determine whether the item is likely to be of interest to them. No matter whether the item is held in the Reference or Lending department of the collection, their attention will have been drawn to its existence. There may only be one item at a particular classmark; there may be many. Hence the device of the first three letters of the main entry element – that is, the filing element, usually the author surname or the title if there is no author – added to the classmark. With this information it is comparatively easy for the user to go with his or her classmark to the appropriate point on the shelves and find the document they seek. The example also illustrates the way in which a catalogue may bring together information across related libraries, in perhaps a public library service with branches to reveal the existence of items regardless of location. This method is far more common now that many catalogues are electronically generated than it was in the days of the card catalogue, when a common criticism was the limitation of the coverage of the catalogue.

The shelf order and the classified sequence of the catalogue do not simply replicate each other. They differ and their value is complementary. The catalogue will reveal more than the shelves and it will also save the enquirer's time in perhaps needlessly consulting several sections of the collection in search of a particular classmark. Another great advantage of the classified sequence is that it solves one of the major problems of shelf subject arrangement: a book can only have one place in the physical sequence. If a book covers more than one subject, then the dominant or most significant subject must be identified by the classifier and the book placed at that point on the shelf. However, in the classified sequence a work can be entered at as many points as there are subjects covered within the contents of its pages, although in practice there are likely to be some limitations placed on the number of entries made. For a work dealing with two subjects the following entries would be made (note that it must be made clear to the enquirer which classmark represents the location of the work on the shelves):

636.0890681
Shelved at 657.8635
Rogers, Peter
Accountancy for veterinarians/by Peter Rogers. – Oxford:, OUP, 1987. 167p: ill; 23cm.
   ISBN 0998754367   Central 1 copy

657.8635
Rogers, Peter
Accountancy for veterinarians/by Peter Rogers. – Oxford:, OUP, 1987. 167p: ill; 23cm.
   ISBN 0998754367   Central 1 copy

and so whichever of the subjects was the first choice of the enquirer, the item would be located. The classified catalogue is thus of enormous assistance to the classifier in overcoming the limitations of the physical arrangement of their collection. The classifier may go even further and create *analytical added entries* for all of the parts of a composite item, such as conference proceedings, where in practice the subject content of the individual papers may vary quite considerably. This is a time-consuming process and it has been argued that it can confuse the user. It means that the subject content of a collection will be revealed to a far greater extent than where such entries are not made. Grace O. Kelley's[1] research many years ago suggests that an enormous proportion of valuable material is overlooked in any subject search simply because it is contained within works and hence is not drawn to the attention of the inexpert user, who will not know where to look. Again the entry must clearly show the nature of the material to be located. If, for example, a work dealt with local government but had a significant section on central government, an entry such as the following would be made:

354.42
Shelved at 352.042
Todd, Victor
The future of central government
In
Local government today; proceedings of a conference held at Lancaster, 15th September, 1993. – London: HMSO, 1993. – pp.265-293.

This present manual might generate an analytical entry under *special classification schemes* in addition to its likely main classified entry under *general classification*.

The classified catalogue has therefore certain advantages over the classified items on the shelves, but because of its low level of usage and because of the twofold approach – that is, that the catalogue and the shelves must both be consulted to locate actual documents – it is not wholly satisfactory as a complete replacement for a subject arrangement on the shelves. They are, as has already been stated, complementary tools, and even by the staff of a library they will be used in different ways in different circumstances. Recent research is indicating that the significance of classification in the online catalogue is greater than might have been expected. The utility and value of the classified catalogue – and hence its future existence and development – are likely to be issues which will continue to be of significance to information science.

In the classified catalogue, the classified sequence has to be supported by an alphabetical subject index for the library user will not know the classmarks which relate to the specific subjects in which he or she is interested. The alphabetical subject index to the classified catalogue serves merely as a key to the classified sequence – and of course to the shelf arrangement – and does not identify individual works. For one of our examples above, then, the subject index entry would appear:

Porcelain: decoration   738.15

It is essential that a subject index is provided and that the published index to the classification schedules of the scheme used by the library should not be employed as an alternative. This happens frequently and the saving in time and intellectual effort which such a course presents tells us why it is such a popular option. However, the index to the classification scheme is not an effective replacement because it will not represent the library's collection and will therefore mislead the user by providing classmarks for all sorts of subjects, upon which the library holds no documents at all. The published index may also have a bias in terminology and approach which may not be helpful in the context of a particular library. Neither should the effort of creating a subject index be exaggerated. The index will grow rapidly in a new or growing library, but, thereafter, the effort involved will diminish, for one entry on, for example, 'the history of art' will stand for all works which are purchased by the library on that subject and it is only when works appear on new and previously unrepresented subjects that a new index entry will have to be created. It is another useful, even essential, complement to the classified approach, bringing together the minor subject associations which the shelf order ignores. Normally, such a subject index does not use *see references* for synonyms but produces two entries for synonymous terms. It is, therefore, described as being *asyndetic* – without references. In such an index, two entries would be found for the synonymous terms:

Poisons   RA1195–RA1270
Toxicology   RA1195–RA1270

In addition the classified catalogue has an alphabetical author index, which lists works for all authors represented in the collection. There are, then, three parts to the classified catalogue:

the *author/title index*, providing actual records of items contained in the library
the *classified catalogue*, providing the actual records of items contained in the library
the *subject index*, providing a link to the classified sequence

Here are two stages to the subject approach: the user must go first to the subject index and thereafter consult the classified sequence in order to locate the records of the items which can be found in the collection. The classified catalogue is therefore sometimes referred to as an *indirect catalogue*.

The *dictionary catalogue* takes a different approach to subject treatment. It has two elements:

The *author/title index*, providing access to works precisely as in the classified catalogue.
The *subject catalogue*, providing direct access to works held in the collection, listed under alphabetically arranged subject headings.

With this method we have, therefore, a direct approach via a single index of alphabetical subject terms to the works which will be of value to enquirers. The argument is also made by many that this is an arrangement which is readily understood and more readily approached and used by enquirers. The dictionary catalogue restricts the role of classification to that of providing a shelf location for works and aiding users in browsing through those shelves. The contention that this is a simpler and more effective system is based upon the notion that a classed sequence is less easily understood and more difficult to construct. However, there are great problems in the construction of a dictionary subject catalogue and the intellectual demands of such a process should be recognized. The construction of subject headings and their standardization are complex and complex rules exist to assist the process and to ensure consistency, via the *Library of Congress Subject Headings (LCSH)* for example. These are even available in a simplified form as *Sear's subject headings*. To try to predict all possible headings, their alternatives and contexts is an undertaking on the same scale as that of creating a classification scheme. Equally it is debatable whether the argument that the subject terms are more approachable is really soundly based. If we consider our previous examples, which were brought together in the classified catalogue, in the dictionary catalogue we would find a number of entries widely scattered in the alphabetic sequence:

Entries in a dictionary catalogue

Porcelain: painting
Mason, Sheila. Painting on porcelain/by Sheila Mason. – London: Batsford, 1992. – 166p: ill; 26cm.

| ISBN 0713433362 | Central | 738.15 Mas |
| | Suburbia | 738.15 Mas |

Ceramics
see also Porcelain
Zanardi, Nicoletta. Guide to decorating ceramics/by Nicoletta Zanardi. – Newton Abbott: David & Charles, 1989. – 114p: ill: 24cm.

| ISBN 0715385399 | Sea Side | 738.15 Zan |

Pottery: European
A guide to European pottery/edited by Sean Cushion. – London: Constable, 1989. – 1004p: ill (some col.); 35cm.

| ISBN 0850973546 | Central | Ref 738.2094 Gui |

Stoneware
Oswald, Adrian. English brown stoneware/by Adrian Oswald. – London: Faber, 1982. – 220p: col. ill; 36cm.

| ISBN 0571119050 | East End | OS 738.37 Osw |

The classified catalogue also provides a subject index for the language approach. To say that the dictionary catalogue is a one stage approach is not entirely valid either, for the chances of the user choosing the correct subject term at the first attempt are slight indeed, given the huge reference apparatus of the dictionary catalogue. It would be uneconomic for the dictionary catalogue to list the works appearing in the collection for each of the synonyms of a subject; that would increase the bulk of the catalogue many times. Therefore, to return to our earlier example for poisons and toxicology, only one of these would be identified as the *used* term, at which the works would be listed; at the other a reference would be made. The user consulting poisons, for example, would not have immediate access to the works available but would rather be directed to the term 'toxicology' in a quite different part of the sequence.

Poisons *see* Toxicology

Toxicology
Smart, A. A toxicological . . .

This is no quicker than finding the classmark for poisons and consulting that. The syndetic system of references in the dictionary catalogue is often very cumbersome and very irritating for the user.

The greatest disadvantage of the dictionary catalogue arises from the fact that there is no possibility of collecting related materials which will be scattered by the alphabetic arrangement. Thus the enquirer who is interested in school libraries may find that they are only directed to specific works, as this is the principle upon which dictionary catalogues operate, that is, that entries are only made for specific subjects. However, a very large proportion of enquiries are not subject specific; it is very rare for an enquirer to be interested only in documents which deal with school librarianship and not in those which deal with particular types of school library. Such a specific entry approach also fails to acknowledge the way in which books are written and information communicated; that it is very likely the case that in a work on, for example, 'library management' or 'book selection' quite considerable attention may be paid to the school library environment. Most enquiries are vaguer than this; the user wants to find information on a group of related themes or may even have in mind a topical approach. Such an enquirer would thus miss works on libraries in infant schools in the subject specific dictionary catalogue. Dictionary catalogues cater for this problem by providing *see also* references to more specific subjects, as is the practice in the *Library of Congress subject headings*. However, they do not make such references to broader related subject headings and therefore potentially valuable works, which might contain significant sections on school librarianship, might be missed. In practice too, in the creation of huge dictionary catalogues inconsistencies and anomalies arise, as they do in the subject headings lists themselves.

The chief arguments for the two forms of catalogue may therefore be summarised thus:

that the classified catalogue better provides for the subject retrieval of materials, as it provides a greater collocation of subject within the hierarchy of a discipline, as well as catering for the subject term approach via its index.

that the dictionary catalogue is simpler in form providing immediate – though the extent of the immediacy may be in debate – access to materials via a single alphabetical and, for the majority of users, recognizable and understandable sequence.

It is sometimes suggested that the dictionary catalogue is better suited for public library collections and the classified for academic and research libraries. This is an attitude that is rather condescending, although it may be realistic. It fails to acknowledge the role the major public library services play in support of research and intellectual activity. Not all such work is linked to a research or academic environment. With the growth of union catalogues, it is ever more likely that few public library branches will stand alone. It is rather the case that they will have a catalogue which will also contain the holdings of their central library, potentially a large and valuable body of material. The value of the classified sequence for such materials is less in question.

It can be argued that one's stance in relation to the advantages of the two forms of catalogue tends to be affected by one's experience of their use and value. Dictionary catalogues are the most common form of catalogue in the United States, while the classified catalogue is more common in Britain. This fact has had an impact upon attitudes to classification on both sides of the Atlantic and may explain the greater interest in classificatory research and in the development of classification as a tool for subject retrieval in Europe. It is important, however, to bear in mind that the development of electronic catalogues in the form of online public access catalogues (OPACs) has rendered the battle between these two great opponents – the dictionary and classified catalogue – apparently extinct, as it has removed the distinction between the two types of catalogue, although the debate may still have an impact upon attitudes to the catalogue and the role of classification in the OPAC. Indeed, there is evidence to suggest that the OPAC and increased electronic access to information are causing American theorists and practitioners to reappraise their attitudes to classification and the catalogue. This is a theme which will be developed in Part Three when we consider classification and information technology.

CLASSIFIED BIBLIOGRAPHIES

Classification is used for the arrangement of entries in a large number of published catalogues and bibliographies. Many of these, for example the British National Bibliography (BNB), use well-known general schemes; in the case of BNB it is DC which is used. Essentially, general bibliographies will use general schemes; their scope and extent being equivalent. The classified arrangement in such a bibliography allows for a form of subject approach and browsing and is supported by an alphabetical subject index which will guide the user to the appropriate section of the classified sequence. In BNB, for example, the user who did not know the classmark for his or her subject would first consult the subject index, where they would find gathered all treatments of their subject, whatever the discipline, with the classmarks for each indicated:

Handicapped children

Care – for parents	362.4088054
Development. Role of play	155.45
Education	371.9
Home care. Behavioural aspects	649.15

Then, having chosen the treatment which best suits their interest or having noted all classmarks, the user would turn to the classified sequence where they would find the full details of the books on their subject:

362.4 – WELFARE SERVICES FOR THE PHYSICALLY HANDI-CAPPED
362.4088054 – Children confined to wheelchairs – for children
Althea. I use a wheelchair / by Althea; illustrated by Maureen Galvani. – Cambridge; Dinosaur, c1983. [24]p: col.ill; 16x19cm. – (Dinosaur's Althea Books)
ISBN 0-85122-381-8(pbk): Unpriced   B83-42441
362.4088054 – Great Britain. Handicapped children
Looking at handicap: information about ten medical conditions / edited by Sarah Curtis. – London: British Agencies for Adoption & Fostering, 1982. – 65p; 21cm. (Practice series)
ISBN 0-903534-42-8 (pbk): £2.30   B83-22432
362.40924 – Physically handicapped persons – biographies
Carr, Marilyn Gillies. Look no hands! / Marilyn Gillies Carr. – Edinburgh: Canongate, 1982. – 151p, [16]p of plates: ill, ports; 23cm
ISBN 0-86241-023-1 (cased): £5.95   B83-15572

As can be seen from the above, the user then finds a sequence of associated materials, within the section on welfare services for the physically handicapped, among which he or she can browse. Such a bibliography provides a number of methods of accessing information:

by subject
 – subject index
 – classified subject sequence
by author alphabetically
by title alphabetically

Depending upon the use which is likely to be made of them, bibliographies will contain all or some of these indexes. Not all bibliographies choose to provide a classified sequence and rely on an extended alphabetical subject approach with references, as in the dictionary catalogue. For example, *Index Medicus* relies entirely on such an approach:

BODY HEIGHT
Maternal height, shoe size, and outcome of labour in white primagravidas.
Mahmood et al. **Br Med J** 1988 Aug 20–27 297(6647):515–7
BODY IMAGE
Body image and eating behaviour in adolescent girls. Moore DC. **Am J Dis Child** 1988 Oct; 142(10):1114–8

More specialized bibliographies, when they have a classified arrangement, are far more likely to adopt a special classification, such as the *INSPEC classification*, which was described in Chapter 4. Often, as we saw there, the classification has been created for the precise purpose of forming such an arrangement in a bibliography. There are several other bibliographies or abstracting services which have developed their own classifications, with varying degree of detail and attention to classificatory principles. Subsequently, the classification may have been adopted for use in shelf arrangement, but where that has happened its original purpose should be borne in mind, for inevitably there will be limitations in such a scheme. The need for a simple and easily handled notation is perhaps less significant in a classification intended purely for use in a bibliography and the attention to systematic arrangement may have been less rigorous overall than in a classification intended for physical location. What is important, in the classified sequence of a bibliography, is that the classmark is supported by a subject heading, as we see in the example from BNB above, otherwise the sequence and the significance of the associations which are made will be meaningless to the user. *Physics Abstracts* provides, for example, descriptive headings and scope notes in the classified sequence:

67.80	SOLID HELIUM AND RELATED QUANTUM CRYSTALS
51388	Nucleation in Vycor under pressure: superfluid . . .
67.90	OTHER TOPICS IN QUANTUM FLUIDS AND SOLIDS (e.g. neutron-star matter)
51389	Parametric excitation of electrons . . .
51390	An approximate theory of interfacial . . .

CLASSIFICATION AND READING LISTS

Any reading list produced by a library may adopt a classified arrangement of its contents and this will prove useful to the user, depending upon the extent and subject coverage of the list. A lengthy accessions bulletin, covering all the subjects represented in the library stock, will be much more readily consulted if it has adopted a classified approach to arrangement. Given that the majority of materials in the library collection will have been classified, then it is most economic of effort and very practical to build upon the classification in providing a subject arrangement in any listing or bulletin which is produced.

Of more interest though is the use that can be made of the classified catalogue in the compilation of reading lists and bibliographies by the library. Where one has access to a classified catalogue, whether in card or electronic form, it is a very simple matter to identify and reproduce a list of readings on a particular subject and its related aspects or subdivisions. The body of relevant material can be very swiftly assembled from a classified sequence. Given that the classification has brought together works by the most significant characteristic, then the classification will aid the compiler of the reading list in identifying the most useful material to be included. Let us imagine that we are producing a booklist on 'the depiction of war in film and television', then the consultation of the relative index will indicate the classmarks at which works can be found on the subject in a number of disciplines:

War in cinema/TV	45[355]
War camps in fiction films/plays	737.19
War films/plays	737
War in fiction films/plays	737.0
War news	762.15
War propaganda	411.13

The consultation of the classified catalogue will then reveal all of the items in the collection, whatever department they are housed in, and will guide us to more general or specific works in each of the classes identified in the subject index which might contain useful material. Turning to the section of the classified sequence, we might find works collocated there on:

737.1	Cavalry
737.116	Commandos
737.117	Parachute troops. Airborne troops.
737.12	Sea forces. Navy.
737.13	Air forces etc.

If we look at the section **45**, we will find works on factors in society in relation to the cinema, which may well contain substantial sections on war and the cinema.

The classified catalogue can also be used to generate the list itself. It is comparatively easy to duplicate catalogue records for inclusion in a book list. Card catalogue records can be photocopied: the electronically produced catalogue allows the tailoring of the output in a reading list much more effectively and swiftly, using the same principle.

READER ADVISORY WORK AND REFERENCE SERVICES

The classified sequence of the shelves and the classified catalogue are inestimable boons in the support of reference services. The reference service, in its provision of materials to respond to the information needs of the library's users, will exploit the subject arrangement of materials in identifying the useful sources to provide the answers to specific questions. Inevitably the reference librarian will turn first to the stock of their collection to deal with such queries. In many instances the classification may not reveal the content of works sufficiently to indicate their potential in response to specific questions. In particular with general reference works, in which the reference department will abound, the classified arrangement will indicate little, beyond helping the reference librarian to get to know their stock and its subject nature. Many answers in reference work do not come from the traditional reference stock, but may be found in any department and in any type of work in the collection. An enquirer interested in Ranulph Fiennes will locate useful information in the biographical dictionaries and the encyclopaedias; but much more detailed information will be located in the library's lending stock, in his autobiography and in accounts of his expeditions. The reference librarian who does not turn to the catalogue will be ill serving his or her enquirer.

When we turn to readers' advisory work, the value of the classified arrangement of materials will truly come into its own. The librarian seeking to guide and assist the user in the location of works on a subject, in support of an interest, an enthusiasm or research, must be able to locate the works on a subject in the collection. They may seek also to guide an interested user to works which can be obtained from other collections; they may seek to guide the user to journal literature to identify more specific in-depth studies of an aspect of a subject or to locate more current treatments. But in the first instance and still for the majority of users it is books, immediately to hand, which are sought. Efforts are at present being made to investigate the possibility of using classification to help to guide the reader to alternative titles, via a form of classificatory link.

Alan MacLennan[2] has devised a model which, from a list of the works of fiction, a reader has enjoyed, can then via classificatory principles move to a group of related titles to suggest others which may be of interest. The practical value of classification in assisting the reader continues thus to be developed.

ONLINE SEARCHING OF ELECTRONIC DATABASES

Classification takes a number of forms in online databases, from a fairly conventional provision of classmarks assigned to subject groupings, to more specialized instances of the classification of particular categories of material. These are useful in the interactive environment for searching. Classmarks can be sought using all of the features available in such an environment: in combination with other fields, such as language or date; several classmarks can be sought simultaneously – these must be combined using *or* and not *and* as a logical operator, for each item will in most cases have a single classmark; and truncation can be used, thus exploiting the hierarchical nature of the classmark – this latter facility must be used with caution, for precision will suffer in such a search. Some examples of the use of classification in online files are briefly described below:

Subject classification   Some databases classify each record to indicate its subject content. Most Online Public Access Catalogues (OPACS) have this facility, although they do not all make the classmark field available to users for searching. In this instance the scheme will be that in operation in the library. The *British National Bibliography* (BNB) and LCMARC (the Library of Congress records) offer both DC and LC classmarks. Some indexing and abstracting services such as Inspec also have classmarks attached. On the whole this tends to be a less popular and therefore less frequent type of approach by most searchers than the subject keyword one. Inspec is a detailed classification; others take a broader view. *Linguistics and language behaviour abstracts* (LLBA) provides a broad classification of headings such as 'speech synthesis' and 'auditory perception' in just 106 categories. These could then be combined with subject terms to ensure that the correct context for the term was retrieved or they may be used for generic searching of a range of material. Perhaps because of its vast scale, it is in the medical and biological sciences that large scale development of the role of classification in searching online has taken place. The control of terminology is particularly important in this discipline, with the range of potential synonyms and the distinction of expert and popular recognition of terms. Medline has, according to the *Manual of online search strategies*,[3] 'the most detailed classification scheme developed for online searching', allowing the searcher to link via the tree or hierarchical structure of the scheme, to other related works. Similarly Embase offers a hierarchical and much more in-depth approach, via a scheme evocatively entitled EMTREES, indicating the structure of its hierarchies. EMTREES identifies 15 facets representing such aspects as 'anatomy', 'diseases' and so on.

Patent classification   Originally developed as national codes for use with paper-based patent collections, the International Patent Code (IPC), introduced in 1968, has been adopted by the majority of countries, although with some variability in the extent of its implementation. It is a very detailed hierarchical classification scheme, which can be searched in full or truncated form. Classification of this sort is particularly necessary for a patent collection for a number of reasons: patent files are frequently searched by subject; what the patent agent or searcher needs to know is whether the idea, the concept, is unique and therefore recall must be total but precision is important for inventions may be in the same field and yet unique; descriptions of the entity are difficult, for terminology and even language of description vary and these may be best overcome by coding – it is of course notoriously difficult to describe an object; if an idea is new then the terminology may not yet be established or widely known.

Chemical compounds   Chemical compounds have an unfortunate tendency to acquire several names over a period of time. Several systems have, therefore, been developed to identify these. Probably the most familiar to online searchers are the *Registry Numbers* (RN) applied in the Chemical Abstracts database, although available in a number of other files. A combination of strategies, that is, of generic name and of Registry Number, is therefore recommended.

Industry codes Again there are a number of industry codes, but the most commonly used system is the *Standard Industrial Classification* (SIC) Code. Of course these are primarily to be found in business databases and prove invaluable in gathering material upon a particular sector of interest. They can be used in conjunction with other elements in records to identify companies, to investigate market strength, to consider the products available, and to check on the market or on current events.

These are some of the better known examples of classification in electronic files. When using any database it is wise to investigate fully the features and options available to the searcher. Such an approach can greatly enhance recall and should certainly be tried in conjunction with other methods.

Having considered the variety of practical uses which are made of classification schemes in libraries and information services, let us now turn our attention to the manner in which these functions are accomplished.

ISSUES FOR CONSIDERATION

1.   In a library with which you are familiar, identify and consider the ways in which classification is used, both by the library staff and by the users. Do these approaches differ?

2.   There are advantages and disadvantages to the parallel arrangement of works in a collection. How is the effectiveness and accessibility of the collection, as far as the user is concerned, improved or worsened by such treatment?

NOTES

1.   Kelley, Grace O., *The classification of books: an enquiry into its usefulness for the reader.* New York: H. W. Wilson, 1938.
2.   MacLennan, Alan, An expert system selector for fiction. [Research in progress, the Robert Gordon University, Aberdeen.]
3.   *Manual of online search strategies*, edited by C. J. Armstrong and J. A. Large. Aldershot: Ashgate, 1992.

7 Classification policy and library administration

POLICY AND THE LIBRARY MANAGEMENT

Much as some might wish it were not so, classification cannot and should not be treated in the abstract but must be seen in operation in the real world. Classificatory policy does not exist in a vacuum; it must fit into the overall policy of the library or information service, within which it is used, and the nature of that service will impinge upon the role classification plays in any particular environment. There are many factors which will have an impact:

Access to the collection If a collection is on closed access to users and is only going to be approached by library staff, then it is possible that a classified shelf arrangement will not be deemed necessary. The role of providing subject access might then be performed by a subject catalogue or index.

User group The nature of the users of the collection may affect decisions about classification in practice. Factors such as age, levels of subject expertise, frequency of use of the service and specificity of approach will all come into play.

Typical user approaches or queries The type of subject or information need commonly encountered by library staff may affect decisions, for example, on broad or close classification.

Priorities or objectives of the library or information service The role which the service assumes for itself may be significant. Whether the priority is upon quick reference provision or the support of leisure interests or the encouragement of local enterprise or the storage and accessing of documentation, the function the scheme is called upon to perform may play a part in deciding upon the form of classification deemed most appropriate.

In addition there will be practical constraints imposed by the structure and administration of the library service, such as the staffing levels and finance available, the attitude of management to classification and the responsiveness of the service to their customer. If we consider for a moment the attitudes of library management, it is not uncommon to find a management with a limited understanding of the value of classification. It may be deemed a necessary but minor operational procedure, not warranting enormous expenditure of resources. Such an attitude does not bode well for the efficient and effective administration of a very valuable weapon in the library's armoury. Where there are clashes of interest, classification may come off poorly. If, for example, staff are finding it difficult to keep up with backlog in the accessioning of new books, then it might be suggested that less effort should go into the process of classifying them and that they should be processed quickly through the system – perhaps even by library clerical staff – accepting uncritically the classmark assigned on the MARC record, rather than letting them be considered individually by professional librarians.

It is important that library managers understand the impact a poorly chosen or implemented classification scheme can have on their collection and upon the satisfaction of their users. Issue statistics are very important to library managers, as they are often a performance criterion upon which the service will be judged. Let us not underestimate the effect that excellent collocation of related materials on the shelf can have on issue statistics. If we acknowledge the significance of browsing in user selection of materials for borrowing, then we must also accept the fact that where items are brought together efficiently by subject, then the borrower is going to borrow more. When we make it easy for him or her to find relevant material, we will be rewarded, whether in the academic, public or special library. Equally, if we provide a sound classified catalogue or good subject retrieval by classmark, reservations and issues are going to be encouraged. Classification provides an underpinning for much of the significant activity which goes on in our library services.

SELECTION AND IMPLEMENTATION OF A SCHEME

In the majority of cases we will find ourselves in a library with an established classification scheme and no intention of changing. However, in setting up a new library service, whether on a small or a large scale, or in a service which envisages change, we may find ourselves in the position where we need to consider the schemes available in order to identify the most suitable and helpful. There are a variety of criteria upon which we might base this choice and by which we might rank the various schemes under consideration. These fall into five broad categories:

1. the scheme's intrinsic qualities
2. its ease of use
3. schedule availability and revision
4. the extent of use of the scheme

5.   the library service's particular requirements

1. The scheme's intrinsic qualities

Under this heading we might include much of the discussion to be found in Part One, but let us briefly remind ourselves of the areas we should examine. How effective is the classification for the purpose we intend; are materials helpfully collocated on the shelf? Examination of an existing collection arranged by the scheme under consideration can help us to judge how well it performs on this score. Is the level of detail sufficient to meet our users' need? How up to date is the scheme in its coverage of rapidly changing subject areas? Is the notation appropriate to the environment in which it will be used? Is the scheme adaptable: does it offer flexibility or alternatives to cater for special requirements; is the citation order fixed or left to the discretion of the library?

2. The ease of use of the scheme

This is a very practical, but nonetheless significant factor in any consideration of alternatives. It depends largely upon the guidance offered within the published editions of the scheme for the classifier. Is the scheme well enough explained, whether in introductory material, via instructions in the schedules, by the provision of manuals, by educational programmes, or by a combination of all of the above, to be used with ease in the library? The result will be reflected in the consistency of application of the scheme in the collection and this in turn will have a major impact upon the effectiveness of the subject arrangement overall. Ease of use may also relate to the ease with which users can approach the scheme. How much explanation will the library service have to provide of the vagaries of the notational filing order, for example?

3. Availability and revision of the schedules

Not all schemes are available for purchase and clearly such may be a major disincentive to adoption in most instances. In a special library environment if an ideal were found to exist and its developers were happy to allow its use then this might be a viable option. With a published scheme, we are looking for the reassurance of a stable revision policy and the guarantee of future updating of the schedules. Most libraries look for a happy medium here: periodic appearances of new schedules but not so frequent as to cause almost continual reclassification of stock. Frequent drastic change is much in disfavour. A scheme should have a predictable cycle of revision, a policy of forewarning users of proposed changes and a system of consultation of users to establish their practical needs and the problems encountered in applying the scheme in practice. Change is vital and gradual change is best in practice for most collections, if we are to avoid major upheavals and staff intensive reclassification projects.

4. The extent of use of the scheme

The acceptance of a scheme as an acknowledged standard and its frequency of use in other libraries should be seen as an advantage. Clearly popularity would suggest intrinsically excellent qualities and the satisfaction of present users. It also assists in the interchange of information between libraries and information services if a standard is commonly used. If the scheme's classmarks are available on centrally created catalogue records such as those provided by the British Library or The Library of Congress, then this may be seen as a further incentive. In a special library a scheme which is used in one of the major abstracting or indexing services may have attractions and such a dual role may encourage use of classification in that environment as well as in the library.

5. The library's particular requirements

Pragmatic factors may intrude upon our abstract consideration of the schemes available. We may find ourself in a library forming part of a larger organizational structure, where it would be wise to adopt the same system as is applied in other parts of the organization. We may have very specialized users, whose needs may not be best served by the system which otherwise holds all of the aces.

It is wise, periodically, for a service to reconsider the classification in use and to match it with the above criteria. Since its establishment a service may have changed and developed in unexpected ways. The original reasons for the choice of a scheme may no longer be valid. The *whole* of the service should also be considered; here we have the choice between the application of a single scheme versus several. Is the scheme appropriate throughout all of the departments in which it is being used? The choice lies largely between overall uniformity and the meeting of special requirements. These should be weighed very carefully. One very practical problem which arises as a result of the use of a number of schemes is that of their treatment in the classified catalogue. Should all of the schemes be included in a single classified catalogue? If so, how can this best be managed so that the sequence will make sense? A classified catalogue containing several schemes is physically possible but such an entity fails to achieve its true purpose as it will not bring together all treatments of a single subject, unless multiple added entries are made – another reason for questioning the validity of the use of multiple schemes. Equally, as was suggested above in the chapter on special classification, the development of special schemes in-house should be considered very carefully before such a project is launched. It is as well to be sure that work is not being duplicated and essential to understand the future commitment to maintenance and development of the scheme involved.

ADAPTATION AND RECLASSIFICATION

It is not uncommon for libraries to customize or amend the scheme in use with the collection to suit their individual requirements. Certain classes may be felt to be awkwardly arranged; they may not reflect the needs of the library's users. Others may be felt to be inadequate because of their lack of detail or their lack of currency in terminology and in coverage of new developments. The debate is really over the unauthorized adaptation. As we know schemes on occasion offer authorized forms of adaptation – such as in BC's provision of *alternative locations* – where modifications and alternatives are suggested in the schedules. It is when the librarian chooses to make his or her own independent changes that subsequent problems may arise, because once the process is undertaken the adaptation will find its own momentum and it and the original scheme are likely to move ever further from each other. Such a course of action may prove very effective for the collection, for so long as the library is content with its independent position. In effect the library is committing itself to what is virtually the maintenance and updating of an entirely new classification for that class. It is when independence is seen as being less desirable that the difficulties are fully revealed. When, perhaps, the advantages of uniformity with other collections or the desirability of a new edition of the scheme in use offer an attractive alternative, the original decision may be regretted for a process of reclassification will be necessary for the adapted section and there will be no assistance from the editors of the published scheme, as there would be with authorized adaptations. To illustrate the point with but one example, many libraries in the 1980s grew tired of waiting for the revision of the Computer Science class in DC and created their own modified schedule. When the phoenix schedule appeared they could not use DC's tables of changes, which linked old to new numbers, and the time and effort involved for staff in the process of reclassification were, therefore, that much greater.

Adaptation should be undertaken with great discretion and caution. Wholesale adaptation is a dangerous business and small scale adaptation of numerous sections is perhaps even more pernicious. It may be that such modifications go uncharted. Where adaptations have taken place these should be meticulously recorded to safeguard the operation of the scheme in future.

SPECIAL CASES AND ADAPTATION

It is perhaps only with a unique collection, perhaps of local material or of ephemera, that adaptation should be recommended. A local studies classification will have a limited scope and potential for application. There are only a handful of libraries likely to be interested in classifying a collection of materials in a locality, although it may well be in the interests of that small group to cooperate in the maintenance of a special scheme to be used by all. There will be no benefit to standardization beyond this level. With an ephemeral collection too, there are likely to be specific limitations on subject content dependent upon the nature and focus of the collection. We might find a collection of local playbills or of timetables for the train services of a railway company. Again uniformity with such a unique resource will not be an issue.

1. Fiction

There are also areas of collection provision where it is the norm in the library for classification to be ignored or amended. We have already considered biography. Fiction is such a case in point. It is almost unheard of for a library to classify fiction – as opposed to literature as a course of study – especially in the public library. This is largely because most schemes treat fiction as an element within the study of literature and that is simply not the way in which it is regarded by the majority of its users. In the general schemes literature would be classed first by language and then by period. The establishment of period for an author is a process fraught with inherent difficulty. How precisely does one decide upon the period of an author? In DC it is 'based upon the scholarly consensus as to when an author flourished'. The other possibility is to base collocation upon date of birth, which although it may not be reflective of the author's period of greatest endeavour, is at least not open to debate. In practice, if the reader of fiction for pleasure had to know the date of birth of an author before finding something to read, then there would be a riot. Indeed, author birthdate is frequently not reflective of our perception of an author's period. Writers can embody an age in a way quite unrelated to their own chronological age. Catherine Cookson, born in 1904, for example, whose output continues to this day with a new work published in 1993, might, if such were the chosen arrangement, stand alongside her contemporary George Orwell (1903). In fact she narrowly escapes the Victorian period. A writer continuing to attract a readership in her nineties is uncommon, and has to be considered alongside an author such as Leslie Mitchell (Lewis Grassic Gibbon), who achieved his total output by the age of thirty.

There can be anomalies in application of the principle of classification according to period. Barbara Cartland, whom many of us would see as a similar figure to Cookson in terms of period and of age, is classified as of an earlier era by BNB. Equally, we tend to think of Christopher Marlowe as older than Shakespeare, although they were in fact contemporaries; this is because Marlowe had lived, written his greatest works and died before Shakespeare achieved stature. Nationality or language is another significant facet in the classification of authors in most general schemes and yet language and nationality can often be confusing, even in debate on occasion. There is likely to be some variation and misattribution – even in the British Library's classification of authors – for we have Vladimir Nabokov being classified in English fiction at one point and in American at another, and in both instances for the same work – if in different editions. Would a reader know where to place Solzhenitsyn or Samuel Beckett? DC's manual has the intriguing instruction, 'Class an author who writes in more than one language with the language which he last used' – surely inappropriate unless the author is dead. There are many problems for the classifier here: for the general reader of fiction the approach is likely to be completely unhelpful.

This emphasis upon language and period, determined in relation to the author, pays no attention to the content of the works in bibliographic classification. We are classifying language and period, treating the author as the subject. John Dixon[1] argues that if fiction is to be classified as to its subject content, then it should be according to a scheme 'especially conceived for fiction', preferring a non-subject arrangement on the shelves supported by an index to enhance access.

Ironically however, despite the fact that more browsing goes on in the fiction section of a public library than in any other class of literature, it is precisely in the fiction section that least has been done to aid and support that browsing activity. Although there has been much debate as to the value of fiction classification, or more commonly fiction categorization into broad groups, very little in practice has found its way onto our shelves. In the vast majority of cases, what we find in practice is a broad general sequence, consisting of hundreds of shelves of books, arranged alphabetically by author, perhaps supported by a small number of special genres, such as science fiction, thrillers, romance and westerns. Such categorization is the limit of what has been attempted by most public libraries. It is found in a variety of guises and to various extents. Some categories may not relate to subject content but be form-based, such as the graphic novel. Some developmental work has been carried out on special classification schemes for individual fiction genres, such as Croghan's *Classification for Science Fiction* (CSF).[2] Croghan presents his scheme with the rationale that science fiction is 'about ideas rather than emotions' – evidently feeling that to have developed a system for a type of popular fiction requires a defence. This is, without any justification, a useful and creditable experiment and may hopefully generate other fruitful attempts to analyse and organize the remaining genres, although there may be debate as to the extent to which *ideas* may be found in much romantic fiction, for example. Science fiction, in which other attempts have been made to develop schemes, really stands alone at present; one suspects because it tends to have an intellectual credibility not accorded to many of the popular genres.

What has foiled most would-be classificationists of the general fiction collection is the unpredictability of selection method on the part of readers. Research conducted by Jennings and Sear[3] investigated fiction selection and, beyond indicating that most of us find it difficult to formulate in words the method used, they revealed that browsing in search of something interesting was the most popular at 34% amongst users, while 20% looked for a particular genre and 27% browsed and recognized an author's name, but had not set out specifically searching for works by that author. The author approach continues to be significant for many readers but when it comes to the traditional desire 'for something good', then we are in deeper waters. We may want books belonging to a certain genre – again this is fairly simple to accommodate – or works on a particular theme. Often it is something more evanescent we seek: a particular style, an ethos with which we are in harmony or a view of the world which reinforces our own attitudes and self-image. The fiction publishing industry finds it difficult to classify fiction in any meaningful way and book shops have little helpful to offer. Jennings' and Sear's research showed that readers were more satisfied with the books located when they had been sought by a particular author: the difficulty in selection comes when authors are not available, are not known to the user or have simply been exhausted by the voracious reader.

Some systems have tried to surmount this problem by the development of schemes specifically for general fiction. The first, in 1933, was an adaptation of the third edition of DC by F. Haigh, wherein the subject classmarks of DC were used to provide a subject arrangement for fiction. A novel based on the life of Christ would thus be classified at 232. A more original general classification for fiction, R. S. Walker's *'Problem Child' System*, was developed in 1958 as a faceted scheme, using a second round of CC's PMEST facets to represent the subject matter of a work and also providing facets for 'author', 'language and literary tradition' and 'narrative style'. Through the use of the facets various elements of the subject content could be shown:

Example

The men's room[4]

P	Author		Ann Oakley
M	Subject		
	P	Characters	Male, female, educated, middle class
	M	Type of life	Academic life, professional and family life
	E	Themes	Marital, sexual relations, romance, feminism, fidelity, adultery, professional conduct
	S	Place/setting of the novel	London
	T	Time period in which it is set	1970–2000
E	Narrative type, form and style		Novel, realistic
S	Language of author		English
T	Time period of author		1980s

As can be seen from this example, the authors of fiction very rarely limit themselves to a single, simple subject in the way that writers of non-fiction do. Finally, in the late 1970s, Annelise Mark Pejtersen developed an indexing method *Analysis and Mediation of Publications* (AMP) which goes a stage further than Walker. AMP created headings allowing access to records in four facets:

subject matter – indicating events, characterization, action;
frame – the time period, geographic location and social environment;
author's intention – the author's aim and view of life;
accessibility – the readability, style, form and physical layout of the book.

This takes us a little further than the conventional genre categorization at a very simple level or than Walker's method as it seeks to provide not just objective descriptive information on the subject matter of the book but also to convey something of the manner of treatment. Some of the information is evaluative, such as *readability* which will require the exercise of the classifier's subjective literary judgement and will relate to the ease with which the work can be understood. The author's aim and view of life may be very explicitly stated or may be subtly conveyed: again to determine and create a precise statement is likely to test the skills of the indexer. In our example, *The men's room*, we may choose to take the obvious and simplistic approach that the author's view is a feminist one, but that would be a superficial response and may well alienate readers who would otherwise enjoy the book. This is, however, potentially a very valuable tool in readers advisory work. Would we all had access to it to guide our bedtime reading! Anara Guard[5] has suggested that analogy software, which links authors who are similar in subject matter and style, should be developed and this too would be a very useful resource which would address the problem of the significance of authorship in reader satisfaction; a problem which cannot be solved by means of a classified arrangement.

Such schemes help us to analyse the ways in which fiction is approached and the criteria the reader often unconsciously applies in selection. Necessarily they imply a good deal of effort at the stage of indexing fiction, an effort which libraries may be unwilling to commit themselves to, with such a traditionally easy route to follow in present practice. It is very encouraging to observe the continuing interest in the classification of fiction indicated by the continuing development of such systems, although they have not been much adopted in practice to date. The 1990 *Guidelines on subject access to individual works of fiction, drama etc.* support this endeavour, setting out the kinds of access points which should be catered for. OCLC and LC are also collaborating on a fiction headings project for use in OPACs and this may provide a practical, working – and tested – model, which would be adopted by libraries. However, an element of complacency might be observed in operation here amongst librarians. People cope with the fiction collection as it is arranged at present. Issues are excellent. More complicated shelf arrangement might cause more problems than it solved. If we are to have only one place, which of course is inevitable for any shelf arrangement, then there are arguments in favour of keeping it at the broadest A–Z level. One of the criticisms of categorization of material into genres is that this will preclude the devotee of romances from encountering more worthy yet attractive titles, as they would were they searching the general fiction sequence.

Libraries have traditionally relied on means other than classification to assist the fiction reader such as: book displays; lists linking one author to others – 'if you liked P. D. James then you will enjoy Ruth Rendell, Ngaio Marsh, etc.'; bibliographic guides, such as the *Fiction Index*, which identifies works on particular themes, such as novels whose central characters are civil servants or which are set in pre-revolutionary Russia; or guides to particular genres, such as those produced by Julian Symons for detective fiction.

2. Non-book material

The problems faced by the classifiers of NBM are further exacerbated by the significance of the physical form to the user. In bibliographic classification the form is usually subsidiary to the subject, but in a collection which consists of a large percentage of non-book media, the form may assume a greater priority in the typical approach. The user is quite likely to want a video to help them stop smoking or slides illustrating the architecture of Devon. In a collection which is totally devoted to a special media, such as the Visnews Film Archive, special systems may be developed: in this particular example physical subject arrangement is eschewed and access is via an alphabetico classified index. Here items are indexed in four facets: country and date of origination of the film; location, as specifically as possible to the level of the individual building; personality; and subject.

A variety of special solutions have been arrived at for such special media. The chief problems arise in a mixed collection, with small but significant proportions of NBM in a variety of forms. The sheer number of forms and their proliferation should not be ignored. The following identifies some of the most common:

filmstrips
slides
microforms
sound tape – reel and cassette
videotape
discs – magnetic
discs – vinyl
transparencies
CD – audio
   – ROM
   – video
   – interactive
Multimedia – kits or composites comprising more than one of the above

The subject content of NBM is not likely to differ fundamentally in its nature for the majority of media. Practically, however, it may be more difficult for the classifier to determine that subject content from, for example, a video than from a book which can easily be skimmed visually. What must be avoided is the classifier taking the easy way out and classifying merely from the title and the promotional material, rather than from the actual content. There may also be a greater need for subject analytics with NBM, where the user may be perhaps looking for a slide of a specific individual subject and in a medium the user cannot readily browse, then greater subject analysis may be deemed paramount by the classifier. Certain media do differ in their subject nature and offer special challenges, as we have already seen with visual images.

Traditionally non-book material (NBM), as we have seen, is held physically in several sequences separate from the normal classified one. These separate sequences may or may not be classified. We may find several schemes in operation, or a mixture of classified sequences with some form of non-subject arrangement, such as by accession number. To cater for the subject approach some other means of access must be provided, either via subject indexes or by including NBM items in the classified catalogue, supported by a subject index and with clear guidance as to their physical location and format. The advantage of their inclusion in a single, classified catalogue is clearly one of collocation with all other materials on a specific subject. It is there that the user will find the comprehensive subject view. It is equally true that in such an integrated catalogue the media must be clearly indicated. Experiments have been made with coloured cards and with codes. Colour coding is impractical in any but the card catalogue and even there problems abound. Any other form of coding of media, by assigning numbers or letters to signify form, is of course easily managed but adds another level of complication for the user who must become familiar with these additional codes. Representational graphical images are simple and helpful, but may be expensive to incorporate in a catalogue. There are now such a variety of media commonly available in library collections that the issue is a serious one and standardized descriptors for form are identified in the second edition of the *Anglo American Cataloguing Rules* (AACR2). If used as instructed, these tend to become lost in the text of the bibliographic descriptions and many libraries choose to highlight the media description more obviously.

NBM and fiction are two obvious examples of adaptations which are commonly made in libraries. In these particular instances adaptation is less dangerous because we can be fairly sure that the general schemes are not about to alter radically their present approach and where that present approach is evidently unhelpful. It is therefore safe to assume that whatever modifications we put in place will not be overtaken by a better option – or at least not in the foreseeable future.

NEW EDITIONS AND REVISIONS

Given that the scheme in use is continually being updated and amended, the library must establish a policy in relation to the implementation of these changes. This may seem a very obvious point, but it is nevertheless one worth making. There are libraries which have failed to keep up with this gradual change for a variety of reasons: the cost of purchase of the new editions might have been too great; the staff commitment involved in the process might have been impossible to achieve; or new editions may have appeared at an inopportune moment, when other demands took precedence. However, ignoring current changes generate potential future headaches. What does the library do when subsequent editions appear? Do they sit back and allow future changes to pass them by unnoticed while their arrangement and provision of detail become ever more dated? As with unauthorized adaptations, when the library does decide to catch up with the rest of the world they will find that effort much complicated by their having missed several stages in the process.

RECLASSIFICATION

Keeping up with new editions of the scheme will involve a certain amount of ongoing reclassification. It is wise to plan ahead for this. New editions do not appear unheralded. There will be plenty of advance warning of the changes which will be made and the library can then plan to carry out the necessary process of reclassification at the most appropriate time and in the most convenient manner. Academic libraries often, for example, take advantage of the summer recess to carry out such work. With each new edition will come assistance in the execution of these changes, with the provision of tables listing changed numbers and linking old numbers to new. The project will need to be carried out with care and with some form of centralized control over its execution, but it is unlikely in this form to cause major upheaval. There will be minor changes, extensions of the scheme in the form of the addition of new numbers in order to provide for subjects where literature has only recently appeared and, possibly, the full revision of one – or if more certainly a limited number – of the disciplines. The whole process, with adequate staff input, can usually be accomplished quickly and is probably best carried out in one short burst of intense activity. When complete, extra short-term guidance may have to be provided for users until the new arrangement becomes familiar.

Much more problematic is the full reclassification of a collection according to a new scheme, particularly in an established library service which may contain many thousands of items. It is an option which would only be considered if the present arrangement was thought to display serious shortcomings or if the alternative scheme was seen to offer major advantages. The effort involved must be weighed very carefully against the benefits likely to accrue. The library service must consider the resources which would be committed to the project and the disruption of service which would ensue in the short term, against the long-term benefits for the service. A costing and feasibility exercise in advance of commitment is to be recommended. Despite these caveats, the process of wholesale reclassification of a collection is one that takes place with greater frequency than one might imagine; there are fairly recent examples of large academic libraries choosing to adopt a new classification.

Such a project is a major one and involves an extended disruption to the classified arrangement. The manner in which it is conducted is significant. It is very difficult, but not impossible, while the library is operating normally. Given the enormity of the operation and its likely time-scale – even devoting all staff resources to the project – it may not, however, be feasible to close the library while reclassifying all stock. A programme of rolling reclassification may therefore be adopted, where separate classes are dealt with consecutively and where upheaval and disruption of normal service can be limited. An alternative suggested by Ranganathan, the *osmosis method*, recommends that all new accessions should be classified according to the new system while old stock remains as it has always been. This ensures that the most current and active works are arranged according to the best possible arrangement. Gradually as the stock turns around and older material is weeded from the collection and replaced by new editions, the new scheme will come to occupy the largest proportion of the collection and eventually the time will come when only a very small body of material is arranged by the old system, which can then be reclassified fairly easily. Major upheaval is avoided but the collection will be arranged according to two radically different systems for a number of years – scarcely an ideal situation for staff and users.

Whenever reclassification, on whatever scale, is carried out there are three elements involved in the process: the linking from the old classmark or subject to the new; the amendment of the catalogue record; and the physical relabelling and arrangement of the new sequence. The first requires professional input and will be affected by the extent to which the new system differs from the old. It is unlikely that a simple *old for new* approach can be adopted, for the chosen system may analyse subject content in a very different manner from the present scheme. If the chosen scheme is one which is available on centrally created catalogue records, then the decision to use these may reduce the level of staff input at this stage very considerably. A library with an automated system may also find the process much alleviated by the ability to identify works on a subject and link to a new classmark for that subject automatically. Changes to the catalogue must be processed as the reclassification proceeds. As an incidental benefit, the project will allow for a stock check to be carried out simultaneously, for clearly items missing from stock will be identified as part of the process. The third stage is a largely manual and clerical procedure, although careful checks will have to be made to ensure accuracy and consistency. Much movement of stock will take place as space is made for the new sequence to begin, as it continues to grow and as the old sequence contracts. When material on loan is returned to the library this too must be reclassified before being returned to stock. It is vitally important that staff and users are apprised of the status of the project at all times, so that their time is not wasted in fruitless searching. Reclassification offers the opportunity to overhaul completely the arrangement of the collection; and to review and amend earlier subject analysis decisions.

THE PROCESS OF CLASSIFICATION AND THE CLASSIFIER

We have so far considered the major issues and the general policy decisions impacting upon the library's use and implementation of classification. Let us now look at the way in which the process of classifying is carried out within a service, for there are a number of aspects of the organization of the classificatory function which affect the effectiveness of the final classified arrangement.

BROAD OR CLOSE CLASSIFICATION

A major consideration for any library will be the manner in which the chosen scheme is to be applied: whether or not it is to be applied rigorously and to the fullest possible extent. We have already examined some of the problems relating to deviation from a scheme in unauthorized adaptation; the library must also decide if all of the detail the scheme provides is needed in order to create an effective and meaningful shelf arrangement for users.

The size of the collection is the influential factor here: not just the present size but the likely eventual size, if we are dealing with a new and potentially rapidly growing collection. Given that collections may grow at an inordinate rate, one should seek to predict the size of the collection in ten or even 20 years. It is often argued that to classify broadly is less time consuming for the classifier than to classify fully. The difference is one of a very few minutes in the first instance: a major reclassification of a whole collection from broad to full specification will be a major undertaking in ten years' time. In a small general collection, full specification of detail may be inappropriate and ultimately unhelpful for users. However, small and completely independent collections of general material are fairly uncommon. Such subject coverage is likely to be found in the public library branch perhaps, but in the era of online catalogues such a branch will not be truly independent; it is likely to share in a union catalogue, covering all of the branches of the service as well as the central service point. It would, therefore, be inconsistent for the small branch to have a different form of classification from the central library, to say nothing of the ensuing problems for the circulation of stock around the various service points, a factor which renders conformity essential.

The same is often true of the small special library: it may be part of a larger organizational structure and standardization may have very practical benefits. In any case, in the special library, as we have seen, the need for full specification of detail is often paramount. It is unlikely that a special library of any size would require less detail than is available in the published schedules of a scheme, certainly than that which is available in the general classification schemes. In the academic library, particuarly in the large university collections, subject coverage may be uneven across the universe of knowledge, but when a subject is represented full detail will be invaluable. The subject approach and the value of browsing is far less in debate in this setting than in any other, although there are those who argue that the author approach is the most common in the academic library. This is less the case today than it may have been in the past. Much emphasis in further education is placed upon student-centred learning and on the encouragement of the student's ability to research and locate materials in the conducting of independent investigation. Students today place less emphasis upon the recommended author, as do their teachers. For the researcher the subject approach to the academic collection is essential.

It is really in the public and school library that the debate still continues. The arguments for a broader approach relate to an extent to the broad subject coverage of such a collection, and also to the needs of the users for an arrangement which clearly identifies the subject areas of potential interest but does not confuse in the length of the numbers and the complexity of the subject specification. This is a somewhat condescending argument and may exaggerate the difficulties of a long and complex notation, which can be overcome by excellent guiding. The broad shape of the scheme and of its classes can be conveyed by signs and shelf guides. These may be all that the user needs to consult: the fact that the books on the shelf have longer and more complex call marks will be of little significance to the browser.

When the library is small, the subjects held in the collection are not very detailed and the needs of the users are for a simply followed grouping of materials, it may be felt that a broad implementation of the scheme is more fitted to the library's requirements. In such a case schemes may be applied to less than their full extent. Some schemes specifically cater for this approach. DC, for example, allows for the application of the classmarks at different levels. Until 1990 DC classmarks appeared on MARC records divided into meaningful segments, indicating the points at which they could be truncated if a broader approach were employed.

The wine and food of Europe   641.2'1'094

However, this feature has now been dropped and numbers are supplied in full with no indication of segmentation. DC is of course also available in an abridged edition; the 13th abridged edition will be published in 1997. The Abridged Bibliographic Classification (ABC) provides another example of an authorized form of broadening a scheme. In all of the other general schemes, if a library wishes to abridge, it must develop its own method of approach – in itself a daunting task and one that should not be taken lightly if it is to be accomplished effectively.

Whatever the approach, what one is left with is the skeleton of the scheme. The major problem with the broad application of a scheme is that the end result is likely to be a number of categories of material on the shelves within which no meaningful subject relationship is displayed. Let us take an example. In a smallish public library branch in which we have a broad application of DC, we may have a section on dogs. Dogs may be as far as our subject specification has gone for pets. Even in a very small branch we are likely to find some 20 to 30 items on the shelves on the subject: are these to be subdivided and if so how? There are three possibilities: we may observe no order whatsoever, which is the simplest method for staff and saves time in shelf tidying and the replacement of works in the correct shelf order; we may subarrange by author surname, an approach which is very common and is used with all classification schemes even when applied in their fullest detail simply to establish a predictable shelf order, but an arrangement which will have no significance for the user who is unlikely to know the name of an appropriate author; finally we may employ alphabetical order by topic. In the first instance we have made no attempt to assist the user beyond pointing to the works on dogs: they will have to scan the 30 titles to find their book. In the second we have a rigidly maintained order but one which does not help the user to find their subject. In the third we have helped the user to find the work on, let us say, poodles, but we have done so by replacing one form of classification with another – if one which we may feel is easier for users to cope with. It is a system which is employed at many points in LC, but it is also one which can be employed in the support of broad classification. The approach is superficially simple, but has hidden problems which confuse the issue. The user approaching the section on dogs must be informed that these are alphabetically arranged by breed: he or she then knows that 'Afghan hounds' will file before 'boxers', which will again file before 'cavalier King Charles spaniels'. We have, however, seen in operation some of the difficulties of the alphabetical subject approach – can one cross-reference a shelf arrangement? – although these may be deemed insignificant with a small category of material. An insidious problem is that often no single stage of division is possible within such a set of works. Within dogs as a category we will therefore find works not only on individual breeds but also works on the care of dogs as pets. Do we add grooming and breeding to our alphabetical list? Alphabetical order has a place within classification and if based upon the principles of true subject division it may operate more effectively than some purely arbitrary order of foci within a facet. It should not, however, be applied randomly and simply to save time and effort, but should only be employed where no other useful means of establishing order is deemed necessary, whether because of the size of the collection or the nature of the subject.

Broad classification and the use of alphabetical subject arrangement are to be regarded with caution. The savings in time are likely to be very small and the saving in effort for the user may be a chimera, one which is more believed in by librarians than based upon empirical evidence. In a sense broad classification and alphabetical subject arrangement of topics challenge the very principles of subject classification and the merit of relating materials by subject. It is to say as librarians, 'we have gone so far along the road, but to go any further would be time consuming and confusing'. In the final analysis it is a contradiction in terms to say that subject arrangement is useful but only to a certain extent. The argument is possibly most tenable in the children's or school library, where the classification provides a broad framework, allowing an introduction to the basic form of a classified arrangement.

Reader interest arrangement systems, originating in the United States, are a form of broad classification, but one which is not linked to a specific classification scheme. The method is really one of categorization, where the categories are identified to accord with the interests and needs of the users in a particular library. The book's placing in the system is linked to its likely maximum use and it is assumed that if the work is not receiving sufficient attention in one category and if it might do better in another section, it will simply be moved. If a work on 'staff training in the health service' is not being used in the section on 'public sector management', then it may be borrowed more if it is placed in the category on 'personnel management and training'. This might be termed the supermarket approach to classification: what is important is where the item will achieve maximum sales. It is not the intrinsic subject matter which determines placing but the likely appeal of the work. To an extent, with such a system, we are classifying the author's intention and the work's potential audience. Such schemes work best in a small collection and in a library service in which the users' needs are very clearly observed and unlikely to be contradictory. It is only in a fairly small organization that needs will be predictable. The development of the system would have to be linked to an intensive and ongoing programme of investigation of user needs and of their methods of accessing information. The scheme would ultimately require of the library or its creators as much effort and input as do conventional systems. This is not an easy option. Rather than objectively structuring knowledge according to the consensus of expert opinion, we are looking at the possibly biased and ever changing attitudes of a group of users. User studies programmes show that the determination of need is a difficult process and one in which, at the end of the day, the best we can hope for is some form of democratic meeting of the needs of the majority. How do we cater for the minorities and their special needs? What do we do about those who don't use the library or are simply less vocal in expressing their needs? As cataloguers and classifiers, many of us will have experience of the vocal critic who wants everything they are interested in collected at one point on the shelves, regardless of the wishes of others. A client-centred approach is ideologically sound but must not be dictated by the desires of a few.

THE ROLE OF THE CLASSIFIER

There are those of us who still retain an image of the dedicated classifier as an isolated – probably by choice – and obsessive individual who sits surrounded by tomes in some dusty and inaccessible region of the library underworld tirelessly and pedantically analysing the works which come to his or her attention. In reality one suspects that there are very few such left. There are still library services in which we may find a single and single-minded individual carrying out all of the classification for the collection but these are in the minority today. In its favour it should be acknowledged that the expertise, knowledge of the scheme and commitment of such a classifier are likely to be very great. There will be other advantages such as consistency, speed and accuracy in the work carried out. Another option is for the twin operations of cataloguing and classification to be associated and centralized departments for the provision of bibliographic services are common in libraries. Increasingly, in recent years such departments have assumed responsibility for the automated elements of the library service, largely because the catalogue was often the first part of the service to be automated and it was then inextricably linked to other operations such as circulation control, book ordering and accessions. The bibliographic link runs through all of these and that process is likely to consist of a number of operational stages:

- The book is ordered and precise details of authorship, title and of devices such as ISBN (International Standard Book Number) are sought in order to identify an item uniquely.
- At the same time a bibliographic record is sought – if centralized services are subscribed to – from the British Library or the Library of Congress.
- The record which has been created for the purpose of ordering the item can provide a base upon which the catalogue record will be built.
- If a MARC record exists – from the Library of Congress or the British Library – then that record will be purchased and will overwrite the ordering information. This record will include DC and LC classmarks.
- The item arrives in the library and the MARC record is checked to ensure that it matches the work in hand (errors do occur) and the catalogue record is amended. If no MARC record exists then the item will be catalogued.
- *The work is classified:* the classmark and details of location and numbers of copies are added to the catalogue record.
- The subject index is checked to ensure that an entry for the subject is included, if not a new entry is created.
- The record becomes part of the catalogue and is linked to the circulation system employed in the library.

The classification of the work may seem like one small stage in this process, but it is arguably the one which will have most impact upon rendering the work accessible to the user. The process of classifying may similarly be broken into stages:

- The work arrives for classification.
- Is there a MARC record? If so then a LC or DC classmark will have been assigned. If the library service employs either of these schemes, this classmark may be accepted. Should it be accepted uncritically? Most classifiers would choose not to. Interestingly the MARC User Group survey of 1986[6] showed that 62% of those libraries which purchased MARC records and whose libraries were classified by DC only used the classmark assigned by the British Library as a guide. Mistakes creep in and there are often

variations of interpretation and of user need affecting a work's classification. The classmark should be considered critically. Even if the library does not use either of the schemes contained in the MARC record, their placing may be an invaluable guide.

- *Subject analysis of the work* via examination of the work itself. This should always be carried out with the work at hand so that it can be physically examined and its contents accurately ascertained, not with a bibliographic substitute.
- *Detailed subject specification of the work's content.*
- Are there other copies of the work in the collection? There may well be earlier editions of a work or even other copies in a multi-site library or of a popular work. Clearly all editions and copies of a work should be classified consistently. This may seem like very obvious advice, but it is amazing how often inconsistencies appear.
- Are there other works in the collection on the same subject? If so, clearly this new addition should be collocated accordingly. Often a trip to the shelves is essential in determining the similarity or dissimilarity of the present work.
- Is there more than one point at which the work might be shelved? If the work is multidisciplinary or its subject is compound then the weight of treatment and its potential use must be considered. At what point in the arrangement would its use be maximized?
- *Analysis of the subject according to the scheme's schedules.* This stage should be carried out whether or not there are other works on the subject in the collection. It is thus that anomalies and errors in earlier classification are revealed.
- Establishment and recording – on the work and for the catalogue record – of the precise classmark together with any other identifying elements, such as author surname or Cutter Number, to provide a unique shelfmark. The necessity of added classmark entries in the classified catalogue should also be considered at this point.
- The work must be processed, that is, labelled for shelving, and should thereafter be checked by the classifier before it reaches its correct place on the shelf. It will subsequently be rechecked many times, as the shelf order of any collection must be checked and tidied in order to maintain the correct arrangement.

As we have seen, there are a variety of possibilities as to who carries out the role of classification. It may be a single individual. It may be the staff of the centralized cataloguing or bibliographic services department. This has for many years been a popular option and has the advantage of a dedicated, knowledgeable and expert group of classifiers who have a broad picture of the classification in operation throughout a library service. Increasingly though the classifying function has been decentralized and is carried out by librarians responsible for individual departments and subject areas. In this scenario, the children's librarian would classify the children's books, the business and technical librarian the business and technical books, and the local studies librarian the material which will form part of that local collection. In the academic library duties are likely to devolve upon subject specialists and so one might find individuals responsible for Arts, Social Sciences, Medicine, Law and so on. The advantages of this approach are that such individuals will have much greater subject understanding, a greater awareness of the needs of their users and greater familiarity with the existing collection. The debate is between the expertise of the expert classifier versus that of the subject specialist. If we accept that the needs of users are paramount, then the second option will win the day. However, there remains a need for some form of centralized checking procedure, which will ensure that the classification scheme is being correctly and consistently applied over the broader picture and that is where the role of centralized bibliographic services will continue to be necessary. Such checks will be for obvious errors in most instances, but where a novice classifier is involved then more careful scrutiny may be necessary for some time.

The bibliographic services department would also have a role to play in disseminating information about the classification scheme in use and how it is to be applied. The creation of an in-house manual of classification is most useful in a large decentralized service to ensure consistency and accuracy and even in a small library such a manual will be invaluable when, inevitably, staff changes occur. The bibliographic services department may also assume responsibility for staff training, the induction of new staff and for ensuring that all library staff are familiar with the scheme and capable of exploiting it to the full. Their role may be one of supervision and of coordination, ensuring that the collection does not suffer fragmentation and that the subject arrangement has a coherence beyond the dispersed and possibly isolated units of special departments.

THE COSTS OF CLASSIFICATION

The costs of classification have still to be fully researched. However, there are a number of factors which affect the costs of classification, some of which have already been touched upon with a different emphasis in mind. It is important that we should be aware of these costs as classifiers in order that we can represent the process effectively in discussion with management, for an imperfect understanding of their significance will lead to the classifying function in a library service being regarded as removed from the practical realities of existence. Such costs include:

- *Staffing* A consideration of the staffing involved in classification must include all of the various elements in the process from the original classification of a work, to the labelling and checking of information thereon. We must also examine the level of staff involved at each stage, for the time of professional staff will cost proportionally more than that of clerical or non-professional. There are also staff costs involved in user education, the provision and maintenance of guiding and in shelf tidying. Manpower is perhaps the most significant single element in such a cost analysis. One major difficulty in breaking down the staff costs arises from the fact that it is impossible to predict the time that will be taken in classifying works; there is no way in which we can predetermine the proportion of works which will cause mental anguish to the classifier, although one can come to an average estimate for the process as a whole. The equation is also complicated by the fact that speed is affected both by experience in the practice of classification and also by familiarity with the nature of the collection and its literature.

- *Purchase of the published schedules of the classification scheme* This is a not insignificant cost. Depending upon the nature of revision of the particular scheme in use, new editions will appear with varying frequency. It is not unreasonable to assume that a new edition will appear every six to ten years. As we saw with DC, the cost of a full set of schedules may be quite high and if we assume that in an average library service containing a number of departments each will require a copy of the schedules, then we are dealing with a figure well in excess of a thousand pounds. In a multi-site library the cost will multiply. Some libraries purchase a limited number of such new editions in a single financial year, although such a policy will mean that different standards are being applied in different parts of the service, scarcely a desirable situation and one which the classified catalogue will reveal to the user. The appearance of electronic schedules will have an impact on costs. At present the CD ROM version of DC, the *Electronic Dewey*, costs over twice as much as the print. Multiple copies or the right to multiple access via a networked system will have to be negotiated with the publishers. Costing policy, involving licence agreements and the charges which will be put in place for the provision of active links to the catalogue itself, has not yet been resolved by the publishers of schemes; nor, at present, have the issues been fully considered by libraries, for we have yet to have a simultaneous publication of a new edition of a scheme in both hard copy and electronic form. The pricing mechanisms will, at that point, have to be compared by libraries to determine the most cost effective and efficient form of purchase.
- *Printed guides and labelling* Again an ongoing cost will be that of updating and maintaining the system of shelf guidance in the library. A shabby and aged system of signs will scarcely convince the users that they are dealing with a well organized arrangement.
- *Purchase of classmarks* This will not be a stand-alone cost, for one can only purchase classmarks with the accompanying catalogue record. It should therefore be considered as part of the overall cataloguing budget. Economies

of effort are also complicated by the fact that few libraries adopt these without critical consideration.

It has been suggested, but not substantiated in fact, that broad classification is less costly than close classification. However, the process remains the same whichever method is chosen and in most instances the problematic complex treatment of subject creates the greatest problem for the classifier and hence the most significant delay in that process. Since the last edition of this *Manual*, 14 years ago, no authoritative research has provided the answer to this question despite the fact that Arthur Maltby suggested then that it was the problem most urgently requiring examination. Indeed the fullest examinations of the issue have been the report of the British Library Working Party on Classification and Indexing[7] in 1975 and Maurice Line's[8] work in 1969. The interesting result of the latter's findings was that the classification of an item was significantly more time consuming than its cataloguing, taking two and a half times as long to accomplish. In 1992, Vesa Kautto[9] conducted a comparative time study of classification and indexing and found less differentiation between the two activities. The three processes of subject analysis, classification and assignation of subject headings each took a roughly equal time. As staff time is such a significant factor in the costs of classification and with the economic cutbacks and tightening of resources which remain a feature of many services, whether in the public, academic or commercial sectors, it is perhaps an issue which is overdue for investigation. In particular – as Line suggested in 1969 – 'some work on the relative times taken for different schemes is surely long overdue'. There remain other points which need to be clarified: the relative speeds of expert classifiers versus subject specialists; the variation in findings which may result dependent upon an analysis of the type of library involved; the nature of the literature and its demands in certain subject areas; the proportion of material which may be deemed difficult and the factors impinging upon this; and the reliability of centrally produced records. We also need to investigate the impact of poor subject arrangement upon the demand for reader's advisory service – a form of service which is very costly in terms of staff time and effort.

THE PHYSICAL LAYOUT OF THE LIBRARY AND GUIDING

As we had occasion to observe in the previous chapter, classification in practice is affected by the design and layout of the library building or buildings. In designing new library buildings attention will have been given to behavioural, ergonomic and aesthetic considerations. The classification employed and the needs of the collection itself should have been analysed, although there is little in the literature of library design specifically on the subject. In this context, classification is likely to be seen as secondary and flexible within the design process. In practice, in most libraries we are not so fortunate as to have specially designed accommodation for our collection: we will find ourself utilizing buildings which may never have been intended as libraries and, in such circumstances, the potential problems multiply. It is not uncommon to find libraries occupying a number of rooms which have been knocked together and where no logical order of shelving is possible. We may find, therefore, a classified sequence meandering around an often attractive but tortuous, even labyrinthian, series of rooms – *upstairs and downstairs and . . .*

The height of shelving is another apparently minor but in practice significant feature. Where shelves are above or below easy reach – where, for example, a user has to use a ladder to reach French poetry – then there are often proportionate drops in the level of usage of stock. If a sequence loses its way, if, for example, a user cannot find his way from the European history section to the French material because the sequence suddenly goes upstairs, then the effect will be the same. There are in addition the problems posed by all of the parallel sequences and instances of broken order, discussed in the previous chapter.

The answer to most of these difficulties in the straightforward implementation of the chosen classified order is the provision of an effective and helpful system of *guiding* the collection. Because the classified sequence is likely to be unfamiliar, even incomprehensible to the user, and it may have been subject to all kinds of deviation and complexity, then the user needs clear and simple guidance on how to find their way around the material. It is not necessary that he or she understand the classification scheme, merely that the sequence and its hidden benefits of collocated material may be exploited fully and quickly. Too many systems designed for guidance become embroiled in the intricacies of explaining the theory of classification and the role of the catalogue and fail to instruct the user in a simple fashion upon their use. It is also most ineffective for the librarian to try to predict what the users' problems and needs in using the collection are likely to be. These should be observed and then responded to, for it is only thus that we will provide guidance which truly addresses the difficulties faced by the totally novice user without making assumptions. The problems, and hence the need for guiding, are exacerbated in a large collection, but there are almost no circumstances in which guiding can be completely omitted without seriously affecting the ability to access subjects.

There are a number of elements which may require the provision of guiding:

- the physical sequence or sequences;
- the filing order of the notation within the sequence;
- materials which are not filed on shelves but in some other form of storage;
- materials not on immediate open access.

There are a number of methods of guiding the user around the classified collection. These should not be used in isolation but rather in a complementary fashion, for they each serve different needs.

THE CATALOGUE

Although the catalogue has been dealt with in depth elsewhere, it is worth reiterating that the catalogue should guide users to works by indicating when these are held in parallel sequences or in a special department or where they take a different physical form. The user's attention must be drawn to the fact that an item is a video or that it is held in basement reserve stacks, otherwise the user may expend considerable time and effort – and goodwill – seeking elsewhere in vain. How many times have we as librarians responded to the cry, 'It's not there on the shelves', to find that the oversize sequence immediately reveals the desired item. We should bear in mind as cataloguers that the user's first question upon discovering an item of interest is where they will be able to locate that document. Such information should therefore be highlighted or given prominence in catalogue records.

PLANS OF THE LAYOUT OF THE LIBRARY

Floor plans of the library which indicate the relationship of the classified sequence to the features of the rooms in which the collection is held are very useful. They show the user the big picture: they provide guidance on where to find the main classes or disciplines and also where special collections or media may be found. Such maps can be very basic or fairly detailed. Whichever approach is chosen they should be aimed at the needs of the user. If, for example, a plan were to be devised for a school library using the *Early Stages Classification*, which as we will recall was based upon a system of colour coding, then colour itself is a simple key to the whereabouts of material. Colour can be a useful way of reinforcing subject sequences, however, in any such plan. Maps of libraries for children may use an imaginative approach, replicating for example the effect of a dungeons and dragons game, perhaps, or a treasure map.

Such a map should guide simply at the bookshelf and bay level and it should be duplicated at various points in the library, not just at the entrance or inquiry desk, where it is of course invaluable. Links also need to be made from the catalogue and with an OPAC it is possible to have such a map available online, perhaps even linking to the chosen subject area which would then be highlighted on the map displayed. Some such automated version of the plan is likely to be highly attractive to users and it might be that a dedicated terminal in an automated library should be devoted to this purpose. Classificatory guiding must take its place as part of any scheme of induction or user education employed in a library service and the development of hypertext systems of user instruction, where the switch to graphical display of images is part of the process, are particularly apt in this context. In a large library service complications may arise and it may be necessary to provide maps of various floors or even of several sites showing the relationship between these across a campus. Once such a map or maps has been designed, then it is a simple matter to reproduce it in a variety of forms: on the walls in large scale; on small cards for user retention and consultation; in pamphlets describing the library collection; in induction material for new staff of an organization or pupils and students in an academic environment.

GUIDANCE ON INDIVIDUAL CLASSES

In a large library it might be thought useful to provide more detailed instruction and guidance on the way in which a particular class or discipline is arranged. Maps or plans may provide details of where in a large collection material relating to business management may be found, for example. Pamphlets or cards may indicate the way in which the class is broken down into its main subdivisions and where these may be found. Such a class guide can also figure in the physical sequence, at perhaps the beginning of a main class in the form of a notice indicating which subjects and topics may be found in the class which follows. We are here dealing with the classes in greater detail and at levels which will vary with the extent and specificity of the collection. In a special library of business information large sections will be found of, for example, company information and comparatively greater description of the content of the various sections may need to be provided:

Company Information

KI	General directories	KIML	Industry sectors
KIM	National directories	KIMM	Professional directories
KIMA	Great Britain	KIMN	Annual reports
KIMB	France		(alphabetically)
KIMC	Germany		
	etc.		

See also FAME on CD ROM and Companies House on microfiche

Such guides need to be prominently and attractively displayed. We might also offer for such a subject a plan of the collection.

BAY AND SHELF GUIDES

It is also necessary to indicate the subjects contained on individual bays and shelves. Notices at the end of each bay are most effective and a consistency of approach to the design of these throughout the library service is preferable. The bay guides should take a simple and easily adapted form, for in a growing library, or indeed in any library where new stock is being selected and which hopes to cater for the changing needs of users and developments in the published literature, the content of individual bays may change quite considerably over fairly short periods. Notices may be constructed from interchangeable plastic letters or of typed notices. The notice should indicate precisely the content of the bay – nothing is more infuriating than being guided to the wrong bay – and should also direct users to other collections and related subjects found at other parts of the classified sequence. Shelves should also be marked to show the particular classmarks which can be found at specific points in the sequence, usually to indicate the starting point for a new classmark; again, these have to be capable of easy change and relocation, as the subject content of the shelves shifts.

SPINE LABELLING

At the individual level, each item in the collection must be clearly labelled to show its classmark and hence its position in the classified sequence. This is fairly simple in a uniform collection of volumes of at least half an inch thick. The spine of the book is the point at which the user will easily be able to read the shelfmark. Where precisely on the spine the mark appears is not significant as long as the label is easily decipherable and there is a degree of uniformity of approach, so that the user can readily scan along the line of books. Such a concern may seem trivial indeed beside the great questions of classification, but in reality the classifier is likely to be beset by more complaints about poorly labelled books than about the main class order of the sequence. It is important because the implementation of classification in practice and the realization of its benefits can only be attained, if the process is carried through to its full extent with care. It is at the individual book level that the user will seek a response and they must be guided through the sequence to that level.

Labelling becomes a problem when the collection comprises a significant proportion of very slim documents or other media, such as microfiche, which have no clearly visible surface when conventionally stored. Then other solutions and aids for the user may have to be found. Greater reliance will be placed on shelf guides and on the interpolation of classmark indicators.

STAFF GUIDANCE AND INSTRUCTIONAL PROGRAMMES

If the library's system of guidance has been effectively designed and well implemented it may in many instances preclude the need for staff assistance, or at least reduce the demand on staff. However, there will still remain many occasions on which such assistance is sought. All staff of a library service should themselves fully understand the system of classification in operation and should be able to guide users around the departments and the various sequences that exist. Whether the user actively seeks assistance or simply looks lost and confused, expert explanation should always be available. More effective still are proactive methods which seek to pre-empt such confusion, via the provision of library orientation sessions, induction courses and user education seminars. These are more commonly found in the academic and special library environment, but it is not unreasonable to expect that upon registration a new library member in a public library should be told about the arrangement and various departments of the service and that they should be encouraged to ask for personal assistance from staff in the future. There will always be those readers who, for a variety of reasons, slip the net of the instruction programme or who are reluctant to approach the staff – and we should acknowledge as librarians that we do not always have the best record for approachability – and for these a stand-alone system of guiding should be in operation which is capable of taking the novice user and directing him or her to the materials desired.

A classified sequence also places demands upon the space required to house a collection. If we have an unclassified sequence of reports filed by report number, with each new report simply being added to the end of the sequence, we can pack our shelves very tightly. In a classified arrangement space has to be left at periodic intervals on the shelves, if we are to retain the correct subject sequence. A growing collection puts extra demands upon the shelves. In academic libraries during the long summer vacation one can find the shelves failing to accommodate all of the returned material, and piles of books lying on top of bays.

EDUCATION AND TRAINING FOR CLASSIFICATION

Of great interest to the present authors is the relationship between classification and education. There are two questions to be asked here. What is the place of classification in the curriculum of schools of librarianship and information science and what form should the teaching of classification take? If we have agreed upon the importance and significance of the classified sequence in the overall utility of the library or information service, if we have acknowledged that even in the non-collection based service that classification has a role to play in accessing information in electronic form, then we must equally accept that classification is central to the future professional life of our students when they eventually become professionals and are in the position of maximizing the effectiveness of their own services. Educational practice does vary. In Britain there is variation. More significantly, many American schools of librarianship and information studies take a different view; there, the cataloguing function may predominate as part of the curriculum. There are signs that this may change with the new emphasis upon the accessing of international information, via the Internet. It is our belief, however, that classification should occupy a central or core place in the curriculum. As Michael Gorman[10] argued persuasively in 1992:

> Learning is, in great part, a matter of training the mind to analyse and organise the data, information and knowledge with which it is presented throughout life. The vehicle for that training should be rigorous, intellectually satisfying, coherently structured and of practical usefulness. By that standard, I would submit that cataloging and classification (a.k.a bibliographic control) is the only candidate to be the centre of education for librarianship.

Certainly the teaching of classification will be of practical utility to the majority of young librarians and information professionals. The principles of subject analysis and retrieval are essential to them whether they will be creating and maintaining bibliographic systems of document storage or simply using them. In order to make maximum use of bibliographic sources it is important that the information professional understands not just what these are and what use may be made of them, but also the manner in which they were constructed and the principles upon which they were based. Only then can we expect search strategies to be developed which truly reflect an understanding of the implications of the methods employed, rather than a hazy and haphazard stab at the most likely approach. To an even greater extent this argument can be applied to the superficially invisible arrangement of the electronic database, where prompts and clues may be hidden. As practising librarians we should be aware of the limitations of classification – something which can only be achieved by fully understanding the principles and the operation of classification – in order to circumvent and provide alternative fall back positions to enable full subject recall.

The theory is important but so too is the practice of classification for that will reveal imperfections both in a specific scheme and in applying any scheme. The librarian must understand how classification relates to the library operation and to other functions of the information service. Otherwise, he or she is like a surgeon who missed the module on anaesthesiology; knowing their own job such an individual will be able to evaluate the effectiveness of their own performance but they will be unable to relate it to the essential underpinning which is provided by the anaesthetist and they will not perceive when that process is letting them down or is in danger of doing so. The expert online searcher may know the subject content of the databases available to him or her, may be speedy and expert in manipulation of the command language and the searchable fields, but if he or she does not know the manner in which the records have been indexed or classified and fully appreciate the limitations and possibilities on offer, then the end result can never be a fully effective search. Some have argued the view that classification is a minor technical process in the scheme of things, 'a bibliographic bingo', in Raymond Moss's memorable phrase. On the contrary, it has been the central tenet underlying this manual that however street-wise, pro-active and socially integrated today's librarians and information scientists may be – and we would certainly not underestimate the desirability of such an image – they and the systems which they serve will only be effective if they meet the users' needs. Classification has a significant and enduring role to play in ensuring that these needs are met.

Classificatory education must, then, cover four elements: the principles of subject classification; the systems which exist across a broad range; the manner in which classification is employed in the information service and its role in the production of bibliographic tools; and the process of classifying. This book has considered the first three of these in some detail, as well as the way in which such systems are put into operation. What it has not attempted to do is to provide practice in the operation of classifying. Finally such practice is essential, both in order to hone the very specialized skills of subject analysis and to get to grips with the intricacies and vagaries of the schemes themselves. Schools can offer such supervized practice, although to a lesser extent within the tight limits of post-graduate education. Many librarians will go on to encounter in-service training and the experience of classifying when employed, although such is likely to be limited to the single scheme in use in the service – or at best to a single general and a small number of special schemes. Schools of librarianship and information studies have, therefore, an obligation to ensure that from the start of their professional careers librarians have the broader picture; that they are familiar with the ideals and the variety of present practice in order to evaluate the subject arrangement they are eventually responsible for offering to their users.

THE LIMITS OF CLASSIFICATION

There are limits to the role a classification can play and there are constraints upon the manner in which a classified arrangement is provided in the library setting. Some of the practical limitations have been dealt with in this setting; others have been identified in discussion of the theory of classification. It is useful to rehearse these finally, for, while we believe in the value of the classified sequence, as classifiers we should not be blind to the limits of what can be achieved by it.

The most significant limitation is that any work can only have one place in the classified sequence, despite some experimentation with the purchase of multiple copies of a work and their dispersal to the multi-disciplines with which they deal. Classification insists that we analyse and place a work according to its major discipline. To an extent this problem is catered for by the existence of catalogues and bibliographies and subject indexes, which will allow for other approaches to the work in hand or may provide added entries for a multi-topical book. However, given that many patrons do not use such tools, the problem still remains.

Shelf arrangement is also by definition a linear arrangement. This means that the physical separation of works in a large collection may still be very great. There is also the problem of coordinate subdivisions of a subject: some of these are going to be farther away from their parent than others in a linear setting. The idea of proximity may therefore suffer.

In such a shelf order clearly *special libraries* are farther away from their immediate division in the hierarchy, *library design*, than is the treatment of *national library design*. The order of the coordinate foci of a subject will therefore have a significance in collocation of subject. The user will have to trawl his or her way through all of the other kinds of library design in order to find those documents on the subject they seek. Expressive notation helps the user here; or it may when its significance has been explained adequately to the user. With such

Library design		National libraries
	Public libraries	
Academic libraries		
		School libraries
	Special libraries	

a notation, the user will be alert to the subdivisions of library design and will continue to seek until they find their subject. Physical nearness or separation is a criterion by which the effectiveness of a classification can be measured on the shelves, although proximity is affected by the size of a collection, as we have seen. In a collection where there are a very small number of works on library design in each of the types of library, the user will quickly find his or her material. In one where there are a large number of items, the separation will be much greater. Good, clear guiding in the form of class, shelf and bay guides will do much to overcome this problem.

The complexity of the system of classification in use will also limit its effectiveness for the user. There are two warring impulses here: the desire for minute specification which will reveal subjects as fully as possible for the user; and the knowledge that such minuteness of specification will necessitate the use of lengthy and possibly complex notation and may confuse the user whose interests we seek to safeguard. There may be no solution to this problem. It is one which has exercised the minds of classificationists and librarians since the development of bibliographic classification. Whichever course is chosen – that of a simple scheme which is easy to use or minute specification in a complex arrangement – there are problems. We cannot afford to ignore the capacity of the user to cope with the arrangement provided, neither can we fail to provide as helpful a definition of subject as possible. More research on the user approach would help us to determine how and why the arrangement fails and may suggest strategies to overcome the difficulties experienced.

Many see the classifying role as a solitary and introspective one; the classifier as an isolated and remote figure. While challenging the general validity of this observation, it should be acknowledged that the emphasis within the process of classification should be upon the ultimate aim of classification and of the classifier, that is, it should assist in the retrieval of information, by providing a map of knowledge and by arranging materials in the most helpful manner. Classification ought not to be regarded as an abstract, intellectual pursuit – akin to the solution of acrostics – but should be seen as a stage in the process of obtaining helpful filing order of subjects. The classifier must have an awareness of the literature and of the users of that literature; far from being isolated the act of classifying must be integrated within that wider vision. Classifiers in practice need to be more concerned with the broader picture, with the improvement of subject retrieval overall, and less preoccupied with the accurate placing of minutiae within single schemes. The vision of Ranganathan, the archetypal advocate of change, suffered as a result of such parochial and procrustean unwillingness radically to review and adapt to new environments, on the part of the classifiers.

The nature of the documents with which classifications must cope continues to present problems. The literature changes. There are varieties of approach depending upon the nature of the document. Classification is subject specific and often books are not. Information science still has difficulties in coping with this concept – as do readers. There will always remain a need for reference and readers advisory services to provide a link between the two: the question and the potential source of an answer.

We have seen the various disruptions which occur, in any but the very smallest collection, to the classified sequence. Very few libraries will truly have brought together all of the materials on a subject in one place, and if they do they will have done so at a great deal of cost in terms of space. A classified arrangement is also one which requires to be spread, with room for the subjects to grow.

A classification is, by its nature, a pre-coordinate system. The citation order of the subjects is fixed prior to its placing on the shelves. It therefore needs to be supported by post-coordinate methods if *all* the material on a specific subject is to be recalled in a search. The process of classification and the eventual physical arrangement are only as good as those who are carrying out the actual classification. Systems are complex to use and the nature of the literature presents many problems to the classifier.

In the rapidly changing environment in which we live, the shape of knowledge is constantly changing. New subjects are taught, the significance of subjects changes, subjects which were thought of as subsidiary may suddenly achieve disciplinary status, more interdisciplinary courses are being developed in our universities and there is, in academic course development, a greater emphasis on the practice within identifiable occupational fields rather than the study of the pure arts and sciences. Our structure and perception of knowledge may change radically and in a fairly short time scale. Either schemes have to be prepared to respond quickly to such changes – a move that is likely to be unpopular with library managers – or educators have a greater role to play in treating the relationship between the subject taught and the various disciplines of knowledge. Indeed, the lack of enthusiasm for rapid and radical change, by the libraries served by the various classification schemes which we have examined, is a major limiting factor. It is largely in acknowledgement of this fact that the publishers of the various schemes have responded in such a ponderous fashion when it comes to revision. Some changes in DC have been 25 years in coming to fruition.

Entrenched attitudes on the part of libraries have hindered many potential advances.

Automated catalogues and online electronic access to databases have not removed the need for the classified arrangement of materials on the shelf, despite their greater popularity with users than their manual predecessors. They form a method of approach in which subject access is post-coordinate and where subject searching may take a greater variety of forms than ever before. Limitations are less apparent to the searcher. The combination of free-text retrieval with retrieval from controlled language fields allows for excellent, if not guaranteed perfect, recall: it does not, however, negate the value of the subject arrangement. These should be seen as complementary approaches. There are signs that, far from rendering classification obsolete, electronic systems are reinforcing the need for soundly-based forms of classified subject retrieval. The extension of access to information, which such systems underpin via developments such as the Internet, may mean that one of the limitations of present classifications may be addressed swiftly, that is, their inequitable treatment of subjects, reflecting, as they sometimes do, a national, philosophic, cultural or religious bias.

As classifiers, we must acknowledge the limitations of classification in subject specification and in practical operation. To do otherwise would be to make claims which classification can only imperfectly fulfil and therefore render it open to justifiable attack from a number of quarters. Classification is not a universal anodyne: it is a useful tool in subject retrieval, but one which must be complemented by the support of others. At the end of the day we must ask, 'Can we do without the classified sequence, despite the imperfections of the systems in use?' The answer must still be a resounding 'No'.

ISSUES FOR CONSIDERATION

1.   What we must seek finally is a happy balance in operation between the ideal of the optimum arrangement, bearing in mind the principles of helpful association of related subjects, and the practical feasibility of housing and managing the collection, given the various constraints which will impinge upon the form and manner of physical storage of the collection. Try to identify these constraints and prioritize them in terms of their significance and their impact upon the subject arrangement.

2.   It is interesting to establish relative times for the classification of works according to different schemes. Variants will of course have to be acknowledged, such as the expertise of the classifier and their familiarity with a scheme. How best might such a test be planned and executed? How would you seek to cost the classifying operation within a particular library or information service?

3.   Inevitably, technology and its impact upon classification – whether in

principle or in practice – have been touched upon frequently in the preceding chapters. That impact is so great that in the final section of this book we will turn to a discussion of the ways in which information technology has affected the development of classification, looking both at the situation as we find it today and, insofar as it is possible. at what the future is likely to hold.

NOTES

1. *Fiction in libraries*, edited by John Dixon. London: Library Association, 1986.
2. Croghan, A., *Science fiction and the universe of knowledge: the structure of an aesthetic form*. London: Coburgh, 1981.
3. Jennings, B. and Sear, L., How readers select fiction – a survey in Kent. *Public Library Journal*, 1 (4), 1986, pp. 43–47.
4. Oakley, Ann, *The men's room*. London: Virago, 1988.
5. Guard, A., An antidote for browsing: subject headings for fiction. *Technicalities*, 11 (12), 1991, pp. 10–14.
6. Lovecy, Ian, MUG questionnaire on the use of subject data, 1984. *MARC Users' Group Newsletter*, 85 (1), 1985, pp, 47–50.
7. *British Library Working Party on Classification and Indexing: final report*. Wetherby: British Library, 1975.
8. Line, M. B., The cost of classification. *Catalogue & Index*, 16, October 1969, p. 4.
9. Kautto, Vesa, Classing and indexing: a comparative time study. *International Classification*, 19, 1992, pp. 205–209.
10. Gorman, Michael, How cataloging and classification should be taught. *American Libraries*, 23 (8), 1992, pp. 694, 696–697.

Part Three
Information technology and classification

8 An introduction to classification and the computer

The impact of automation on libraries has been far-reaching and classification has not been immune from change. In this section we would like to consider how computers have affected the theory and practice of bibliographic classification.

The past two decades have seen a pervasive rise in the degree of library automation. The main factors which have influenced technical services departments of libraries have undoubtedly been associated with the introduction of the 'standard' MARC format – an internationally recognized format for communicating the bibliographic record, the development of sophisticated OPACs which facilitate easy access to the library's own catalogue and the tremendous developments in communications hardware and software which now provides the librarian (and in some cases the end user) with almost unlimited access to an enormous international information network.

MARC is a variable field record format and while the bulk of the variable fields are provided for bibliographic description there are those which are reserved for class numbers. In the United States and Great Britain LC and Dewey are provided as standard fields in both US and UK MARC record formats. This is an important factor when considering adopting a new scheme.

In theory a library using either of these schemes and acquiring a MARC record for a work has no need to classify the work. However, the degree to which the classmark can be taken from these fields and used 'unmodified' varies greatly depending on local practices as the MARC user group survey discussed earlier in this work indicates. Research is currently being undertaken at the Robert Gordon University in Aberdeen to provide an up to date picture of how classification is being used in British public and academic libraries and in particular whether economic constraints affecting professional staff time have meant that the classmark provided in the MARC record is being used less critically. Currently we are seeing the development of a standard MARC format for classification, although the way in which this will be integrated into online systems is not yet fully developed (see Chapter 9).

Since the early 1980s many libraries have been providing fully online catalogues (OPACS) and there can be little doubt that this has had a profound effect on library technical services departments. Major changes have been more obvious in the sphere of activity concerned with descriptive cataloguing rather than with classification or subject cataloguing, but the scale of the changes and the very obvious benefits in this area has led to a willingness to question some of the basic assumptions we have hitherto made about the value of classification to the user and the practical methods by which we can make full use of the effort being expended on this task. The proliferation of automation has provided the means as well as the reason for studying the way in which users approach the catalogue to find information. Classification has traditionally been seen to have as its main objective the ordering of material on the shelves to facilitate browsing and giving context to a user's search for information. Increasingly the focus is turning towards an examination of the role of classification as a search tool. In this connection it has been used fairly extensively by librarians, for example, in the production of SDI profiles or for analysis of use of pre-defined subject areas of a library's collection but it has not until recently been considered as a serious tool for end user searching of online files. The availability of major bibliographic classification schedules in machine readable format has been an important factor in prompting more research in this area.

The most obvious example of this is the interest generated by the production of *Electronic Dewey* – a CD-ROM version of the 20th edition of the Dewey Decimal Classification which is annually updated to reflect additions and revisions to the scheme. Such a tool makes classification easier to use and to apply correctly. In addition to supporting searching for the appropriate area of the schedules via the index and schedule terminology itself *Electronic Dewey* also provides up to five Library of Congress Subject Headings, a sample bibliographic record and online help to assist the librarian in selecting the most appropriate classmark. Search methods incorporated include keyword, phrase and number searching, Boolean search options, truncation, the ability to browse through hierarchies and the ability to limit searches to particular major subdivisions of the scheme. It is a DOS based product but has access windows and a notepad which makes number building online easier. More of course can be done – in particular it should be possible using such a system to provide automatic number building by using a suitable expert system shell. A facility for annotation of local schedules could also be incorporated. Such improvements are in fact being actively considered.[1] Also under consideration are mechanisms to use classification to enhance subject retrieval in online catalogues and the use of classification in automatic indexing and thesaurus construction. (This is discussed in detail in the next two chapters.)

As the volume of information increases it becomes harder and harder to provide comprehensive organization of that information. Classification certainly has a major role to play in this area and in fact UDC is currently being used as an information retrieval tool for accessing and controlling the vast amount of information available on the Internet and research is proposed to explore a similar role for DC. The quantum leap in communications technology has made vast networks of information available to many libraries, but if libraries are fully to exploit the potential of such networks they must be actively involved in their organization.

NOTES

1.   Dewey Decimal Classification Research Agenda (Draft). Dublin, OH: OCLC Forest Press, June 1993.

9 Classification and the OPAC

If we assume that the current structure of general classification schemes is not likely to change much then it is important to examine the approaches which can be made to modify the ways in which library users access such systems – or indeed to question whether the systems themselves are of any value in modern information retrieval practice.

INTRODUCTION

There has been considerable research in recent years into the manner in which users approach searching for information using the online public access catalogue (OPAC). Some of the findings of the research should make us question the basic assumptions we have hitherto made about how we should organize information in order to maximize access to it. OPACs became increasingly widespread in the 1980s and were generally seen to offer an enormous potential for improving subject access to library collections. Many writers predicted that there would be an increased trend towards subject searching as opposed to known item searching, the latter being estimated as accounting for anything from 60 to 80 per cent[1] of all catalogue searches in manual catalogues. The change to subject searching would be prompted by the ease with which the user could retrieve and manipulate bibliographic records and the potential for automated systems greatly to increase the number of access points provided.

What Seal referred to as the 'hidden need for subject access which has not been easily met in the card or COM catalogue'[2] could now be delivered. Research by Larson, Hancock and others[3] confirmed that this was in fact the case. A majority of user searches were now based on access to subject information and in automated systems which lacked a formal subject approach title searching supplemented by shelf browsing was frequently employed.

DIRECT CLASSMARK SEARCHING

Almost all OPACs have some facility for searching by classmark. This can take the form of direct browsing of classmark headings. Using this option the user is prompted to input a classmark and is then presented with a browsing screen from which he can select and display titles (Figure 1). This facility is of course very limited as the user is generally unaware of the specific classmark or range of classmarks which the OPAC uses to define his subject enquiry. Furthermore, the browsing display is of little value if the classmark notation is either not fully expressive, or the user does not appreciate the expressive nature of the classification which the notation is designed to convey.

An advance on this approach is the direct browsing of titles in classmark order. The result when using this approach is that, if the user identifies a classmark, he is then presented with a series of bibliographic references (Figure 2).

Again, of course, the facility depends on the user knowing an appropriate classmark at which to begin his search. This also presupposes that the user can clearly distinguish classmarks and shelfmarks and that the automated system will recognize and accommodate problems arising from the use of a variety of prefixes and suffixes appended to classmarks when constructing a sorted classmark sequence. The system used must allow the librarian a large degree of flexibility over determining filing sequences to cater for the existence of more than one classmark sequence in cases where a library, for example, uses more than one classification scheme (commonly UDC and DC). It should also allow the preferred branch library holdings or special collections to be displayed according

```
16 NOV 93              ABERDEEN UNIVERSITY LIBRARY          03:40pm
                         PUBLIC ACCESS CATALOGUE            PORT 96

    Your search:  006.33
         CLASS (May be truncated)                          Titles
     1.   006.3 Wal                                          322

     2.   006.31 Gol                                          35

 >  3.   006.33 Mum                                          131

     4.   006.34 Gas                                           1

     5.   006.35 Gaz                                          28

     6.   006.37 Dew                                          75

     7.   006.4 Koe                                           36


  Enter a line number :
  Commands:  SO = Start Over, B = Back, P = Previous Screen,
                <Return> = Next Screen, ? = Help
  Esc-chr: ^] help: ^]?  port:2 speed: 1200 parity:none echo:rem  VT100 ....
```

Figure 1   Direct classmark search option (DYNIX at Aberdeen University Library)

224

```
CLASSMARK search
Type H for help; M for main menu.
Classmark : QP351
Now scanning list of          46 index points

  1  Frontiers in physiological psychology. 1966.
     QP351.R8 =EWKA=
     Psych QP351.R8

  2  Advances in clinical neuropsychology.
     Psych QP351.A3;1

  3  Annual review of neuroscience; editors: W. Maxwell Cowan ... [et al.].
     per/QP351.A6R4 =A4KN=
     Gatty per/QP351.A6R4 (v. 1-8)

  4  Journal of Neurochemistry.
     per/QP351.J7N4 =A1RT=

Press RETURN to continue with this list, R to restart the list,
C to change display format, S to start new search or menu :
Esc-chr: ^] help: ^]? port:2 speed: 1200 parity:none echo:rem  VT100 ....
```

Figure 2   Direct title display from classmark search (SAUL at St Andrews University Library)

to location of the terminal from which the user is accessing the system. Some turnkey systems (for example LIBERTAS) offer very sophisticated facilities for user parameterization of classmarks but others give the librarian very limited control. Even with sophisticated systems for handling classmarks, however, direct classmark searching is obviously not a useful approach for the majority of library users. A number of researchers have pointed to the very limited use made of the facility. At the University of Sussex, Lee, for example, notes that the option accounts for only 4 per cent of the searches made on the OPAC.[4] Such a result should hardly surprise us. Only the expert user can begin to make sense of the direct classmark option.

SUBJECT SEARCHING IN OPACs

Direct classmark searching as Walker says is 'harmless and occasionally useful'.[5] Before going on to consider the way in which this option could be improved to make classmark searching more useful it is salutary to look first at the alternative approaches to subject searching on the OPAC, that is, using keywords or subject headings. In many ways these approaches were more enthusiastically received by librarians in the early stages of catalogue automation. They appeared to offer the versatility of searching which had hitherto only been practicable using remote databases online. The application of similar tools to in-house bibliographic collections, however, soon raised a number of problems and questions related to the appropriateness and efficiency of the tools. Walker draws attention to the significant differences between searching a library OPAC and using an online database host such as DIALOG to interrogate a large commercial database. He suggests that these are that the end user searching the database is untrained, the range of subjects covered by the typical library OPAC is far wider (often encompassing the whole spectrum of knowledge) and, perhaps most significantly, the subject description in OPAC records is inadequate and sometimes non-existent.[6] We could also add to this the fact that in all but the largest libraries the volume of data being accessed by the user of the system is much smaller and the contents of the database (that generally restricted to the library's collection of monographs) is more intimately known to the librarian and he is therefore more sensitive to any inadequacies in the retrieval mechanism used. Also when the collection being searched is monographic rather than primarily journal articles successful searching of the OPAC may well rely much more heavily on the user being able to contextualize his search – particularly in his having the ability to broaden or narrow his search since much useful information will be contained in works which have often (because of the arbitrary manner in which we generally confine our subject analysis to the 'book' as a bibliographic unit) been assigned very broad subject descriptions.[7]

As has already been said subject searching was regarded as an essential feature of the OPAC by librarians and in the initial stages of the development and proliferation of OPAC's transaction log analyses appeared to confirm that users were attempting a large number of subject searches. Estimates varied but sometimes were as high as 70 per cent. However, it was quickly realized that subject searches made in online catalogues were not satisfactory. As Markey reported in 1984, in most online catalogues 'an unacceptable proportion of subject searches fail to find anything at all'. It is important to examine reasons for this failure.[8]

The main mechanisms for providing subject access in OPACs hinge on the use of a controlled vocabulary in the form of subject headings (generally always Library of Congress Subject Headings) or the use of keywords derived from one or more fields of the bibliographic record. In terms of the potential afforded by automated systems current subject analysis as provided by LCSH is extremely limited. The vocabulary and syntax of LCSH is often just an alternative and formalized mechanism for paraphrasing the title of a work. Many headings in fact duplicate keywords which could easily be extracted from other fields in the bibliographic record. What is required for efficient subject searching is increased depth of analysis and indexing. Current subject headings systems simply do not support this; the vocabulary used is too restricted and is not responsive enough to linguistic changes and neologisms. In addition, in the United States where subject headings have historically been more widely used, research indicates that a major problem has in fact been the lack of them. A high estimate given by Byrne and Micco in 1988[9] is that on average only 1.7 headings are assigned to each bibliographic record. Furthermore, grave doubts have been expressed over the ability of the user to handle searching using LCSH and their confidence in the results. Users who are looking for books on a particular subject are rarely able to describe it in a form which gives even a partial match with the appropriate subject heading. The fault here lies in the indexing system. Classifiers are trained to index the whole document not parts of it and a result of this is that pre-coordinate strings are inevitably required to express fully this content. An important rule in the assignment of Library of Congress Subject Headings is the rule of specific entry, that is, each book must be indexed to a heading specific to content – neither broader nor narrower than the scope of the work. Often this results in subject headings which are simply not specific enough and the use of inverted word order and application of subdivisions adds to the confusion.

The syndetic structure of Library of Congress Subject Headings is very weak. Cochrane has pointed out in particular that it tends to lead the user out of a search. It is not suitable for refining a user's search as it tends to broaden the search to related topics rather than assist the user to find more precise topics. While *see references* to broader topics are specifically forbidden when constructing LCSH, in practice the option to create references to more specific terms is also often ignored.[10] Marcia Bates examined the effects of two variables on success in searching an academic library subject catalogue, 'subject familiarity' and 'catalog familiarity', and the latter was found to have a very significant effect on whether searches were successful.[11] Subject knowledge was found, surprisingly, to have a detrimental effect (though not a statistically significant one). A clue to the reason for this lies in the fact that the librarians and library users who had conducted the searches as part of this experiment expressed the view that the subject headings in their field were not specific or precise enough. Bates concludes that 'to be successful in searching a catalog it is more important to have a knowledge of cataloging and in particular LCSH than it is to have knowledge of the subject on which information is sought'. Le Loarer reports exactly the same problems using RAMEAU (Repertoire d'Autorité-Matière Encyclopedique et Alphabetique Unifié – the system used by the Bibliothèque Nationale) stating that 'unless the user knows the lexicon [terms existing in the list] and the syntax used to assemble the terms, it becomes very difficult to find the headings that described the content of the document he or she is looking for'.[12]

Long-term analysis of transaction logs such as the very thorough research done by Larson[13] in this area confirm the view that subject headings are a major problem because users do not know enough about their structure to make successful searches. He points to an evident trend away from subject searching back to known item searching.

PROBLEMS WITH KEYWORD SEARCHING

Current research suggests that keyword searching (particularly of title keywords) is the users' preferred method of performing subject searches on the OPAC. The ability of modern OPACs to provide comprehensive keyword indexes to the whole of the bibliographic record (including classmark fields) and the existence of full text retrieval systems where the same facility is available has caused some commentators to express the view that there is no longer a need for assigned indexing and in particular that classification is a pointless exercise. The increased number of access points provided, it is argued, enhances the value of unstructured searching and there is consequently a decline in the value of structured indexing models.[14] The user cannot easily search such systems, however, unless his search formulation is as varied as the input used to create the index. We are therefore transferring the onus to search successfully onto the user who must be able to formulate complex search strategies.

Enamoured by the possibility of 'getting everything', advocates of free text searching fail to recognize that bigger is not necessarily better and the tools available for reducing and refining search results can prove to be very blunt instruments. The main options available to the OPAC user to manipulate keyword searches are the use of Boolean logic and truncation. Research and experience of use of OPACs suggest strongly that these are not tools which users are comfortable in using and are only really effective when a trained intermediary is present to assist with searching. Hildreth and other writers, moreover, cast doubt on the effectiveness of Boolean operators. All too often the AND operator proves too restrictive in defining a search while the OR operator gives results which are too broad. Reliance on co-occurrence of single words or keywords is not sufficient because the search takes no account of the significance or weight given to each word defining the search. Linguistic analysis is required to recognize phrases, terms have to be assigned weights according to their significance in defining or limiting the search and syntactical relations must be taken into account. When discussing OPACS the issue is not whether or not all of the user's requested terms result in a specific match but often whether there is anything similar in the catalogue or database which would answer the question implicitly posed by the user's use of these terms. Put in this way it can be seen to be exactly the function which the classification system purports to perform.

CLASSIFICATION SCHEMES AS SEARCH TOOLS

The classification scheme is itself the product of much intellectual effort and the allocation of a particular classmark to a work reflects (or should reflect) considerable intellectual input in to the subject analysis of the work's content. Classification, as Markey observed, offers a logical approach to subject searching and increases the amount of subject information included in the bibliographic record. Furthermore, because the classification assigned to a document by definition gives the main focus of a work, it should increase the precision of searches. Thus it appears that it would be fruitful to pursue the means by which this could be exploited. Classification schemes should be given strong consideration as the choice for an information retrieval language in an automated environment.

As early as 1968 Richmond proposed the compilation of a thesaurus derived from a classification index, schedule terms and subject headings.[15] In a seminal article on the use of classification in online systems Elaine Svenonius[16] highlighted a number of areas in which searching could be enhanced using classification. Classification, she contended, could be used to improve recall and precision of searches, save user time inputting search terms, contextualize the user's search and allow for the search to be broadened or narrowed (particularly in those areas of the schedules which are susceptible to systematic taxonomies). She highlighted the function of classification in permitting browsing, stressing the fact that browsing is not a function which we should see as being confined to the open shelves. As she points out, many national bibliographies – including the British National Bibliography – are arranged in classified sequence to provide for ease of use in scanning for new works on a subject. As the trend towards more remote access to library catalogues continues her arguments gain even more force. The role of the classifier according to Foskett is 'to arrange human knowledge so that it facilitates the discovery of the unknown'[17] and the browsing function is an important element in contributing to this. If the user cannot physically browse the shelves of a collection then it is important that the same sort of facility is retained in an online form. Thus if we systematically display our collection online the user should gain substantial benefit. These are not features which are necessarily confined to the OPAC and Svenonius also extrapolated her views on the usefulness of classification to encompass its use in non-bibliographic databases and to its development as a switching language. In 1978 the results of Atherton's research on the subject access project were published and they strongly underlined the need to improve subject access. The Council on Library Resources Unit sponsored a number of online catalogue projects between 1982 and 1984 which all emphasized this theme in their conclusions. Research into requirements of users by Markey, Kaske and Sanders and Weiss Moore, likewise, all pointed to the need to improve subject access. Specifically, they suggest improved access by the following methods:

- Provision of alphabetical displays of subject headings to promote ease of browsing;
- keywords displayed in context in subject headings;
- online displays of related subjects;
- augmented subject access (using the document's summary or preface, tables of contents and index);
- automatic linking of free text to controlled headings;
- inclusion of subject headings in bibliographic displays.

In 1982 Hildreth proposed that there be automatic links between subject headings and classmarks to allow users to browse through subject headings in a systematic rather than alphabetic manner,[18] but the exact mechanism for providing this on OPACs and its usefulness in practice were not fully explored until the latter half of that decade.

CLASSIFICATION AS A 'PIVOT'

Benefits accrued from using classification in online systems in recent experimental work mainly revolve around development of direct classmark searching which has been termed the use of 'classification as a pivot'. The feature can be implemented in a variety of ways and has variously been incorporated into functions described as navigational searching or related term searching. Essentially the function leads the user from a particular work identified from a natural or controlled language search of the catalogue to records with the same or related classmarks. From the user's viewpoint the problem of access using 'meaningless' notational devices is thus resolved and the problem for the cataloguer then revolves around the viability of the thesaurus being created, in particular its capacity to match natural language input by the user to the most appropriate classmark or classmarks. The future effectiveness of the classification system in an online environment would therefore appear to be essentially dependent on the principles related to the 'classified catalogue' as opposed to the dictionary catalogue. Indeed as Chan observes, 'It is in many ways tantamount to the reintroduction of the classed catalog in American libraries'.[19] The problem in the OPAC, as for any classified catalogue, is how best to provide natural language access to the classified sequence. Some form of index is required to direct the user to the appropriate point (or points) in the classified array. This may be provided offline, using any of the approaches already described in Chapter 5, or could take the form of an online index. The latter alternative is generally viewed as being preferable and could be implemented in a manner which is transparent to the user. In some OPACS a thesaurus record can be provided to direct the user from a natural language phrase to a classmark. (This is done, for example, on the LIBERTAS OPAC.) This allows users to search an alphabetically arranged browsing screen and select headings which they deem to be appropriate. The user can then elect to go directly to the full display of bibliographic records associated with a particular heading. It is anticipated that this broadening of the initial search will produce a rich source of additional related references.

OKAPI

Chan clearly demonstrates that the use of classification as a pivot increases recall.[20] However, use of classification alone as a means of enhancing recall will almost certainly decrease the precision of the search. Walker's work in the OKAPI (Online Keyword Access to Public Information) experiments casts some doubt on the relevance of the records retrieved.[21]

The OKAPI system was developed at the Polytechnic of Central London between 1987 and 1988 to provide an experimental framework for testing OPAC performance. It has been used by Stephen Walker and a team of researchers on various British Library funded research projects. In a project to examine the effects of relevance feedback on retrieval Walker used three experimental systems – 'dumb', 'query' and 'full'. The dumb system performed subject searches in a 'conventional' manner as presented in earlier versions of OKAPI, that is, best match on words and phrases from user input. The 'query' system allowed the user the option to expand an initial enquiry to 'look for books similar to' those deemed relevant. The 'full' system also incorporated an option to look at 'books shelved near to . . .' those found using classification as a pivot. The full option thus offered what was effectively a shelf browsing option. The user was, by means of an inverted file of classmarks, allowed to browse indefinitely either forwards or backwards.

The bibliographic database for the systems was essentially the Polytechnic of Central London's monographic collection. Experimental subject searches were devised to allow various test groups of users to assess the systems. Those searches were presented to the users in the form of task sheets which required the user to find bibliographic references to answer a number of enquiries, some of which were general and some related to broad subject areas – the Arts, Computing, Engineering, Life Sciences and Social Sciences. The researchers used questionnaires, interviews and transaction log analysis to collect, evaluate and analyse feedback from the users relating to how they had performed searches of the system and their degree of satisfaction or otherwise with the various options. Analysis of these clearly showed the users preferred the query expansion system and the full system over the dumb system. Classmark searching was seen to be helpful and an initial analysis of the results of the experiment – looking purely at the recall of bibliographic records – seemed to suggest that it was the most successful approach. In the query system two-fifths of the records retrieved came from the query expansion. In the full system one-fifth of the records retrieved came from the query expansion and an additional two-fifths came from classmark browsing. Significantly then, the initial list of retrieved records was more than doubled using the full system's additional option which allowed browsing via classmarks.

A more detailed examination of how users approached classmark browsing was made and it became apparent that the option as implemented in the full system required the user to browse a very large number of screens of potential records. Although an overall analysis showed browsing to contribute over 42 per cent of records in 54 per cent of cases, the user chose no records from the browsing displays. Classmark browsing displays were shown to be much more erratic than those presented by query expansion and could at times be confusing. Walker thus concludes that the use of classification as a pivot is a very inefficient source of records. For every 17 records retrieved only one was deemed to be relevant.[22] The views of some users expressed in the project report confirm this with comments such as: 'I had to discipline myself not to waste time looking at everything' and 'Just because books were on the same shelf didn't mean they were really relevant'. Walker identifies a problem with classmark browsing that for a large number of questions used in formulating the experimental searches there was no single Dewey classification number. For 24 of the topics used in the research the

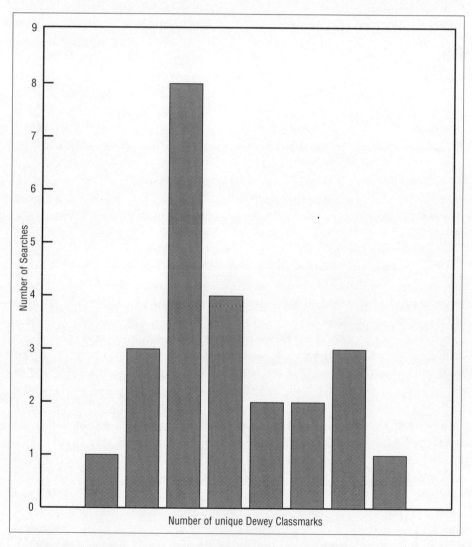

Figure 3   Number of searches performed related to number of unique classmarks present in retrieved record set

distribution of class numbers is summarized in Figure 3.

In other cases the lack of specificity of the classification scheme was identified as causing a problem. This was particularly evident in searches involving computing science where the bulk of the Polytechnic of Central London's collection was classified using pre-18th editions of Dewey and therefore several thousand records were classed at the very general number 001.64.

The success of direct classmark searching (and indeed any technique incorporating use of the classified sequence) is obviously very much dependent on the efficiency of the scheme used and in particular how well the scheme collocates material on a given subject and how consistent it is in dealing logically with placing related subjects. Note that this is not to say that the classification scheme must collocate all material on a given subject. Much criticism of classification as a retrieval device derives from the erroneous presupposition that a single classmark search should retrieve all material on a given topic. However, as Koerner observes: 'The function of library classification is not so much to exhibit the fundamental relations among the things classified as it is to exhibit the relations that are helpful in locating information being sought'. The point at issue is how we can assist the user searching for information by clearly demonstrating the separation of aspects of concrete subjects implicit in assigning works to different areas of the classification schedules.[23] In particular, can this feature of a bibliographic classification scheme be used as a precision tool by the user by clearly contextualizing his search?

CLASSIFICATION SCHEMES

THE UNIVERSAL DECIMAL CLASSIFICATION (UDC)

The question of how well particular classification schemes can be used in an automated environment has been the subject of considerable research. As early as the 1940s Brish, in an article entitled 'Adaptation of the UDC form of notation to punched card techniques,' reported on the use of punchcard equipment to express and sort UDC classmarks. In the mid 1960s the full UDC schedules were for the first time put into machine readable format and this facilitated a series of extensive investigations into the use of UDC in computer systems. In 1968 and 1970 the FID organized two seminars on 'UDC and mechanized retrieval' and the American Institute of Physics sponsored a series of nine research reports on the subject.

Many of the problems were purely technical ones. The very complex punctuation used in UDC and the inevitably lengthy notation consequent on using the classification to denote a subject analysis which was coextensive with the subject of the document posed severe problems in computational manipulation available on computers at that time. Typically problems were caused, for example, in recognizing the significance of notational devices which required two symbols (for example '=' to denote the language facet) or differentiating between the use of the decimal point purely to improve readability of classmarks and its use in devices such as .0 (special auxiliary) and .00 (common auxiliary denoting point of view). Nonetheless, Freeman was able to report confidently that UDC could be used as an indexing language in a mechanized environment (thus refuting Kyle's assertion that this was an impossibility). The synthetic nature of the classification scheme – in particular its adoption of unique facet indicators – made it suitable for searching in a post-coordinate manner while the hierarchical structure it inherited from the Dewey Classification promised to be useful in establishing search context.

Apart from correct interpretation of facet indicators, difficulties in searching via the classmark notation itself centre around the use of ranges of classmarks to denote a broad subject area (either linked consecutively '/' or non-consecutively '+' in the classification schedules). Perhaps more problematic is the enumeration of subjects which could have been synthesized using the auxiliary tables. Numerous examples can be cited of how the UDC notation has been developed as an access mechanism to online information systems. Several databases accessible via the ESA-IRS (European Space Agency – Information Retrieval Service) can be searched using UDC numbers; the HELPIS file on BLAISE-LINE which is provided by the British Universities Film and Video Council can likewise be searched by UDC number (and this system allows truncation of numbers). The CD-ROM Electre Biblio covering French Books in Print provides a menu option to search by UDC number and another to perform a hierarchical browse of the UDC classes.

Perhaps more significant is the application of the scheme in online interactive retrieval systems. The earliest work of importance in this respect was that conducted by Freeman and Atherton in their experiments using UDC as an entry vocabulary for an online bibliographic system. The AUDACIOUS (Automatic Direct Access to Information with the Online UDC System) study was the first experimental study which concerned itself with accessing an online bibliographic database using classification. It ran on an IBM 7044 with only 32K of core memory. A file of classmarks was created for documents concerned with nuclear science and scope notes and descriptors for these were cross-referenced to the bibliographic records. AUDACIOUS was a command driven search system designed for use by library staff to assist retrieval of relevant documents. Freeman and Atherton's conclusions were that the experiment was successful, demonstrating that the UDC could be used as effectively as EURATOM keywords to access the collection of documents dealing with nuclear science. It was further claimed that the results obtained using UDC as an online indexing language could be successfully generalized to encompass use of other classification schemes.

Fox and Palay incorporated the classification system used by Computing

Reviews into the menu based search system, BROWSE. The system was used at the Carnegie-Mellon University Computing Science collection. An interesting feature of this system is that the user is not given a direct classmark search option but is forced to travel from a general part of the schedules to a specific area of interest, that is, he is forced to perform a hierarchical browse of the system. In 1987 a UDC Computerisation Working Party was established 'to facilitate the revision, publication and computerised application of the UDC'.[24]

In 1988 the FID conference in Helsinki reported a number of new developments in the use of the scheme. One automated system of some importance is ETHICS, implemented at the ETH (Eidgenossischen Technischen Hochschule) library in Zurich. The system operates using a separate file of verbal descriptors linked to the document file through UDC numbers. The verbal descriptors (or alphabetical subject register) form a hierarchical system. Each concept corresponds to one and only one UDC schedule number or auxiliary (forming the standard register). Descriptors and synonyms are used to expand the table of concepts and this includes equivalent terms in French, English and German. The system can thus be used fairly easily with a knowledge of any of these languages. When verbal concepts cover more than one UDC number one classification number is chosen and any others are used as references to the chosen classmark. The user dialogue with the system can be initiated by using words or phrases or UDC numbers. If the latter is given the user is taken immediately to the display of the systematic subject register. If a word is given the user is presented with an alphabetical display of the subject register.

On selecting a phrase from this display the user is then given a display which shows:

- Total number of titles
- Total titles with search term as a single concept
- Numbers of titles combined with other search terms (that is concepts which have been coloned onto the basic UDC classmark)

The system also allows free combination of terms and the use of the Boolean operators AND and NOT. Within the ETHICS system the standard UDC schedules are expanded by extending the UDC classmark where more specificity is required.

There has been no systematic testing of the system to gain user feedback but the system appears to be performing efficiently in a practical environment. From a study of the system descriptions available it is hard to avoid the conclusion that the classification system *per se* is being distorted to accommodate search by what are essentially subject headings and it would be useful to have some feedback on the efficiency with which users are able to gain access to the classified array using the alphabetic subject register.

A similar, but somewhat more advanced system is that used by the Scott Polar Research Institute Library in Cambridge. The system is designed around a piece of software called MUSCAT which allows free text searching in English and searching via UDC classmarks. It is a sophisticated system incorporating probabilistic retrieval techniques and relevance feedback with a similar objective to that provided by one of the experimental OKAPI systems. Buxton reports that 'a copy of the classification [the UDC for use in polar libraries – an officially recognized abstract of the full UDC] is kept near the terminals to allow users to check the meaning of the UDC numbers, but regular users are said to become familiar with the ones most relevant to them'.[25] The overt use of classification schedules in this manner is obviously not appropriate in general libraries but in the special library environment it seems to operate very efficiently.

THE DEWEY DECIMAL CLASSIFICATION (DC)

In the United States the major classification schemes used are Dewey and Library of Congress and, while these may not at first sight appear to be as useful for retrieval as the more synthetic UDC, their widespread adoption has generated considerable interest in research into their suitability as online indexing languages. Of the two classification schemes, Dewey is generally seen as having a greater potential and as early as 1976 at the Allerton Park Dewey Centennial there was much speculation as to its potential for retrieval in an automated environment. At the National Online Meeting in 1983 Geller and Lesk[26] reported on the use of Dewey at the Bell Laboratories in a test to determine whether using a hierarchically structured menu-based search strategy defined by the Dewey Classification Scheme was preferable to coordinate searching using keywords. However, the design of the menu-based system was not particularly sophisticated and the experiment's conclusions were basically a comment on the suitability of using a menu-based dialogue to search for information rather than using a keyword approach. The DDC online project – supported by the Council on Library Resources, OCLC and Forest Press – provides one of the most important pieces of OPAC research of the past two decades.[27] The project made use of the DC schedules (produced using the 19th edition photocomposition print tapes). The first objective was to establish the optimum strategy for searching and displaying the DC schedules in an online catalogue. Subsequently the research attempted to demonstrate empirically the effects of incorporating the schedules on subject access and browsing and to test the effectiveness of DC as a search tool in these respects.

The DC schedules were included in an attempt to examine the effectiveness of DC as a search tool in a catalogue which was enriched by the inclusion of subject terms draw from the DC Relative Index and Schedules. It was decided that it would be overly complicated to incorporate the DC tables. A high percentage of DC numbers contain synthetic elements drawn from use of the tables (which act as common facets) or from special instructions embedded within the schedules which generally led to the use of a previously enumerated section of the classification (effectively treating this part of the scheme as a differential facet). The work began with the design of two online experimental catalogues which were created from three data sources:

1. MARC catalogue records collected from four libraries participating in the project (the Library of Congress, the New York State Library, the Public Library of Columbus and Franklin County Library and the University of Illinois at Urbana Champaign),
2. the DC 19th edition Schedules and
3. the Relative Index.

One can scarcely but be impressed by the scale of the project. Each of the four libraries taking part in the project contributed between 8 000 and 15 000 records in the following particular subject areas defined within bands of the DC19 schedules – economics 330–339, commerce 380–382 and management 658 (Library of Congress), New York State history/geography 974.7–974.799 and 917.47–917.4799 and United States colonial history 973.1–973.2 (New York State Library), sports, recreation and performing arts 790–799 (Columbus and Franklin County) and mathematics 510–519 (University of Illinois). Throughout the project the team had access to a whole range of project consultants and advisors who were experts in the fields of classification and systems analysis and design. The project team was unable to implement all recommendations of the experts who had an input to the design of the experimental system but none of the self-imposed limitations were judged to have a significant effect on the research team's findings in the subsequent stages of the project where the experimental system was tested and user feedback analysed. Two online catalogues were created for each of the four test sites. (Technically there was in fact only one online catalogue in which bibliographic records and selected indexes were shared.) The Dewey Online Catalogue (DOC) in which DC classification schedules and index had been included and the Subject Online Catalogue (SOC) which was not enhanced in this manner. The computer readable files created from the Dewey print tapes had to be subjected to considerable editing and manipulation by the project team, for example, to remove Dewey's not used captions (for redundant classmarks), to expand ranges of DC numbers where a single caption referred to a range and to remove terms and phrases used in the schedules which, though understandable to classifiers, would be meaningless to library users.

Both DOC and SOC were designed as menu driven systems to provide as simple as possible an environment for novice users who were expected to gain familiarity with the systems fairly quickly. The SOC menu contained the conventional subject searching options common to most modern OPACs while the DOC menu gave additional subject access options. A very much abbreviated summary of the menu options extracted from Markey's final report is given below:

SOC

Menu Operation Code	Function	Index source
SA	Subject search and browse	Assigned subject headings
SD	Direct subject search	Implicit Boolean AND searching of keywords from title, subject headings, series and notes fields of the bibliographic record
SC	Call number search	Classmarks fields

DOC

SA	Subject search and browse alphabetical index	DC Relative Index
SS	Subject search and browse schedules	Keyword implicit Boolean AND on DC Relative Index Schedules and notes, and first Subject Heading from bibliographic record
SD	Direct subject search	Keyword, implicit Boolean AND search of title, subject headings, series, DC schedules and notes
SC	Call number search	class numbers from DC schedules directing users to classification areas

Two online retrieval tests were conducted involving staff and users of the four participating libraries. The first was a comparison search – users conducting the same search on both catalogues – and the second a controlled experiment in which project supervisors assigned equivalent searches for library staff to perform on both the DOC and SOC catalogues. Quantitative measures related to the search time and volume of data retrieved were analysed. In addition qualitative analyses of responses to more open-ended questions related to ease of use of the system and general user satisfaction were conducted using an input questionnaire and interview responses.

The results showed increased search time recorded using the DOC system. This may have been attributable in part to the unfamiliar search mode and users needing time to familiarize themselves with novel system features and display characteristics. The comparisons between the DOC and SOC catalogue searches themselves, however, prove somewhat inconclusive. As Markey points out in the report, recall and precision and relevance measures as used in the project were not seen as reliable performance measures and were not used to evaluate the findings quantitatively. They were used to identify problems in the performance of the catalogues but not for comparison or detailed evaluation.

The result of DOC searches which allowed the user to browse through the schedules were not satisfactory. This was deemed partly to be owing to the nature of the wording of the DC schedules captions, particularly those for three-digit numbers. A second contributing factor was seen to be the lack of specificity in certain areas of the schedules. Alphabetical browsing of DOC was likewise not a successful option. Searchers were generally critical of the Relative Index entries in DOC as compared with subject headings.

The overall picture which emerged showed that librarians as users preferred DOC and library users preferred SOC which seems to indicate that there is a considerable way to go in making the classification schedules understandable to the general user.

Markey's own conclusion to the report is as follows:

In online catalogues the DDC can be a searcher's tool for subject access, browsing and display. The DDC enhances subject access to the online catalogue. The DDC provides new strategies for subject searching and browsing that are not possible through the alphabetical approaches of subject headings and/or keywords presently supported by on-line catalogs.

To what extent this confident conclusion is justified given the findings of the research is open to debate. Much of the positive comment on the DDC online project is confined to a discussion of how the subject searching vocabulary was considerably enriched by adding terms from the schedules. The table given overleaf shows how the number of subject terms was on average incremented by different fields used in the DOC catalogue.

Statistics provided by the research do in fact show that for each bibliographic record the Relative Index contributed on average 3.44 unique words and schedule captions a further 5.72 words, thus considerably enhancing the number of access points available to the user. However, these are raw figures based purely on unique words and do not take account of the reliability of these words as indicators of the work's subject content. As Markey points out, subsequent analysis shows that 25 to 52 per cent of subject terms added were in fact poor indicators. Far from having a beneficial effect on retrieval these may in fact have been detrimental. As Mitev points out 'The language of the Dewey Schedules, being designed to help cataloguers rather than users, is rather far from the language of many search queries'.[28] In addition, some of the other claims for the inclusion of schedules to enhance retrieval are not so convincing. It is, for example, easy to underestimate the amount of editing and manipulation the schedules require in order to be usable online. This was only carried out in the project for the classmark ranges of the subject fields involved in the experiment and this represents only a small percentage of the whole schedules (and the more recently revised parts at that). Failure to provide some form of analysis of

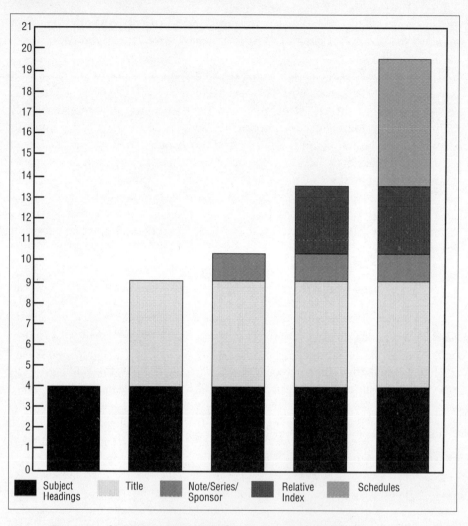

Figure 4 Contribution of different fields to index vocabulary (DDC Online Project)[29]

synthetic numbers is also seen as a weakness. The automatic analysis of these distinct subject elements implied in the classmark is not easy though each element obviously merits consideration as a search key or access point. It is not an easy matter to deconstruct synthetic DC numbers. Unlike UDC, facet indicators are not apparent in the notation. (For shelving and comprehensibility this is a considerable advantage of the Dewey Classification over the UDC.) Wajenberg[30] has proposed a scheme to perform automatic analysis of synthetic Dewey classmarks and it is generally assumed that this would make the classification more effective as a search tool. Empirical research into this is required before any firm conclusions can be reached. A particular weakness of the research project is that the capacity of the DC schedules to provide hierarchical scanning of subjects, notwithstanding Markey's confident conclusion to the contrary, is not convincingly demonstrated. Certainly, controlled experiments are very difficult to carry out because, by their very nature, information systems are extremely complex. Some answers, moreover, look so obvious that they do not require justification. In order to draw conclusions about the performance of systems it is necessary to conduct rigorous experimental tests which can be easily repeated. From the content of the report itself Walker surmises that 'The results were not encouraging enough to suggest that work on hierarchical browsing should be given a high priority'. While the online project provides a great deal of invaluable data on how users approach searching the catalogue there are a number of practical issues which require careful scrutiny before it can be concluded that the inclusion of the DC schedules justifies the considerable investment which would be required in a working library environment.

THE LIBRARY OF CONGRESS CLASSIFICATION (LC)

In 1987 the Library of Congress began actively to investigate automation of the Library of Congress Classification schedules and in January 1988 at the ALA midwinter meeting a formal announcement was made of a project to set the framework for achieving this objective. Researchers at the University of Toronto undertook a detailed content analysis of the schedules in order to provide experimental data to support the project's four clearly identified goals. These were to provide a system which would:

1.   provide online editorial support
2.   allow librarians to work online with the schedules
3.   provide for the production of LC schedules in a variety of physical output formats – in particular to investigate production on CD ROM
4.   enable use of the schedules as a catalogue search tool.

Of these the most complex problems encountered will be in implementing the fourth goal. Williamson, Mandel and others who have long advocated the use of the LC classification scheme as providing a useful platform for research have thoroughly discussed the major difficulties in implementation. LC was designed and continues to be maintained primarily as a shelf location device, stability being the primary consideration. The classification is based very much on literary warrant rather than on theoretical precepts and is the most enumerative of all general bibliographic schemes.[31] Tables used for expansion are not uniformly employed and the various indexes to the schedules are inconsistently constructed. In particular, hierarchical force which is a major feature of Dewey Classification is not a dominant feature in the Library of Congress Classification scheme. Thus searches cannot be broadened or narrowed easily. Furthermore, where hierarchies exist, the notation is not expressive so one cannot use the simple expedient of iteratively truncating the classmark by one digit in order to broaden the search. Nonetheless, it is argued that the ability to browse schedule captions, explanatory notes and the indexes which are designed to assist classifiers would also provide assistance to users in allowing them to contextualize their searches or as browsing aids. Many more machine readable bibliographic records contain LCC numbers than DC numbers and the LCC schedules and indices themselves can be complemented by Library of Congress Subject Headings as a source of vocabulary enhancement.

MARC FORMAT

A significant outcome of research into use of the LC schedules has been the recognition of the need to develop a standard MARC format for classification. Class numbers in schedules contain several data elements, thus the format adopted includes fields not only for notation and schedule captions but also accommodates fields for *see references*, notes, index terms, preceding hierarchies and previous history of the notation. The USMARC format has been agreed upon and work is currently going on to define a UNIMARC format. Williamson's[32] article of 1989 describing current research provides many useful examples to illustrate the problems of converting the LCC schedules into this form. She instances, for example, notes which read 'in case of doubt see', 'class elsewhere' and 'f.i.' (for instance). She also notes many typographical errors and curiosities (for example, Marx, Karl *see* Karl Marx) but concludes that there is a large degree of conformity in the schedules and is optimistic about the prospect for full automation. Hierarchical linking and construction from LCC tables is seen to be particularly problematic. To express the meaning of a classmark fully the complete hierarchy of which that classmark is a part is required. Cochrane and Markey[33] discuss this in terms of 'nesting of unit records'. The procedure they describe is in fact very similar to the chain indexing procedure and this hierarchy encoding cannot be easily applied automatically.

PRACTICAL CONSIDERATIONS

Much effort is being made and there is a definite commitment to providing automated versions of major schedules but, without wishing to detract from the quality of research and the progress made to date, much more is required to determine the benefit of the approaches currently being pursued. There exists in practice a fundamental dichotomy between the use of classification as a shelf ordering device and its use as a retrieval tool. The many relocations and complete revisions of sections of any of the major schemes which would be required to enhance the scheme's online retrieval potential are simply not practical. Notational complexities which would be required explicitly to denote superordination and subordination of topics to assist online browsing would almost certainly undermine the effectiveness of schemes as shelf location devices.

Librarians must be able to demonstrate not only that information retrieval can be enhanced using classification but also that it is worth making a significant monetary investment to make it work. Included in this cost would be the requirement to reclassify stock to ensure that the most recent version of the classification scheme being used is uniformly implemented throughout the library and the necessity to ensure that the reclassification is conducted in a timely manner in order to keep pace with any revisions of the published classification schedules. Currently many librarians would argue that it is financially impossible to maintain large bibliographic collections to keep pace with schedule revisions. (As Swan Hill points out, the fact that the University of Illinois at Urbana Champaign received government support for reclassification of its mathematics collection to Dewey 19 was a reason for Markey's research being located there, but in the current financial climate it is hard to imagine libraries being voted funds for reclassification exercises.) Suggestions put forward by Gorman[34] and others to enhance classification as a retrieval device by the use of analytical classmarks, while sound theoretically, are not a practical option which is available to most major libraries.[35] Nor does the answer lie in transferring this task to central record suppliers such as the Library of Congress or the British Library. They themselves are not immune from the economic pressures which proscribe the activities which are possible in other libraries. In addition, in many large academic libraries it is not uncommon to find two or even three editions of the classification scheme being used concurrently. Some libraries may have stripped the MARC record of fields which hold classmarks assigned by central agencies such as the Library of Congress and the British Library or have introduced their own local amendments to the schedules to incorporate what they have seen as peculiarly local requirements.

Considerable research is also required into the instructive and relational approaches which must be available to integrate schedules into current commercial OPACs. As Swan Hill states, 'Even if classification were immediately and overwhelmingly recognised as a top priority for subject access in online catalogs, there is a considerable inertia of present practice and staffing to overcome in order to achieve this desired end'.[36]

FUTURE USE OF CLASSIFICATION

Definitions of the OPAC have essentially been based on their function as access tools. Fayen, for example, describes the online catalogue as 'a mechanism for providing real time access to the bibliographic records for a library's holdings' and Walker reinforces this view in his description of the OPAC as 'the end user interactive information retrieval system by means of which users try to find references to materials held in libraries'. It is important to broaden this functional description particularly when one considers the problem of subject access. The purpose of an information storage and retrieval system, if one looks beyond a basic functional description, is essentially to answer questions. This presupposes a dialogue between the system and the user of the system and the structure of the classification scheme should be able to form a framework for entering into this dialogue.

The work by Walker into query expansion which makes use of relevant feedback from users to provide enhanced search results is very significant in this respect and is a step towards recognition that the searching behaviour of users is partly probabilistic and partly indeterminate. Walker's research in this area centres on probability theory.[37] Users are invited to search for subjects using a free language approach. Records retrieved as a result of the user's initial enquiry are assessed for relevance and the system then repeats the search using subject terms and classmarks from the chosen record. These terms are weighted, the actual weight given to a term being inversely proportional to the frequency with which the word occurs in the database. The system then performs a new search and produces a ranked list of bibliographic references.[38] The results are very promising and Walker has demonstrated that this approach provides consistently better results than other techniques. The use of ranked output in response to a subject search is extremely useful and may be an important factor in motivating users to browse through lists of retrieved items. While Walker's work has treated the use of classification somewhat obliquely it seems very likely given the initial findings of his work on relevance feedback and catalogue browsing that a fuller investigation of the way in which such search techniques can make use of the classification scheme would bear fruitful results. One of the most interesting results of recent experiments using classmark searching online to provide additional records is that it in fact provides different records from those provided using keyword approaches. The problem of how to provide access to these records without increasing the number of false drops incurred to an unacceptably high level, however, remains unresolved.

Ultimately there is no one technique which will provide satisfactory subject searching on the OPAC. Text handling techniques such as stemming, truncation, automatic spell checking and cross-references have been investigated and found to be very useful. Le Loarer gives examples of the dramatic improvements which could be possible by incorporating techniques based on linguistic analysis – elimination of silence (that is, tackling the very serious problem of when users get no hits in a search on a given subject because one of the terms input is not contained in the system's indexing vocabulary), the elimination of noise (where recall is excessive and not precise), filtering or focusing user enquiries, use of contextual analysis and recognition of phrases. Artificial intelligence techniques currently being investigated are essentially based on language processing – queries being processed by word recognition followed by syntactic then semantic analysis. Slack, Matthews and others have demonstrated that improvements in searching can be brought about by providing better help facilities and improving screen presentation. Hancock-Beaulieu has written extensively on the subject of enhanced transaction logging facilities, in particular OLIVE, a system available from several commercial OPAC suppliers which also provides the ability to incorporate online questionnaires.[39]

These techniques provide very powerful means of analysing user requirements and elucidating the way in which the user searches for information. Researchers can, for the first time, accurately quantify use of the catalogue and demonstrate changing patterns of use. Results of research currently being undertaken confirm that central issues which must be tackled are the inadequacy of indexing languages, the problems associated with use of Boolean logic and the need to support browsing. Other more theoretical research in the field of information retrieval generally concludes that changes in the technology we use to access information systems have outpaced work on the principles used to store and access information. In 1982 Richmond, expressed pessimism about the future of subject searching, stating that 'It is my considered opinion . . . that there is not a very great future in the use of keywords, Boolean algebra or Library of Congress Subject Headings in online searching'.[40] She then went on to draw attention to the potential use of hypertext as a solution to providing the essential links between bibliographic 'chunks of data' held in machine readable form. The most interesting work in this area is currently being conducted in Scandinavia. Hjerppe has reported the work of the HYPERcatalog project at Linkoping in Sweden[41] and Pejtersen described the BOOKHOUSE project in Denmark.[42] Also of interest is Noerr's research on alternatives to the linear nature of classificatory arrangements.[43] These researchers basically work from the same premise that attempts to describe a document by objective summation of its content is not sufficient. There is no perfect indexing language or means of describing documents which will produce adequate content description of documents. The attempt to index by subject is in practice impossible as we cannot find a language which will adequately define what the subject of a document is. The emphasis on constructing information retrieval systems must therefore be moved to de-scribing the relationship between documents. In this sense the system designed is that which conforms to Vannevar Bush's 'memex' system where the human mental associations are projected onto the information system to create a web which the information seeker can navigate and from which he can 'discover' rather than 'find' information. The implications of this for practical maintenance of a documentary collection are of course enormous. Each new document added to the collection must be treated not as a discrete entity but must be processed in a manner which explicitly links it to other related documents in the information system, that is, the catalogue as a whole, allowing the document to be present not only in a single hierarchical structure but in an interconnected web of information nodes. It would appear, therefore, that classification which by definition seeks to expose relationships between documents, far from being redundant in online catalogues, could prove to be very important in tackling these problems.

NOTES

1. See for example K. Markey's review of major studies of card catalogue use: *Subject searching in library catalogs before and after the introduction of online catalogs.* Dublin (Ohio): OCLC Inc, 1984.
2. Seal, A., The development of on-line catalogues. In *Introducing the online catalogue.* Bath: Bath University Press, 1984.
3. Larson, R. R., Evaluating public access on-line catalogs. Berkley (Calif.): UC Division of Library Automation, 1983.
    Markey, K., Subject searching experiences and needs of online catalog users. *Library Resources and Technical Services.* Vol. 29, 1985, pp. 34–51.
    Hancock, M., Subject search behaviour at the catalogue and at the shelves. *Journal of Documentation.* Vol. 43, 1987, pp. 303–321.
    Lipetz, B. and Paulson, P. J. A study of the impact of introducing an online subject catalog at the New York State Library. *Library Trends*, Vol. 3, 1987, pp. 597–616.
4. Lee, S., On-line keyword catalogue at the University of Sussex. In *Keyword catalogues and the free language approach,* edited by P. Bryant. Bath: Centre for Catalogue Research, 1985.
5. Walker, S., Views on classification as a search tool on a computer. In *Computers in Libraries International 91. Proceedings of the fifth annual conference on Computers in Libraries. London: February, 1991.* London: Meckler, 1991.
6. Walker, S., *Improving subject retrieval in online catalogues 1.* London: British Library, 1987. BL Research Paper; 24.
7. While in theory the broad subject description implicit in the classification assigned to a book should be supplemented by more detailed subject specification or depth indexing it is rare to find this degree of detail in a practical situation.
8. Markey, K., *Subject searching in online catalogs.* Dublin (Ohio): OCLC, 1984.
9. Byrne, A. and Micco, M., Improving subject access: to ADFA experiment. *College and Research Libraries*, 49 (5) September, 1988, pp. 432–441.
10. It should be noted, however, that amendments have recently been made and continue to be made which provide a more comprehensive thesaural structure to LCSH and should certainly increase its retrieval performance in an online environment. See in particular Dykstra, M., LC Headings disguised as a thesaurus. *Library Journal*, 46 (3), 1990, pp. 193–217.
11. Bates, M., Factors affecting subject catalog search success. *Journal of the American Society for Information Science*, 28 (3), 1977, pp. 161–169.
12. Le Loarer, P., OPAC: opaque or Open, Public, Accessible and Co-operative? Some developments in natural language processing. Program, 27 (3), 1993, pp. 251–268.
13. Larson, R., The decline of subject searching: long term trends and patterns of index use in an online catalog. *Journal of the American Society for Information Science*, 43 (3), 1991, pp. 197–215. Interestingly the findings of this recent research which represents a large survey covering a six-year period and representing about 15.3 million searches on the University of California MELVYL system seem to show a reverse in the trend reported by Larson in 1983 which noted a general enthusiasim for subject searching. The fact that the trend has been reversed and users are now emphatically expressing dissatisfaction with subject searching is a cause for considerable concern.
14. The holistic approach to bibliographic indexing is typified, for example, by the replacement of PRECIS by COMPASS by the British Library.
15. Richmond, P. A., General advantages and disadvantages of using the LC classification. In *Use of the LC classification: proceedings of the Institute on the use of LC classification,* edited by Richard H. Schimmelpfeng and C Donald Cook. Chicago: ALA, 1968.
16. Svenonius, E., Use of classification in online retrieval. *Library Resources and Technical Services*, 27 (1), Jan–Mar, 1983, pp. 76–80.

17. Foskett, D., *Library classification and the field of knowledge*. London: The Library Association, 1958.

18. Hildreth, C., The concept and mechanics of browsing in an online library catalogue. In *Proceedings of the 3rd national online meeting*. New York: 1982, pp. 181–96.

19. Chan, L. M., The LC in an online environment. *Catalogue and Classification Quarterly*, 11 (1), 1990, pp. 7–26. Before British librarians become too complacent about this, however, they should pause for a moment to consider how successful the classified catalogue has actually been as an information retrieval tool in their libraries and recognize the enormous work required to make this a successful means of subject searching online.

20. Chan, L., The LC in an online environment. *Cataloguing and Classification Quarterly*, 11 (1), 1990, pp. 7–25.

21. Walker, S., OKAPI: evaluating and enhancing an experimental online catalogue. *Library Trends*, 35 (Spring), 1987, pp. 631–645.

22. Walker concedes that the classmark browsing option as implemented in the full system was not very sophisticated and that better design might well improve results. However, it is also worth noting that the manner in which the option was implemented on the OKAPI system was certainly as good as, and in some cases better than, the manner in which several commercial systems incorporate a classmark browsing option. The simple expedients of truncation and string searching on parts of the classmark may offer some potential advantages for expert users.

23. A useful discussion of this topic is to be found in Cochrane, P., Subject access – free text and controlled: the case of Papua New Guinea. In *Online Public Access to library files: Conference proceedings*, edited by J. Kinsella. Oxford: Elsevier, 1985.

24. 'UDC computerisation working party'. *Information Hotline*, 6 (March) 1987, p. 12.

25. Buxton, A., Computer searching of the UDC. *Journal of Documentation*, 66, 1990, pp. 193–217.

26. Geller, V. and Lesk, M., An online library catalog offering menu and keyword interfaces. In *National Online Meeting Proceedings*, 1983, Compiled by M. E. Willis and Thomas H. Hogan. Medford (NJ): Learned Information, 1983.

27. Markey, K., DDC Project. (OCLC/OPR/RR–86/1) Dublin (Ohio): OCLC, 1986.

28. Mitev, N. W., Venner, G. and Walker, S., Designing an online public access catalogue. *BLRD Report No. 39*. London: BL, 1985.

29. A similar chart given on page 305 of the report does not in fact correspond to the figures presented by Markey in the Executive Summary of the Report (p. XXXIX). The chart here has been based on those figures.

30. Wajenberg, A. S., MARC coding of DDC for subject retrieval. *Information Technology and Libraries*, 2, September 1983, pp. 246–251.

31. Chan actually argues that because of this direct classmark searching using Library of Congress Classification can sometimes be a useful option, with LC numbers providing complete call numbers for books. However, her example of a simple call number search, JN6598.K7W4671984, is not convincing.

32. Williamson, N. J., The Library of Congress Classification and the computer: research in progress. *International Cataloguing and Bibliographic Control*, Jan/Mar 1989, pp. 8–12.

33. Cochrane, P. and Markey, K., Preparing for the use of classification in online cataloging systems and in online catalogs. *Information Technology and Libraries*, 4, 1985, pp. 91–111.

34. Gorman, M., The larger the number the shorter the spine . . . *American Libraries*, 12 (8), 1981, pp. 489–499.

35. While many American commentators see lack of analytical classification as a particular failure associated with use of the dictionary catalogue it is in fact a more general problem and British libraries have not in fact been significantly more successful in providing this feature in their catalogues.

36. Swan Hill, J., Online classification number access: some practical considerations. *Journal of Academic Librarianship*, 10, 1984, pp. 17–22.

37. For the mechanism used to provide relevance feedback see Harper, D. J. Relevance feedback in document retrieval systems: an evaluation of probabilistic strategies. Cambridge: Ph.D. Thesis, 1980.

38. Mathematical techniques for document classification are discussed more fully in the next section on automatic classification but it is interesting to note here that these techniques, which

have proved largely unsuccessful when applied to large document collections, appear to be efficient and cost-effective mechanisms for improving retrieval performance when applied to sets of documents in databases and OPACs retrieved using conventional Boolean approaches.

39. Hancock-Beaulieu, M., A comparative transaction log analysis of browsing and search formulation in online catalogues. *Program*, 27 (3), 1993, pp. 269–280.
40. Richmond, P., Futuristic aspects of subject access. *Library Resources and Technical Services Quarterly*, Jan/March 1983, pp. 88–93.
41. Hjerppe, R., HYPERCAT at LIBLAB in Sweden: a progress report In: *The online catalogue development and directions*, edited by C. Hildreth, London: LA, 1989, pp. 177–209.
42. Pejtersen, A. M., A library system for information retrieval based on cognitive task analysis and supported by an icon based interface. SIGIR Forum, 23 (1), 1989, pp. 40–47.
43. Noerr, P. L., Browse and navigate: an advance in database access methods. *Information Processing and Management*, 21, 1985, pp. 205–213.

10 Automatic Classification

The preceding chapter discussed in some detail how in practice and theory classification and classificatory structures have been seen as useful techniques to assist users in retrieving information from a computerized file. This chapter will explore computers and classification from a different perspective – the use of the computer itself to classify, or assist in the classification of documents.

INTRODUCTION

The question which must be answered is whether classification by human intellectual effort can be superseded by computerized techniques. On first examination it would appear that the question should obviously be answered in the negative. The computer is not a 'thinking' machine. Classification requires the basic intellectual capacity to understand likeness and difference between subjects and the ability to determine sometimes subtle and complex relationships between them. How then can we make use of the computer to highlight relationships between subjects if it is incapable of 'understanding' the meaning of even the most elementary of these. The computer is incapable of conceptualizing relationships, that is, of making associations between concepts, and, as this is fundamental to classification theory, it would appear computers have no role to play in this sphere of activity. It seems that the work of the classificationist,[1] and to a certain extent the user of classification schedules, need not be affected in any fundamental manner by the ubiquitous spread of automation. As long as libraries find it necessary to use shelf classification schemes there will be a need for someone to classify documents. (Universal Bibliographic Control has not yet advanced sufficiently to ensure that the first description of a document in terms of subject content and format needs to be its last.) The computer's incapacity to make the complex associations required to classify even in a fairly simple manner would seem to negate the possibility that it could ever provide a substitute for intellectually derived maps of knowledge which modern bibliographic classification schemes seek to provide.

However, what computers are able to do is count and compare, and they can perform these functions at incredible speeds. In order to harness the power of the computer to provide 'meaningful' classification we must use these two basic functions. That these can in fact be used to provide what appears to be a degree of intelligence is illustrated in fairly recent developments in 'artificial intelligence' and its application in, for example, the automatic detection of a document's authenticity, in language translation and in the design of complex expert systems which perform a whole range of tasks previously seen to be completely in the domain of the human expert.

DEFINITION OF TERMS

First, it is important to make a distinction between the two terms automatic indexing and automatic classification. Automatic indexing deals with the automation of the process whereby we assign index terms to documents, that is, terms we will later use in order to retrieve a subset of documents from a file. Automatic classification deals with the way in which we group either the index terms assigned to documents or the documents themselves in order to highlight the relationship between documents on similar subjects. Automatic classification is concerned with procedures and systems which can make comparisons between terms used to index documents and from this draw conclusions concerning the degree of similarity of the keywords used to index documents or the degree of similarity of the documents themselves.

If we consider a matrix – each row of the matrix representing a document using the terms which define its subject content and the columns representing all potential indexing terms used to describe documents in a collection – it can be seen that we can approach automatic classification either by considering the relationships between documents (that is, rows of the matrix) or by considering the relationship between terms (the columns of the matrix). Thus, automatic classification, as it will be discussed here, will refer to the measures of similarity (or dissimilarity) to provide one of two distinct arrangements: grouping of index terms or grouping of documents themselves. The former of these is usually referred to as keyword clustering and the latter as document clustering.

DOCUMENT REPRESENTATIONS – ELEMENTAL ANALYSIS TECHNIQUES

The simplest techniques using the computer to provide automatic indexes can be considered to be those which deal with the automatic production of title indexes, or keyword enhanced title indexes (KWIC, KWOC, Double KWIC, etc.). But precision and recall from these techniques alone leaves a great deal to be desired. Classification is a tool which can be used dramatically to improve the efficiency of such systems. Much of the work on automatic indexing proceeds from the basic premise that classes must have a semantic unity, hence it is suggested that linguistic analysis can potentially provide the key to the way in which these classes can be automatically identified and defined and some key ideas are borrowed from this field. In order to be able to apply classification automatically it is important that we first establish how we can construct representations of documents capable of computer manipulation. Before going on to look at experimental systems which have been constructed in this field it is useful to look at some of the basics of elemental analysis techniques which underpin much of that work. Of necessity the following descriptions are simplifications of what is essentially a very complex area of study.

WORD FREQUENCY

We could begin by making the not unreasonable assumption that the words contained in a document are a strong indication of what the document is about. This was the assumption made by Borko and Bernick in their work on automatic document classification[2] and earlier by Luhn who in an article written in 1958 stated that 'It is here proposed that the frequency of word occurrence in an article furnishes a useful measurement of word significance', that is, significance in terms of establishing the subject of the document.[3] If we begin from this standpoint we could reasonably assume that we can to an extent 'classify' a document on the basis of comparing the words used in the document with words used by other documents – documents which contain similar words should be classified together. Such a measure is obviously too simplistic to be employed in a serious attempt at analysing a document's content. Over one third, and in some subject areas as much as 46 per cent, of words employed in documents are function words, words with no lexical meaning such as 'and', 'of', 'the', etc. They belong to the set of words in any language which serve a syntactic function – prepositions, conjunctions, articles, etc. – but do not serve directly to express content. Consulting a copy of Kucera and Francis' *Computational Analysis of American English* we would be led to the conclusion that on the basis of simple word counts alone the vast majority of printed documents are about 'the'.

RELATIVE WORD FREQUENCY

Obviously we need to use a more refined technique than simple word frequency counts if we are to use the words contained in a document as a basis for determining its 'subject'. Zipf demonstrated that the product of the frequency of use of words and the rank order is approximately constant.[4] Thus if we plot a graph of frequency of occurrence of words against their rank order we obtain a hyperbolic curve. Using this distributional property, Luhn proposed that the ability of words to discriminate content was restricted to those words which fell within an upper and lower cut-off point on this graph. (The way in which these cut-off points are determined, however, is rather vague.) The usual way in which the upper cut-off point is implemented is to compare the input text with a stop list of words which are to be removed. A neater solution to the problem, and one which tackles both high frequency and low frequency words is put forward by Edmundson and Wyllys.[5] Instead of simply looking at the number of times a word occurs we should concern ourselves with the relative frequency of occurrence of normalized terms, relative, that is, to the frequency with which such terms occur in a standard sample of text written in the same language. We are therefore looking not at frequency of occurrence of a term but at its frequency of occurrence in relation to its expected frequency. Thus, for example, a word which occurs 20 times in 1 000 in a given document but only once in 1 000 in our standard would be judged to be a significant indicator of the content of the work whereas a word which occurs 30 times in 1 000 in a given text and 30 times in 1 000 in our standard would not be considered significant.

Thus words belonging to the closed set of syntactic or grammatic words are eliminated from consideration.[6] The actual computation used to determine which words are significant indicators of meaning must, of course, be much more complex than simply examining relative frequency calculated in the manner implied by the above example. Techniques used may well involve complex mathematical theorems making use of hypergeometric significance or the Poisson standard deviate but the objective is essentially the same, to derive a set of terms which serve the function of making the particular document being examined distinctive from a piece of normal text because of the inordinate frequency with which they occur. This of course begs the question, what is 'normal text'? How do we identify the corpus of text which we are going to use as the basis for comparison? It seems probable that in fact we would need to use several 'standards', each being peculiar to a particular broad subject area. In addition, there is an implicit need to ensure that the standards are regularly updated because of inevitable linguistic changes over a period of time. Such questions have not yet been given satisfactory answers and have, in fact, been largely ignored in research into automatic indexing and automatic classification. The issues raised by these questions are seen to be more in the domain of linguistic approaches to automatic text analysis. Effectively this is concerned with how to generate a description of a document automatically, that is, how to index a document automatically or prepare an automatic abstract of a document's content. These concerns are evident, for example, in literature dealing with text analysis. Some of the work by Luhn and Borko and Berneir, for instance, despite purporting to deal with classification, deals more explicitly with automatic abstracting or automatic sentence analysis. The ultimate objective of research in this area is the development of a theory of language which allows us to provide automated systems which are capable of interpreting the meaning of documents and which can be used as the basis for determining relationships between documents. As van Rijsbergen pointed out in 1979, 'Undoubtedly a theory of language will be of extreme importance to the development of intelligent IR systems. But, to date no such theory has been sufficiently developed to be applied to IR'.[7] The statistical approach is therefore still very much more prominent in current investigations into automatic classification and in the majority of experiments conducted in this field, including those of Salton, Sparck Jones, Borko and Bernick, and Larson, discussed below, a large measure of intellectually derived indexing terms have been used as the basis for constructing keyword or document classifications. While Salton and Sparck Jones both argue that their experimental approaches on automatic classification can be widened to embrace natural language processing there is as yet no empirical proof that this is the case.

STEMMING AND TRUNCATION

If we were to browse through an alphabetically ordered list of words extracted from any document we would immediately note another problem associated with the use of simple word counting as a measure of a document's 'thought content', that is the frequency with which we encountered words which are obviously related but on which the computer has performed distinct counts, for example:

COMPUTER
COMPUTERS
COMPUTING

This problem is, of course, familiar to anyone who has to search an online database. Most database search interfaces provide a truncation option which allows us to compensate for this at the stage at which we formulate our search. Truncation allows the searcher to input an arbitrary symbol at the end of part of a sought after term to be used to indicate that any sequence of characters occurring in this position should constitute a match if preceded by the input term. When using the DIALOG host to search the MEDLINE database, for example, the symbol '?' can be used at the end of words to indicate truncation. The search command

S EMPLOY?

will thus retrieve EMPLOY, EMPLOYMENT, EMPLOYING, etc. Stemming on the other hand is a more sophisticated technique. Stemming algorithms have been developed which recognize and eliminate common inflectional suffixes and prefixes and thus facilitate the identification of morphologically distinct but conceptually related families of words. For instance, by removing suffixes such as:

-s	-ing
-es	-ible
-tion	-able
-ism	-ization
-ism	-ability

we can reduce words to a common root or stem. Stemming is termed 'weak' or 'strong'. Strong stemming refers to the removal of longer and more 'meaningful' suffixes. A useful description of one specific algorithm to provide automatic stemming is given by Porter[8] and this has been used in several online systems, for example in the OKAPI system developed at the Polytechnic of Central London. Some writers, notably Salton, Cleverdon and Keen, contend that the grouping or conflation of semantically related words in this way is a form of automatic classification. Although strictly speaking this is correct the term automatic classification will not be used in such a restrictive manner in this chapter.

SYNONYMS

A third problem raised when using frequency counts of words is that, if we simply look at word frequency, we take no account of use of synonyms. This is compounded by the attempts of authors (even in scientific texts) to introduce 'style' into their writing by avoiding repetitiveness by the use of synonyms or analogues. The normal method of controlling synonyms is through use of the thesaurus but even fairly basic thesauri are the product of considerable intellectual effort. To automate this procedure, that is, to produce a system which could use the computer to generate a keyword classification, it is essential to be able to identify similar and related terms. The technique of automatic generation of thesauri or keyword classifications will be dealt with in detail in a later section in this chapter.

DOCUMENT CLUSTERING

A clear statement of exactly what is achieved by document clustering is that given by Hayes who states that:

> We define the organisation as the grouping together of items (e.g. documents, representations of documents) which are then handled as a unit and lose, to that extent, their individual identities. In other words, classification of a document into a classification slot, to all intents and purposes identifies the document with that slot. Thereafter it, and all other documents in the slot are treated as identical until they are examined individually. It would appear, therefore, that documents are grouped because they are in some way related to each other; but more basically because they are likely to be wanted together, and logical relationship is the means of measuring this likelihood.[9]

In document clustering we perform classification of documents and use our classification scheme in the same manner as it is used in conventionally created systems, that is, we use it so that we can reduce the size of the file being searched and focus more accurately on the subject on which we wish to retrieve material. But the basis for deriving classes is not that used in traditional classification. The classical Aristotelian view of classification is based on the definition of a class with reference to a set of properties which are necessary for inclusion in the class. This has been termed monothetic classification. This is the philosophy which pervades most current information retrieval systems. Boolean formulations, which have become accepted as the basis for conventional retrieval, essentially function by allowing the user to specify his search by creating classes based on single concepts or combinations of concepts exhibited by individual documents in a collection. The user himself is required to deal with vocabulary control, for example, the use of synonymous terms and the identification of variant forms of words. Response time in systems created around this method of searching are fast because of the construction of auxiliary inverted index files (linked to document descriptors), searches being performed only on the index. The major problem which is immediately apparent in such systems is that by their very nature 'all terms are created equal' and all documents retrieved are deemed to be equal. Search formulations and resultant output are necessarily very rigid. The introduction of term weighting and the use of 'fuzzy set logic' may improve retrieval performance of such systems. However, we can approach the problem of retrieving useful classes of documents in a more satisfactory manner by recognizing the fact that commonly in bibliographic classification we are not concerned with documents which deal with a closed set of discrete well defined subjects – all of which must be present to define the document class – but with groupings of documents which are acceptable substitutes one for the other because the degree to which they deal with subjects is sufficiently similar. Most documents are essentially multi-topical and, rather than insisting on exact coincidence of all topics contained within the documents, we have to recognize what are termed polythetic classes, that is, classes having common properties but no single member of the class necessarily possessing every property, to construct useful bibliographic collocations satisfactorily. The purpose of library classification should not be seen to be concerned purely with the need to identify and exhibit fundamental relations or taxonomies of concepts but is more immediately concerned with providing helpful groupings of documents which contain a large degree of similarity in their subject content. The detailed examination of the document collection to reveal and create these classes is achieved by using document clustering techniques.

SIMPLE CLUSTERING OF DOCUMENTS

The basis for document clustering relies on examining the frequency with which terms co-occur in documents but the method of analysis of the data derived from this will obviously determine to a large extent the efficiency of the classification obtained. Thus the important issue when considering the viability of automatic document classification is to determine how efficient are the clustering algorithms used to obtain the classification, and in particular if they are as efficient as intellectually derived classification of the document collection.

First, the most obvious question to be addressed is how is the computer capable of making associations between various keyword sets derived from individual documents in a collection in order to measure how closely the subject matter of different documents relates.

The methods used to measure the strength of association between documents can be very complex. Therefore, a fairly simplistic approach to the way in which document or keyword clustering is achieved will be given in order to introduce the issues involved in this field of study. The following discussion builds on and extends the method of treating the subject given by Buchanan.[10]

If we assume that we have a very small collection of documents we might consider that they contain a variety of keyword identifiers. For example:

	Keywords					
Document	*Maps*	*Public*	*Academic*	*Libraries*	*Scotland*	*Cataloguing*
1	0	0	1	1	1	1
2	0	0	1	1	1	0
3	0	1	0	1	0	0
4	1	0	0	0	0	1
5	0	0	0	0	1	0
6	1	0	1	1	0	0

The ones and zeros in the above matrix represent the presence or absence of the concepts named at the top of each column of the matrix in six documents. The rows of the matrix thus provide us with six binary vectors representing each of the six documents. Note that at this point our indexing of the document's content is binary indexing; the components of any vector representing a document are given a value of either 1 or 0 depending on whether the concept is present or absent. This, of course, does not reflect in any manner the degree to which the concepts are central or essential in the description of the document's content.

We can now analyse the vectors created to determine the extent to which they are similar. The degree of closeness is going to be influenced to a large extent by the mathematically determined measure used to compare pairs of documents. This is variously termed the similarity coefficient, the correlation coefficient or the matching coefficient. Having decided on the way in which this is to be done we can construct a matrix of similarity coefficients by determining the extent to which documents share the same index terms. The basis on which we are going to derive our similarity coefficients is to consider first the number of index terms presented in a pair of documents and then to look at the number of such terms which are shared or common to the pair of documents being considered. Mathematically we can represent the manner by which we will derive our similarity coefficients as follows:

$$\frac{|\,x \cap y\,|}{|\,x \cup y\,|}$$

(i.e. Jaccard's coefficient)

From the above matrix of document descriptors, therefore, we arrive at the following:

	Documents					
	1	*2*	*3*	*4*	*5*	*6*
Documents						
1	1	0.75	0.2	0.2	0.25	0.4
2	0.75	1	0.25	0	0.33	0.5
3	0.2	0.25	1	0	0	0.25
4	0.2	0	0	1	0	0.25
5	0.25	0.33	0	0	1	0
6	0.4	0.5	0.25	0.25	0	1

Although we obviously do not wish to create six clusters (the objective of creating clusters being to limit the size of the file we need to search) we now have the basis for forming six document clusters. If we look, for example, at the third row of the above matrix we see that we could construct a cluster of documents based on document 3 which excluded documents 4 and 5. Possible clusters are summarized below:

Cluster basis	Documents included
1	1, 2, 3, 4, 5, 6
2	1, 2, 3, 5, 6
3	1, 2, 3, 6
4	1, 4, 6
5	1, 2, 5
6	1, 2, 3, 4, 6

One of the most important concepts in clustering is the determination of the centroid vector (also termed the cluster profile, the classification vector or the cluster representative). Ideally this should be 'close' to every other vector in the cluster. The purpose of creating clusters of documents is to allow us to limit the number of documents we need to examine when we make an enquiry on the bibliographic file. We obviously do not wish to create as many clusters as there are documents in our collection so we have to examine the potential clusters and determine which grouping is most likely to provide a useful classification of similar documents. To do this we have to assess potential clusters with respect to two criteria: How many documents does the cluster contain? How strong is the association between documents in the cluster?

Almost all clustering algorithms depend on empirically derived parameters which will be used to determine the above conditions. In addition a working system will require parameters to be obtained which place limits on the total number of clusters and control the degree of overlap of documents between clusters. Using very simple parameters then we may impose conditions on the analysis of potential clusters in our example to state that a cluster can only be formed if it contains more than three documents with a similarity coefficient with the centroid vector of greater than or equal to 0.5. The only cluster to satisfy these conditions is based on document number 2. We therefore have a cluster containing documents 1, 2 and 6. The same procedure for identification of clusters is then repeated on items left unclustered until the process terminates itself when associations between documents are too weak to fulfil the criteria for cluster creation. Documents can then be left unclustered or assigned to a 'rag bag' cluster which consists of documents which do not fit easily into any of the established clusters. (Those with even a basic familiarity with practical construction of faceted classification schemes will immediately recognize this problem.)

SEARCHING CLUSTERED FILES

When a search is made on a system in which the documents have been classified in the above manner the user's input is processed in the same way in which vectors were constructed for documents. The enquiry vector thus derived is then matched against the centroid vectors and then against each vector in clusters which are considered to provide a close enough match. Output from such a system can be presented in 'rank' order of nearness of match to the enquiry vector or cut-off points can be established when it is considered that the set of documents being retrieved do not display a sufficiently close match to indicate a required degree of relevance. (Note that the question of relevance and its determination in this context is a complex problem in its own right.)

CLUSTERING METHODOLOGIES

This, of course, is a gross over-simplification but it serves the purpose of introducing the manner in which mathematical measures of 'similarity' or 'association' and 'dissimilarity' are used when attempting automatically to classify a document collection. There are numerous examples of other methods of determining similarity of documents based on different clustering methodologies and a whole range of clustering algorithms are thoroughly discussed in the literature. Sparck Jones and Jackson describe the use of graph theoretic methods to define clusters using a graph derived from the measure of similarity of a group of objects.[11] From a Cartesian graph corresponding to the set of similarity values for a set of documents a graph can be derived by linking objects whose similarity is above a certain threshold. The following example, using the sample documents above and the similarity co-efficients already established, illustrates the use of graph theoretic methods.

Document Similarity Coefficients

1					
2	0.75				
3	0.2	0.25			
4	0.2	0	0		
5	0.25	0.33	0	0	
6	0.4	0.5	0.25	0.25	0
	1	2	3	4	5	6

Setting a threshold of 0.5 we can establish the following structure:

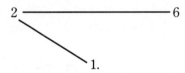

Lowering the threshold to 0.33 the following cluster can be established:

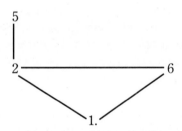

Various graphic representations are possible. Examples of these are shown in the discussion of Sparck Jones' work on automatic keyword classification (see below).

There is also a large class of hierarchic clustering methods, the most important of which is the single link, based on a dissimilarity coefficient. The output from this method is a tree type structure (or dendogram) in which clusters are represented by nodes on the tree. A very comprehensive treatment of this method and of other hierarchic methods (for example, the use of MSTs – maximum spanning trees and minimum spanning trees) can be found in van Rijsbergen's textbook *Information Retrieval*. These are also the subject of a British Library Research and Development Report by Griffiths and Willett who attempted to make comparisons between several methods: single linkage, complete linkage, group average and Ward clustering. The results of the report are, however, fairly inconclusive.[12] Some authors, for example, Maron and Kuhns and, more recently, van Rijsbergen and Harper, have based their work on what they see as more theoretically sound solutions using probability models. Given the nature of relevance judgements which characterize the purpose of classifying a document collection, no deterministic relationship exists between the terms used in indexing documents and the relevance of a particular document. This suggests that probabilistic solutions are more appropriate. The answer would therefore appear to be to construct a probability model by measuring association in terms of deviation from independence in the occurrence of index terms in two representative strings for document pairs. Examples of this can also be found in the research of Bookstein and Robertson.

SMART

One of the earliest extensive research programmes into the application of various mathematical theories related to document clustering was carried out by Salton and is embodied in his experiments using the SMART system. The system was designed at Harvard University between 1961 and 1964 and has been used largely as an experimental tool for measuring the effectiveness of many different types of analysis and search procedures on a variety of document collections, including a collection of about 780 abstracts on computer science (IRE-3), the Cranfield collection of documents related to aerodynamics and a collection of about 270 documents on medicine extracted from the MEDLINE database. This work is described extensively in a collection of monographic reports (the Information Storage and Retrieval (ISR) reports).[13] In the SMART system documents are represented by a set of concept numbers which refer to subject terms (reduced to a standard form by the control of word forms and synonyms). The analysis of documents into what Salton terms concept vectors in this way is achieved using a variety of techniques; it is not fully automatic. A variety of intellectual aids in the form of synonym dictionaries, hierarchical thesauri and statistical and syntactic phrase generation methods were used to provide content identifiers for documents. Many experimental approaches were made in various SMART projects to design an optimum clustering algorithm based on the descriptions of documents obtained from these techniques. The most successful of these was the Rocchio clustering algorithm.[14] This determines a number of objects which can be used as cluster centres. Starting from the premise that all documents are unclustered it performs what is termed a region density test on each document in the system to determine which documents are similar. As in the simple example given above a cut-off point is used to determine how many documents are permissible in a given cluster and the degree to which they must correlate. Centroid vectors are then established for each document cluster created. The centroid vector for each cluster is then matched against the whole document collection to create an altered cluster. At this stage there may be a large degree of overlap in the clusters formed (several documents may appear in many clusters). Additional stages are therefore executed which reduce the degree of overlap and minimize the number of documents left unclustered. Centroid vectors can themselves be grouped into clusters reflecting broader subject areas and this process can be continued to produce a hierarchic or multi-level cluster model. These can be shown to be most effective when the amount of document overlap between clusters is minimized.[15] When a user searches the system to retrieve documents the user's request is processed in a similar fashion to produce an 'enquiry vector'. The task of the system is to match the enquiry vector against concept vectors and produce the best match. Measures of association commonly used in experimental IR research are Dice's coefficient, Jaccard's coefficient, the Cosine coefficient and the Overlap coefficient. As van Rijsbergen points out they can all be considered as normalized versions of the simple matching coefficient which is simply the number of index terms shared between two documents. Normalization takes account of the size of the sets of index terms themselves.

Salton made use of the cosine correlation to determine degree of association between concept vectors and enquiry vectors in the SMART system as this appeared to give best retrieval performance. The cosine correlation considers documents to be represented by binary vectors embedded in an n-dimensional Euclidian space (n being the total number of index terms) and interprets the degree of association of any two documents using the cosine of the angular separation of their corresponding binary vectors. The SMART system was tested in a comparison with the commercial MEDLARS (Medical Literature Analysis and Retrieval System) in a series of experiments which led Salton to the confident conclusion that the SMART system worked so well that 'no technical justification appears to exist for maintaining controlled manual indexing in operational retrieval environments'.[16] However, more than 20 years on, the impact of the initial experimental systems on modifying these conventional retrieval environments gives us justification in using Salton's own words out of context to say that 'such a belief reflects sentiment rather than fact'.[17]

Salton continues to work and publish in the field of automatic document classification and many other authors have contributed towards research in this field. An extended version of the SMART system is currently running on a Sun 3/50 workstation under Unix at the University of California Berkeley Library School. CHESHIRE (California Hybrid Extended SMART for Hypertext and Information Retrieval Experimentation) has been used for work on the clustering of classification numbers themselves as reported in the work of Larson and discussed below.

IMPACT OF RESEARCH ON CURRENT PRACTICE

The ultimate objective of research in this field is the provision of an automatic self-organizing database but currently this goal still eludes researchers.[18] One major problem is the amount of computing power which is required to provide document classification and retrieval systems on a large scale. There are various reports in the literature of algorithms designed specifically to operate more efficiently. Investigations are currently being made into the use of neural net models rather than hierarchic models. A claim has been made in one recent article that neural networks have the potential to overcome the computational 'bottleneck' which characterizes implementing document clustering algorithms using sequential architectures.[19] The performance of such algorithms in document retrieval, however, does not present a dramatic improvement. For systems based on clustering and enhanced query techniques to make an impact on the currently entrenched methodologies for offering access to large scale bibliographic databases (including library catalogues) their retrieval performance must be proven considerably to better that of conventional systems and at present this is still not the case.[20]

KEYWORD CLASSIFICATION

Another avenue for research in this field is the automatic construction of classification schemes through an examination of keywords used in indexing documents. Automatic classification of keywords does not seek as its primary objective to cluster the document collection but, through an examination of the distribution of keywords within a document collection, to derive groupings of keywords. One of the most important pieces of research into automatic classification of keywords is embodied in the work of Karen Sparck Jones and her associates at the Cambridge University Language Laboratory.[21] Sparck Jones' investigations into keyword classification can be viewed as being basically an attempt to provide an automatic method of producing a thesaurus. The arguments for the use of thesauri in information retrieval are based on the fact that they provide means of normalizing terminology which we use to characterize documents or requests for documents. Thus they can be seen as devices for promoting recall and as such prove extremely valuable in assisting retrieval from automated systems. Traditional thesauri are extremely labour intensive to construct and maintain, however. Automatic grouping techniques to provide thesauri would not only save time but would provide groupings which were potentially more objective than manually created ones.

In particular, keyword classification would not be based on semantic properties but on shared contextual references. The classification derived should consist of 'connected words which are intersubstitutable in retrieval', that is, keywords which should be equally good in retrieving the same set of documents. Synonyms obviously have this property but, as Sparck Jones observes, 'These words need not be synonyms or even near synonyms and they need not be generically related either . . .'[22]

THEORY OF CLUMPS

The idea that a clump type classification could be developed on a large scale was strongly suggested by experimental work which had been conducted on the use of a lattice type of keyword network in information retrieval. This derived from work based on the CLRU collection of off-prints on articles on automatic language processing. Clumps were created using terms used to index the document collection. The basis for forming these clumps or groupings of keywords was to be fully automatic. We cannot consider the question of 'meaning' if we are to be able to accomplish this using fully automated techniques. Although not rigorously tested the application of clumps appeared to give useful collocations. While some such groupings looked rather like traditional classificatory divisions others grouped words in a less conventional manner. Examples of some terms derived from the indexing of the CLRU collection which formed clumps are:

Associative, Compound, Element, Magnetic, Memory, Recording, Storage

or

Adjective, Ending, Grammar, Phrase, Style, Text, Tense, Thesaurus

These clumps are formed from groups of words which can be shown to occur together regularly. They were thought to produce much more efficient retrieval than the use of simple keywords. The use of clumps rather than single keywords would obviously lead to an improvement in recall, as is evident from the diagram below:

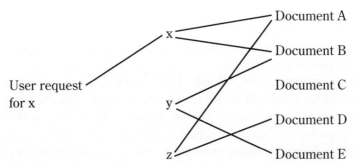

If we consider x, y and z to be members of a clump then enquiries for a document indexed using keyword x retrieves documents ABCD and E. Without the clumping retrieval is restricted to documents A and B. Likewise keyword classification or clumping was seen as a device which could improve precision. If we consider the following diagram for example,

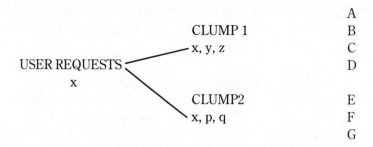

the keyword appears in two different clumps. However, the context in which the keyword is requested can be derived from the content of other keywords in the clumps selected. Using only one input search term determining the appropriate context would have to be done interactively, the user perhaps being prompted to select the appropriate clump by being given a brief description of content of the clumps. When using more than one term it is possible for the system itself to process the request correctly. Thus in the case of the diagram below documents retrieved would be A B C and D and documents E F and G would not be retrieved.

	A
CLUMP 1	B
x, y, z	C
USER REQUESTS	D
x	
and also	CLUMP2	E
	x, p, q	F
		G

TYPES OF KEYWORD CLASSIFICATION

The test results from using the clumping technique proved to be disappointing but work continued to refine the model for clumps further by using statistical and probabilistic techniques to derive weightings for keywords which would serve as an indication of the reliability with which they contributed to the definition of the clump and by inference their usefulness as terms in context of the user's search. Further research was conducted using the set of documents used by Cleverdon in the Cranfield II experiment. Cleverdon's test collection,[23] consisting of 200 documents dealing with aeronautics, which had been indexed in detail for the Cranfield experiments, was used to test the efficiency of different methods of constructing keyword classifications and standard recall/precision mechanisms were used to measure the effectiveness of the different structures used. During the course of this research Sparck Jones' ideas developed from an initial standpoint which assumed working with one type of clump or keyword cluster to use four different types of clusters (all non-hierarchical), which were characterized by their complexity (according to which keywords are included or excluded from groups) and the search procedures typically associated with them. Thus different methods of treating keywords were built into the classification process itself, by varying the way in which similarities of keywords was computed. These variations are shown diagrammatically below:

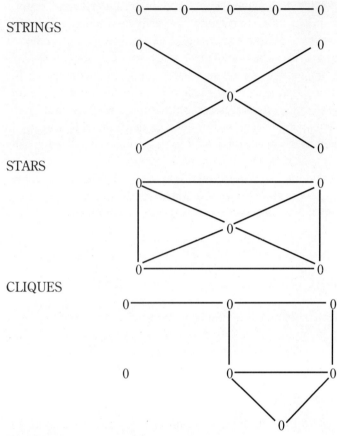

STRINGS

STARS

CLIQUES

CLUMPS

Strings are the simplest form and are constructed by starting from one specific keyword and finding a second keyword strongly connected with it. The process is repeated with the second keyword. A maximum length of seven terms was permitted in the construction of strings. Stars take as their starting point a single 'central' keyword, and keywords connected with this central keyword are included on the basis of their strong association with this term. Size of star cluster can thus vary and in Sparck Jones' research three sizes of star were used containing either four, six or eight terms. Cliques are obtained by identification of a set of fully interconnected keywords. Limits on cliques were set at 13, 16 or 21 links. Clumps depend on the existence of stronger relationships between keywords within the clump than those excluded.

Techniques used in the evaluation were complex and results are difficult to interpret clearly. However, the conclusion that information retrieval systems can be enhanced through the use of keyword classification is clearly demonstrated.

Sparck Jones' work is particularly important because it questions many of the assumptions which have always been made about classification. From a theoretical point of view her work stands on its head the traditional view of how a classification scheme should be constructed. The traditional practice, whether facilitated using faceted or enumerative approaches, proceeds from pigeon-holing concepts to provide a structure which contains a place for each document likely to be added to our collection, meanwhile attempting to ensure that the construction so achieved is as nearly as possible ideal in terms of collocating documents which are likely to be acceptable substitutes. In automatic classification the relationships between documents are determined by the way in which the concepts themselves are represented in the document collection. The classification scheme is specific to the documents contained in the collection and will be affected by any additional acquisitions. Inevitably the document subset retrieved in response to requests in a system constructed in this way may well differ significantly from those retrieved using a system based on conventional classificatory principles.

REQUIREMENTS OF AUTOMATIC KEYWORD CLASSIFICATIONS

This does not in itself mean that such methods of creating classification schemes are intrinsically superior to manual systems. Indeed the results of research into clustering techniques appears to show a 'rediscovery' of exactly the problems which confront the construction and use of manual schemes. These may be summarized as follows:

- clusters must be stable, that is, they should not be affected drastically by the addition of new documents (this was a problem which was particularly apparent in early experiments into the formation of clusters by Needham and Sparck Jones). In any manual classification system the same holds true. The classification schedules must be capable of incorporating concepts represented by adding new documents and should be able to tolerate a certain level of addition of 'new' concepts before substantial revision is required;
- clusters must not be affected by errors in document description. Small errors in the description of documents should not necessitate radical revision of the classification scheme;
- clusters must not be biased by the order in which documents are processed. Likewise, in a manually created scheme (for example, in a scheme created using faceted principles) the scheme should be consistent irrespective of how the documentary literature is sampled when the scheme is devised.

A number of studies have claimed to demonstrate the feasibility of techniques, but an examination of these claims throws serious doubt on their validity. For automated methods to replace fully the manual creation and use of classification schemes implies the following:

1. that a classification system for the whole subject range of bibliographic material can be automatically devised,
2. that there are automated procedures which correctly allocate any document to the classes provided by the scheme created, and
3. that the system fully satisfies the requirement by users to find material on a specific subject and related subjects easily and quickly.

DOCUMENT CLASSIFICATION

Clustering methodologies present us with a dynamic approach to the use of computers in classification; they are concerned with similarity of document content without reference to pre-defined classes. Experiments on document classification on the other hand attempt to make use of clustering algorithms to generate 'traditional' classes and then to assign documents automatically to these classes. A widely quoted early example of a method of document classification is that provided by Borko and Bernick.[24] Their research with automatic classification was reported in the *Journal of the Association for Computing Machinery* in 1963. However, it begins with the false premise that 'Classification means the determination of subject content' and fails to explore in a systematic manner the use of automatic determination of classes. The discussion centres more on the ability of the computer to index documents automatically and thus to assign them accurately to a set of predefined subject classes. A total of 405 abstracts derived from articles published in the *IRE Transactions on Electronic Computers* were used to provide two test groups. The first group (the experimental group) consisted of 260 abstracts and these were used to derive rules for classification. The second group (the validation group) were used to test the validity of the procedures adopted to classify the items contained in the experimental group. From a previous experiment conducted by Maron (using the same test documents) 90 index terms were devised and used as the basis for devising the classification scheme. Counts were made of how frequently the 90 terms appeared in documents and these were then arranged in the form of a data matrix. This was then factor analysed to reduce the original correlation matrix to a smaller number of factors providing 21 classification categories for the collection. The derivation of these 21 categories was not in fact fully automatic, the judgement of the experimenters playing an important role in their determination. The documents in the experimental collection were then classified into the categories as follows:

1. a list of index terms and their frequency of occurrence in each document was

1. a list of index terms and their frequency of occurrence in each document was recorded;
2. each category containing the index terms present in the document was given a 'score' derived by taking the product of the number of occurrences of an index term multiplied by a 'factor loading', that is, a weighting which determines the reliability of the index term as an indicator of the document's subject;
3. after considering each index term in the document the category having the highest score was judged to be the most probable subject classification.

The method used is demonstrated in the figure below which has been constructed using data given in Appendix D of Borko and Bernick's paper.

Clue word	Frequency in document abstract	Categories				
		1	14	8	16	21
Analog	1	.0773	.1363			
Coding	1			.2408	.1259	
Conversion	2			.1211		
Translation	1					.3325
Sum of products		.0773	.1363	.4830	.1259	.3325

Categories used
1   Differential systems of equations and inequations
8   Code compression and conversion
14 Digital and analog control systems, analog computers, function generators
16 Data transmission
21 Computers and programs applied to scientific and engineering problems, mechanical translation

This procedure was repeated on the validation group. Although not stating the basis of the standard on which he measured 'correct classification' Borko's work asserts that in the experimental group only 154 of the original 260 documents were correctly classified (63.4 per cent) and in the validation group the results were even worse, only 44 of the 145 documents being correctly classified (48.9 per cent). Considering the small size of document sample and of the 'classification scheme' the results of the experiment cannot be said to have been encouraging. Other examples of attempts to use automatic techniques to construct broad classification categories and automatically assign documents to those categories were conducted by Hoyle[25] and by Kar and White. Results of these were likewise inconclusive in establishing automatic methods as being a workable alternative to manual classification.

More recently researchers have been concerned with comparing the classes created using some of the more advanced clustering techniques referred to above with approaches used by conventional schemes. Enser, indeed, claims to have demonstrated that automatically generated clusters are in fact more effective than assigned Dewey classes for retrieval.[26] Enser's work centred around the creation of a clustered database of 250 books. The content representation of the books was determined from the indexes. While noting the many defects of the index as a source of subject information Enser concludes that it is nonetheless sufficiently reliable to enable the production of classification schemes which are superior to a conventional library classification of the same material. A major problem Enser himself notes in his report on this research concerns the way in which assessment is made of the performance of the classification schemes. Descriptive phrases from the DC schedules were used as query surrogates but the methods devised to determine relevance of items retrieved were very subjective and as Enser states 'imposed considerable limitation on the evaluation phase of the project'. Indeed one would be justified in going further and stating that they inevitably throw doubt on the validity of the conclusions reached. Garland describes the use of single-link clustering method to generate clusters based on LCSH and document titles.[27] Her findings that LC assigned classes and automatic clusters derived on this basis are strongly related should not, however, be viewed as surprising given the strong functional correspondence between LCSH and LC classmarks. The LC rules for classification in fact state that the classmark assigned to a document should be based on the first subject heading assigned. Larson[28] reports on more extensive research currently being conducted into generating classification clusters based on a large sample of MARC records (over 30,000 records were used). The clusters are created automatically using a variety of elements, and combinations of elements, extracted from fields of the USMARC records. The following fields have been used as the basis for providing data elements for research into the effectiveness of automatic generation of classification clusters:

    all title and LCSH subject fields
    title and first LCSH subject field
    all LCSH subject fields
    first subject heading field only
    title only

Clusters were created to represent LC classes using the following procedure:

1. Information required to form a document representative was extracted from the MARC record using the LC number, the title and all subject headings;
2. The LC number was normalized – typically by retaining only the $a subfield giving the topical part of the subject heading;
3. Documents were sorted by classmark;
4. Documents with the same classmark were combined to provide cluster text

records consisting of the classmark, title proper data, subject heading (6XX fields) and statistical information related for example to number of documents used to form the cluster and frequency of occurrence of subject headings;

5.   A unique ID was assigned to the cluster.

Clusters were then processed, words being reduced to common stems, stop words being applied and the resultant concepts used to form a vector form of the classification cluster.

From a document collection of 30,471 MARC records representing books in the field of Library and Information Science (LC class Z) 8435 classification clusters were created. Four query mechanisms involving simple coordination, term frequency and probabilistic modelling were used as the basis for assigning classmarks to a test collection of 283 MARC records. Effectively the vector representation of documents to be classified were treated as queries on the clustered file and the classification process was treated as a search process. Identification of the correct classification cluster provides the 'correct' classification. Larson acknowledges the inevitable problems associated with poor assignment of classmarks in the collection used to create the clusters which will distort results. Even taking this into account the results when using the clustered file give disappointing results. The single method with best performance was only able to select the 'appropriate' classmark for about 46 per cent of new records. The major significance of this research lies in its comparison of different query methods on clustered files rather than as a working system which can be used to generate the 'correct' LC classmark using bibliographic or index data contained in the MARC record. As Larson states, 'These results, while good considering the size and diversity of the LCC scheme, indicate that fully automatic classification may not be possible'.

CONCLUSION

Although research has been ongoing for over two decades now there is no sign that automatic procedures are sufficiently developed to replace manual classification. There is a lack of theoretical justification for the vector type approach which underpins much of the research which has been conducted to date on clustering techniques. This, compounded by the lack of any significant findings to the contrary, have led Sembok and van Rijsbergen's to conclude that 'this [the keyword] approach with statistical techniques has reached its theoretical limit and further attempts at improvement are considered a waste of time'. Certainly, a major drawback of clustering techniques based on keyword representations of documents is that they make a basic assumption that the keywords used to index a document form a mutually exclusive class of terms –

greater numbers of matches on terms implies closer similarity of documents. However, in document classification it is necessary to recognize the inter-relation of terms and devise a mechanism to measure and compensate for this in algorithms designed to compute similarity. Salton draws our attention to several methods by which improved automatic classification techniques can be constructed. These involve the use of such techniques as advanced language processing, Bayesian inference techniques, the calculus of generalized vector norms and the Dempster-Shafer belief theory. The main barrier to successful implementation of such techniques is that we have as yet no complete theory of knowledge representation, and it is this area of research which appears to offer most promise. Research in these fields, it is argued, gives richer representatives for text to provide a relational based framework in which to place documents and queries and thus to allow the user to go 'beyond the keyword barrier'.[29] Classification currently demonstrates the relational information amongst primitive concepts which these systems seek to provide. Current schemes may not do so perfectly but there is as yet no single approach which provides a viable alternative. The literature currently shows a convergence of approaches. Hypertextual mapping techniques are being developed which have as their ultimate aim the discovery of 'new concepts for old'. The design inputs for these are provided by a range of different subject fields. Cognition theory, linguistic analysis, expert systems research and classification theory are all recognized as playing an important role in developing knowledge based systems with inference rules which will allow users to traverse complex conceptual networks. This may well validate Salton's conclusion in a recent article on developments of automatic text retrieval that 'The time is at hand when sophisticated searches can be conducted with large collections of natural language text in unrestricted subject areas that can provide high quality rapid file access for interested users'. But from a survey of the recent literature on the subject of automatic classification it is apparent that this is as yet a goal rather than a reality. The concluding comments by Wellisch in his survey of the field in 1981[30] are as valid today as when they were written:

> All these quasi-operational 'automatic' projects share a characteristic that might be compared with reports on the manufacture of mechanical birds: after a quarter century of trial and error, some models begin to look bird-like, a few can imitate chirping noises, some can flap their wings, but so far none can really fly or sing – a fact carefully hidden behind some dense verbiage, generally in the last but one paragraph of such reports.

It seems more fitting, therefore, to conclude this discussion on automatic techniques with a quote from the previous author of this manual in which Maltby, discussing the role of manual classification in general asserts that 'The real issue confronting . . . critics is to find a constructive and viable alternative to classification that can serve most library situations so well – for despite the difficulties classification is a good servant'.[31]

NOTES

1. Ranganathan's term for the compiler of a classification scheme as opposed to the user of such a scheme.

2. Borko, H. and Bernick, M., Automatic document classification. *Journal of the Association for Computer Machinery*, 10 (2), April 1963, pp. 151–162.

3. Luhn, H. P., The automatic creation of literature abstracts. *IBM Journal of Research and Development*, 2, 1958, pp. 159–65.

4. Zipf, H. P., *Human behaviour and the principle of least effort*. Cambridge (Mass.): Addison-Wesley, 1949.

5. Edmundson, H. P. and Wyllys, R. E., Automatic abstracting and indexing survey and recommendations. *Communications of the ACM*, 4, 1961, pp. 226–234.

6. It is important to note here that these 'little words' which have syntactic function are not insignificant in information retrieval theory. The Cranfield project clearly recognized the role of the syntactic or syntagmatic elements in an indexing language – in particular in relation to the way in which they improve precision. This has been clearly demonstrated in Gardin's work on SYNTOL. There are indeed certain automated procedures which are devoted to assigning words of text to their appropriate grammatic classes, for example the Economic Parser and Klein and Simmon's Computational Grammar Code. The discussion of these, however, falls more into the scope of linguistic analysis and will not be considered in detail here.

7. van Rijsbergen, C. J., *Information retrieval*. 2nd Edn. London: Butterworths, 1979.

8. Porter, M. F., An algorithm for suffix stripping. *Program*, 14 (3), 1980, pp. 130–137.

9. Hayes, R. M., Quoted in van Rijsbergen, *Information Retrieval* 2nd Edn. London: Butterworths, 1979.

10. Buchanan, B., *Theory of library classification*. London: Bingley, 1979.

11. Sparck Jones, K. and Jackson, D. M., The use of automatically obtained keyword classifications for information retrieval. *Information Storage and Retrieval*, 5, 1970, pp. 175–201.

12. Griffiths, A., Evaluation of clustering methods for automatic document classification. *BLRD Report 5837*, 1984. See also *Journal of Documentation*, 40 (3), September 1984, pp. 175–205.

13. A useful collection of 27 studies from various ISR reports is given in Salton, G., *The SMART retrieval system: experiments in automatic document processing*. Englewood Cliffs (NJ): Prentice Hall, 1971.

14. Rocchio, J. J. (Jr), *Document Retrieval System: optimisation and evaluation. ISR 10*. Cambridge (Mass.): Harvard Computation Lab., 1966.

15. In exactly the same way manually constructed hierarchic schemes function most efficiently where the document collection corresponds closely to a well established natural taxonomy.

16. Salton, G., A new comparison between conventional indexing (MEDLARS) and automatic text processing. *Journal of the American Society for Information Science*, 23, 1972, pp. 75–84. Quoted in Foskett, A. C., *The subject approach to information*. 4th Edn. London: Bingley, 1982.

17. Salton, G., Developments in automatic text retrieval. *Science*, 253, 30th Aug. 1991, pp. 974–980. (Salton is in fact here referring to claims that it was pointless to refine statistical techniques further based on single term indexing representations for documents.)

18. See for example the work of Prywes, Lang and Zagorsky on programs designed to process textual databases and produce searchable directories and class number ordered output. Prywes, N. S. *et al.*, A posteriori indexing, classification and retrieval of textual data. *Information Storage and Retrieval*, 10, 1974, pp. 15–27.

19. MacLeod, K. J., A neural algorithm for document clustering. *Information Processing and Management*, 27 (4), 1991, pp. 337–346.

20. That is to say, experienced searchers familiar with Boolean logic, term truncation and search heuristics can obtain results from online searches using conventional means which are better or as good as those achieved by the best 'intelligent' systems. However, as the trend towards end user searching continues the need for the intelligent interface will undoubtedly increase.

21. Sparck Jones, K., *Automatic keyword classification*. London: Butterworths, 1971.

22. Sparck Jones, *op. cit.*

23. The Cleverdon collection, the Keen (ISILT) collection dealing with information science and the

INSPEC collection dealing with electrical engineering have now become standard document samples for testing projects related to retrieval efficiency and effectiveness. An interesting paper by Sparck Jones notes the marked difference in retrieval effectiveness when using these test collections and poses interesting questions related to the basic assumptions we make when evaluating both manual and automated retrieval techniques. See Sparck Jones, K., Collection properties influencing automatic term classification performance. *Information Storage and Retrieval*, 9, 1973, pp. 499–513.

24.   Borko and Bernick, *Op. cit.*

25.   Hoyle, W. G., Automatic indexing and generation of classification systems by algorithm. *Information Storage and Retrieval*, 9, 1973, pp. 233–242. Hoyle makes use of probabilistic methods based on Bayes theorem and claims that his algorithm is 90 per cent accurate although the sample size is very small. Interestingly, he notes a clear similarity between the classes he derives automatically and those produced manually but fails to comment on reasons for this.

26.   Enser, P. G. B. Automatic classification of book material represented by back of book index. *Journal of Documentation*, 41 (3), 1985, pp. 135–155.

27.   Garland, K., An experiment in automatic hierarchical document classification. *Information Processing and Management*, 19 (3), 1982, pp. 113–120.

28.   Larson, R. R., Experiments in automatic Library of Congress classification. *Journal of the American Society for Information Science,* 43 (2), 1992, pp. 130–148.

29.   See for example Maulin, M., Beyond the keyword barrier: knowledge based information retrieval. *Information Services and Use*, 7 (4/5), 1987, pp. 103–117.

30.   Wellisch, H. Year's work in subject analysis: 1980. *Library Resources and Technical Services*, 25, July/Sept 1981, pp. 295–309.

31.   Maltby, A., Classification – logic, limits and levels. *In* A. Maltby (ed.), *Classification in the 70's: a discussion of development and prospects for the major schemes.* London: Clive Bingley, 1972.

Further reading

Rather than provide lists of reading for the individual chapters of this book, these have been brought together in order to direct the reader to useful sources and writers. This is not a comprehensive bibliography; rather it seeks to identify potential sources of further investigation. Some of the works listed are old but are still irreplaceable to the enthusiastic student of classification. The majority of the items listed are monographs although significant journal articles have also been identified to reflect very current attitudes, developments, issues and thinkers.

One of the best sources for the study of classification is the schedules themselves, their introductions and manuals. These are not included in this bibliography, but are readily enough identified and located.

GENERAL WORKS

AACR, DDC and MARC and friends: the role of CIG in bibliographic control, edited by John Byford. London: Library Association Publishing, 1993.

Bliss, H. E., *The organisation of knowledge in libraries*. New York: H. W. Wilson, 1933.

Buchanan, Brian, *Theory of library classification*. Bingley, 1979.

Classification research for knowledge representation and organization: proceedings of the fifth international study conference on classification research, edited by Nancy J. Williamson and Michelle Hudon. Amsterdam: Elsevier, 1992. Has appeared in various years and locations.

Downing, Mildred H. and Downing, David H., *Introduction to cataloguing and classification*. 6th Edn. Jefferson, NC: McFarland, 1992.

Foskett, A. C., *The subject approach to information*. 4th Edn. London: Bingley, 1982.

Hunter, Eric J., *Classification made simple*. Aldershot: Gower, 1988.

Kautto, Vesa, Classing and indexing: a comparative time study. *International Classification*, 19, 1992, pp. 205–209.

Langridge, D. W., *Approach to classification for students of librarianship*. London: Bingley, 1973.

Langridge, D. W., *Classification: its kinds, elements, systems and applications*. London: Bowker-Saur, 1992.

Langridge, D. W., *Subject analysis: principles and procedures*. London: Bowker-Saur, 1989.

Maltby, Arthur, *Classification in the 1970's: a second look*. 2nd Edn. London: Bingley, 1976.

Mills, Jack, *A modern outline of library classification*. London: Chapman and Hall, 1960.

Palmer, Bernard, *Itself an education: six lectures on classification*. London: Library Association, 1971.

Ranganathan, S. R., *Elements of library classification*. London: Association of Assistant Librarians, 1959.

Rowley, Jennifer E., *Organizing knowledge: introduction to information retrieval*. 2nd Edn. Aldershot: Ashgate, 1992.

Saye, Jerry D., *Manheimer's cataloguing and classification: a workbook*. 3rd Edn. New York: Dekker, 1991.

Turner, Christopher, *Organising information: principles and practice*. London: Bingley, 1987.

Vickery, Brian C., *Faceted classification*. London: ASLIB, 1960.

THE HISTORY OF CLASSIFICATION

Richardson, E. C., *Classification: theoretical and practical*. New York: Charles Scribner's Sons, 1901.

THE GENERAL SCHEMES

Major classification systems: the Dewey Centennial, edited by Kathryn Luther Henderson. Urbana, IL: University of Illinois, 1976.

THE DEWEY DECIMAL CLASSIFICATION

Batty, David, *An introduction to the twentieth edition of the Dewey Decimal Classification*. London: Bingley, 1992.

Dewey: an international perspective; workshop on the Dewey Decimal Classification and DDC 20. London: Saur, 1991.

Dewey international: papers given at the European Centenary Seminar on the Dewey Decimal Classification held at Banbury England, 26–30 September, 1976. London: Library Association, 1977.

Liu, Songqiao and Svenonius, Elaine, DORS: DDC Online Retrieval System.

Library Resources and Technical Services, 35, 1991, pp. 359–375.

Markey, Karen, DDC as a library user's tool. *MARC Users' Group Newsletter*, 85 (1), 1985, pp. 19–26.

Osborn, Jeanne and Comaromi, John P., *Dewey Decimal Classification 20th edition: a study manual*. Englewood, CO: Libraries Unlimited, 1991.

Spriggs, Beatrice, *A comparative guide to the Library of Congress and Dewey Decimal Classification Systems*. Bowling Green, OH: BGSU Library, 1984.

Vizine-Goetz, Diane, The Dewey Decimal Classification as an online classification tool. *OCLC Research Review*, Jan. 1991, pp 1–2.

MELVIL DEWEY

Melvil Dewey: his enduring presence in libraries. Englewood, CO: Libraries Unlimited, 1978.

Dewey, Melvil, Decimal Classification beginnings. *Library Journal*, 115 (11), 1990, pp. 156–157.

Rider, Fremont, *Melvil Dewey*. Chicago, IL: American Library Association, 1944.

THE LIBRARY OF CONGRESS CLASSIFICATION

Chan, Lois Mai, *Immroth's guide to the Library of Congress Classification*. 4th Edn. Englewood, CO: Libraries Unlimited, 1990.

La Montagne, Leo E., *American library classification with special reference to the Library of Congress*. Hamden, CON: Shoe String Press, 1961.

Library of Congress, *Guide to the Library of Congress*. Washington: Library of Congress, 1982.

Miksa, Francis L., *The development of classification at the Library of Congress*. Urbana, IL: University of Illinois, 1984.

THE COLON CLASSIFICATION

Batty, David, *Introduction to Colon Classification*. London: Bingley, 1966.

Satija, M. J., *Colon Classification: 7th edition: a practical introduction*. New Delhi: Ess Ess Publications, 1989.

S.R. RANGANATHAN

Binwal, J. C., Ranganathan and the universe of knowledge. *International Classification*, 19, 1992, pp. 195–200.

Gopinath, M. A., Summary of the work and achievements of Dr S.R. Ranganathan. *Library Science with a slant to Documentation*, 29 (2), pp. 47–57.

Libri, 42, whole issue devoted to Ranganathan.

THE UNIVERSAL DECIMAL CLASSIFICATION

Brown, A. G., *Introduction to subject indexing: Volume 2: UDC and chain procedure in subject cataloging*. London: Bingley, 1976.

Gilchrist, Alan, UDC: the 1990's and beyond. In *Classification research for knowledge representation and organisation: proceedings of the 5th International Conference on Classification Research, Toronto, Canada, June 24–28, 1991*, edited by Nancy J. Williamson and Michelle Hudon. Amsterdam: Elsevier, 1992.

The UDC: essays for a new decade, edited by Alan Gilchrist and David Strachan. London: ASLIB, 1990.

Williamson, Nancy J., Restructuring UDC: problems and possibilities. In *Classification research for knowledge representation and organisation: proceedings of the 5th International Conference on Classification Research, Toronto, Canada, June 24–28, 1991*, edited by Nancy J. Williamson and Michelle Hudon. London: Elsevier, 1992.

THE BIBLIOGRAPHIC CLASSIFICATION

Maltby, Arthur & Gill, Lindy, *The case for Bliss: modern classification practice and principles in the context of the Bibliographic Classification*. London: Clive Bingley, 1979.

Mills, Jack, The Bibliographic Classification. In *Classification in the 70's: a second look*, edited by A. Maltby. London: Bingley, 1976.

Thomas, Alan R., Bliss Bibliographic Classification, 2nd edition: principles forms and applications. *Cataloging and Classification Quarterly*, 15 (4), 1992, pp. 3–17.

SPECIAL CLASSIFICATION, THESAURI AND INDEXING

Aitchison, Jean, A classification as a source for a thesaurus: the Bibliographic Classification of H.E. Bliss as a source of thesaurus terms and structure. *Journal of Documentation*, 42, September 1986, pp. 168–181.

Foskett, Douglas J., Concerning general and special classifications. *International Classification*, 18, 1991, pp. 87–91.

Guard, Anara, An antidote for browsing: subject headings for fiction.

Technicalities, 11 (12), 1992, pp. 10–14.

Hunter, Eric J. and Bakewell, K.G.B., *Cataloguing. 3rd edition*. London: Bingley, 1991.

Mahapatra, M, Design of special classification schedules based on the principles of Colon Classification. *Libri*, 29 (2), 1979, pp. 169–188.

Olderr, Stephen, *Olderr's fiction subject headings: a supplement and guide to the LC thesaurus*. Chicago, IL: American Library Association, 1991.

Vickery, Brian, *Faceted classification: a guide to the construction and use of special schemes*. London: ASLIB, 1968.

INFORMATION TECHNOLOGY AND CLASSIFICATION

Chan, L. M., The LC in an online environment. *Catalogue and Classification Quarterly*. Vol. 11, (1), 1990, pp. 7-26.

Dym, E. D. (Ed.), *Subject and Information Analysis*. New York: Marcel Dekker, 1985.

Kinesella, J., Classification and the OPAC. *Catalogue and Index*. (Autumn/Winter), No. 105/6, 1992, pp. 3–10

Larson, R. R., Experiments in automatic Library of Congress classification. *Journal of the American Society for Information Science*, 43 (2), 1992, pp. 130–148.

Markey, K., *DDC online project. (OCLC/OPR/RR-86/1)*, Dublin Ohio : OCLC, 1986.

Rigby, M., *Automation and the UDC 1948–80*, 2nd Edn. The Hague: FID, 1981.

Svenonius, E., Use of classification in online retrieval. *Library Resources and Technical Services*, Vol. 27 (1), Jan–Mar 1983, pp.76–80.

Sparck Jones, K., Notes and references on early automatic classification work, *SIGIR Forum*, Vol. 25, 1991, pp. 10–17.

Sparck Jones, K., *Automatic keyword classification*. London: Butterworths, 1971.

USMARC Format for Classification Data: including guidelines for content designation. Library of Congress, Network Development and MARC Standards Office, 1991.

van Rijsbergen, C., *Information Retrieval*. 2nd Edn. London: Butterworths, 1979.

Walker, S., *Improving subject retrieval in online catalogues 1*. London: BL, 1987.

Walker, S., *Improving subject retrieval in online catalogues 2*. London: BL, 1990.

Williamson, Nancy J., The role of classification in online systems. *Cataloging and Classification Quarterly*, 1/2, 1989, pp. 95–104.

Index

The index uses the same abbreviations for the main general classification schemes as have been employed in the text and is alphabetized on the letter-by-letter principle. It excludes references to books and articles referred to in reading lists.

Effective Library and Information Centre Management

Jo Bryson

Library and information centre managers have to be innovative and knowledgeable to manage their services strategically to meet increasing demands within complex environments. This book describes the modern management techniques needed to do this, thereby providing ideas which can be used to stimulate entrepreneurial and effective solutions to management concerns. Considerable management expertise is required to achieve goals whilst being cost effective. Special attention is paid in the book to the concepts of managing in times of economic restraint, changing work attitudes, environments and management styles, and to the influence of technology, corporate culture, and commercialisation. The influence of a library's external and internal environment must also be taken into account. A systems approach to strategic management has been selected as the basis for the design and layout of the book, which allows the library manager to move systematically from considering the library and its parent organization's external environment, and its influence upon the management of the library, to an examination of its internal environment. A sub-systems approach is taken for the information centre's internal environment allowing the manager to again move through these topics systematically. This book is also a management textbook for students of librarianship and information studies, it should act as a reference tool on management issues throughout their future working lives.

1990   432 pages   0 566 05640 2

Gower

Information Management and Library Science
A Guide to the Literature

Ray Prytherch

Information management embraces the strategies and technologies of acquiring, organizing, retrieving and exploiting information in any context. Increasingly it is used to describe those processes found in corporate environments where the efficient and accurate handling of internal and external data can give vital competitive edge. Such techniques are common to the professional concerns of librarians and information personnel. This book analyses and discusses the standard sources in this field. International activity, particularly in Europe, is reflected, and sources in CD-ROM and online formats are included.

This is a complete revision of the first edition, published as *Sources of Information in Librarianship and Information Science*. Coverage has been extended to encompass new areas such as records management and document imaging, and to include telecommunications and networking, which now form a basic infrastructure in the information world.

A new feature of this edition is the annotated bibliography of standard texts, reports, and background reading that would support readers in unfamiliar areas. The list of key journals which appeared in the first edition has now been restored in an expanded, categorized format, and a list of key organizations has been added.

This volume will offer guidance in core and fringe areas to information workers in industry, the professions and the academic context. Librarians, trainers and students in all branches of librarianship will welcome this revision of the only standard British source in their field.

1990   331 pages   0 566 07467 2

Gower

Manual of Archival Description
Second Edition

Michael Cook and Margaret Procter

The *Manual of Archival Description Second Edition* aims to provide standards which will control the production of finding aids and finding aid systems in archival repositories and archives services. It is, therefore, primarily intended as a guide to normal descriptive or cataloguing practices carried out by archivists in general repositories. Users of the first edition of MAD will see that the principles established there have been maintained but have been developed in nearly every direction. The rules and recommendations have been extended and made more precise whilst authoritative and important refinements have been introduced.

Contents

Scope of the manual • Organization of the manual. The Nature of Archival Description: What are archives? • Archival arrangement • The function of a finding aid system • Level and depth of description • The multi-level rule • Fitting levels together • The two modes of archival description • Depth of description • Other aspects of archival description. The Data Structure of an Archival Description: The purpose of data structure • How the table of data elements is made up • Summary table of data elements • General rules • Specific rules. Recommended Description Formats: Macro and micro descriptions • Paragraph or list mode • Description formats • Management heading • Group descriptions • Subgroup descriptions • Class descriptions • Item descriptions • Piece descriptions • Composite descriptions • Standard listing conventions. Typology of Archival Descriptions. Special Formats: Introduction • Title deeds • Letters and correspondence • Photographs • Cartographic archives • Architectural and other plans • Sound archives • Film and video archives • Machine readable archives • MARC for archives and manuscripts • Dictionary of technical terms • Sources used in the dictionary • Brief bibliography • Index.

1990   304 pages   0 566 03634 7

Gower

Organizing Knowledge
Second Edition

Jennifer Rowley

This book provides an integrated overview of information retrieval. The common principles associated with the storage and retrieval of information in databases of all kinds are introduced. Catalogue databases, bibliographic databases, (with and without abstracts) and full text databases are all considered. The book is divided into five main sections: records, authors and titles, subjects, systems, and general issues. The first edition was designed as a standard introductory textbook for students on postgraduate and undergraduate courses in library and information management. It has been exceptionally well received both in the United Kingdom and many other countries and has established itself as a standard text. The second edition retains the objective approach and structure of the first edition but has been significantly revised since the compilation of the first edition.

Contents

Introduction • Part 1 – Records • The tools of information retrieval and the organization of knowledge • Records in printed indexes and catalogues • Description of documents: principles and monographs • More on bibliographic description: nonbook media, periodicals and analytical cataloguing • Summaries, manual files, and full text databases • Computerized record formats and database structures • Part 2 – Authors and titles • Problems in author cataloguing and in name indexing • Cataloguing codes: purpose and development • The Anglo-American cataloguing rules and author access • Catalogue and index access points for the works of corporate bodies • Titles • Part 3 – Subjects • The subject approach, introduction, processes, tools and simple evaluation • The theory of bibliographic classification • Bibliographic classification schemes • The alphabetical subject approach • Alphabetical indexing languages • Indexing systems: principles and printed indexes • Indexing systems: computer-based systems • Part 4 – Systems • Online information retrieval systems: external services • Optical disks • In-house information retrieval and cataloguing systems • Cataloguing systems: networks • Part 5 – Generalia • Research and the future • Filing order in indexes and catalogues • Document arrangement • Physical forms of catalogue and index • Glossary • Index.

1992   530 pages   1 85742 004 7 Hardback   1 85742 005 5 Paperback

Gower

Records Management Handbook
Second Edition

Ira A Penn, Gail B Pennix and Jim Coulson

Records Management Handbook is a complete guide to the practice of records and information management. Written from a multi-media perspective and with a comprehensive systems design orientation, the authors present proven management strategies for developing, implementing and operating a "21st century" records management programme. Where most available titles are biased toward dealing with inactive records, this book gives a balanced treatment for all phases of the record's life cycle, from creation or receipt through to ultimate disposition.

The *Records Management Handbook* is a practical reference for use by records managers, analysts, and other information management professionals, which will aid decision-making, improve job performance, stimulate ideas, help avoid legal problems, minimize risk and error, save time and reduce expense.

Special features of the second edition include:
- new chapters on record media, active records systems and records disposition
- new information on management strategies and programme implementation
- revised guidance and material on records appraisal and record inventorying
- expanded and increased information on retention scheduling, records storage and electronic forms.

1994   320 pages   0 566 07510 5

Gower